Movies, Modernism, and
the Science Fiction Pulps

MOVIES, MODERNISM, AND THE SCIENCE FICTION PULPS

J. P. Telotte

OXFORD
UNIVERSITY PRESS

OXFORD
UNIVERSITY PRESS

Oxford University Press is a department of the University of Oxford. It furthers
the University's objective of excellence in research, scholarship, and education
by publishing worldwide. Oxford is a registered trade mark of Oxford University
Press in the UK and certain other countries.

Published in the United States of America by Oxford University Press
198 Madison Avenue, New York, NY 10016, United States of America.

© Oxford University Press 2019

Library of Congress Cataloging-in-Publication Data
Names: Telotte, J. P., 1949– author.
Title: Movies, modernism, and the science fiction pulps / J.P. Telotte.
Description: New York : Oxford University Press, [2019] |
Includes bibliographical references, filmography, and index.
Identifiers: LCCN 2018046803 (print) | LCCN 2018059207 (ebook) |
ISBN 9780190949679 (updf) | ISBN 9780190949686 (epub) |
ISBN 9780190949693 (oso) | ISBN 9780190949655 (cloth :alk. paper) |
ISBN 9780190949662 (paperback :alk. paper)
Subjects: LCSH: Science fiction, American—20th century—History and criticism.
Pulp literature, American—20th century—History and criticism. |
Motion pictures in literature.
Classification: LCC PS374.S35 (ebook) | LCC PS374.S35 T44 2019 (print) |
DDC 813/.509—dc23
LC record available at https://lccn.loc.gov/2018046803

9 8 7 6 5 4 3 2 1

Paperback printed by Webcom, Inc., Canada
Hardback printed by Bridgeport National Bindery, Inc., United States of America

CONTENTS

ACKNOWLEDGMENTS

As ever, a great many people contributed to the creation of this book and deserve special note. My wife, Leigh Ehlers Telotte, once more listened to many ramblings about science fiction and provided valued comments. Members of the International Association for the Fantastic in the Arts sat through several papers on this material, asked the usual smart questions, and helped me to pull ideas together. Several faculty members and my students at Georgia Tech humored my blathering about forgotten pulp fiction, film industry trade papers, and film advertising and reviews from another era that had no clear relevance to their lives or interests. Among the faculty let me especially thank Lisa Yaszek for encouraging an interloper in the literature of science fiction, which is more her area of expertise. From among the many bright students in my Science Fiction Film and Television courses, I would especially single out Wyatt Bazrod, Andrew Lippens, Lexie Scott, and Ryan Fadell for their insightful comments and discussions. And for her first efforts as a research assistant, let me especially thank Lauren Moye who displayed great patience as she surveyed numerous pulp magazines, discovered some intriguing cinematic images lurking there, and called my attention to the key pulp term "scientifilm." While perhaps a bit skeptical of her assignments at first, Ms. Moye's efforts helped assure me that the cinema-pulp connection was well worth detailed investigation. As usual, my School Chair Richard Utz was supportive, and Jacqueline Royster, Dean of the Ivan Allen College of Liberal Arts at GT, provided timely support by awarding me one of the College's research grants. And once again I want to make special mention of the editors at *Science Fiction Studies* who saw and published an early article-length treatment of these ideas and whose readers pointed me in profitable directions. I am also thankful to have once more had the opportunity to work with the outstanding editorial group of Oxford University Press: Norman Hirschy who recognized the appeal of this material and enthusiastically supported the project, Lauralee Yeary who skillfully handled the early details of the publication process, and the reviewers who helped sharpen my thinking on this material. Finally, the production team at OUP deserves mention, especially copy editor Suzanne Copenhagen who demonstrated a fine feel for language, and the ever efficient Alphonsa James who kept the project on schedule. This book was a pleasure to work on, and the entire professional team at OUP contributed to that pleasurable experience.

CHAPTER 1

Introduction

Science Fiction's "Composite" Project

As has often been noted, film was one of the most important translators of twentieth-century modernity. At a time that old verities were rapidly disappearing, when it seemed like, as Marshall Berman reminds us, "all that is solid melts into air" (15), the new medium of the movies, which is itself little more than light, was providing audiences with what Francesco Casetti terms a much-needed "script for reading the modern experience," one that "not only proposed a reading of that experience, but at times imposed a pattern"—a highly visual one—"for its expression and communication" (5). It is a description and an assessment that might well be applied to another form that was born, took shape, and found its identity during the same late modernist era—science fiction (SF). Certainly, an early champion of and midwife to that birth, editor and author Hugo Gernsback, saw this burgeoning genre, which he initially labeled "scientifiction," as offering its own kind of "script" for modern technological life: providing writers with a tool for "imparting knowledge" about science and technology, while giving readers "inspiration" or a pattern for the sort of new thinking and development that this modern age was going to require of them ("A New Sort of Magazine" 3). In fact, he underscored that kinship when, in describing what he termed the "science saturated atmosphere" of the 1920s, Gernsback suggested that SF's concerns were essentially the same as those of several other "wonders of modern science," including "talking motion pictures" ("Science Wonder Stories" 5). Besides citing another highly modern subject that might be explored and turned into subject matter for his magazines,

Gernsback was recognizing film as an integral part of the climate that had engendered the SF imagination and had produced an SF literature that was embarked on its own project of "reading" and shaping the late modernist experience.

I note this relationship because it is one that, despite Gernsback's lead, has all too often been overlooked or simply been taken for granted as we write our histories of SF. Perhaps the issue is that, as Paul E. Wegner offers, SF has been perceived as "always already as modernist as . . . film" (141), so some of the specific intersections or influences have been seen either as not needing exploration or as so obvious that they are not particularly note-worthy. But a more likely explanation is that our sense of modernist prac-tice is, as Andrew Milner puts it, a "distinctly slippery" one (27), subject to very different interpretations from within different disciplinary or media borders, resulting in some of those interpretations leaving SF outside of or apart from our considerations of other modernist forms that seem ei-ther more experimental or more radically realist. Thus Milner observes that we have often approached SF in terms of a conceptual cleavage, that is, as inhabiting some "other" category, somewhere between realist and mod-ernist literatures, mass culture and high art, conventional representation and the avant-garde. But consequently, those who associate modernism largely with "a combination of aesthetic self-consciousness and formalist experimentalism," that is, with explorations in aesthetic form or narrative style rather than with what Milner terms "a modernism of content" (28), usually view SF as having little in common with film, which, by contrast, often seems to fit both measures. For even in its earliest efforts film freely capitalized on a self-conscious presentation of "content," foregrounding its edited or plastic nature, as when the Lumiere brothers' *Demolition d'un mur* (1896) was projected in reverse, thereby reversing our sense of time by making a crumbled wall seem, without agency, to reconstruct itself; and as film crafted unusual or striking images, typically described as "attractions," that exploited what Laura Marcus describes as the "intensity of its appeal to the eye" (4). As several commentators have argued, though, we might well see SF, marked as it is at times by an overtly different, even tech-nical discourse and by a fantastic content that inevitably challenges con-ventional cognition (Wegner 142), as staking a similarly modernist claim. This is the claim that is implicit in the *felt* connections and influences that Gernsback and others both acknowledged and fostered through the litera-ture published in the various SF pulp magazines that they helmed.

While SF might well be seen from the vantage Milner suggests, as "nei-ther realist nor modernist, but rather an entirely distinct third" type of literature (30), I want to take a more pragmatic approach in trying to add a dimension to the genre's history. Following Gernsback's lead and allowing that film and SF—however we "locate" it—breathed the same modernist atmosphere, we shall here consider how the work of SF and the work of film often coincided in that heady pre-war period when both were coming of age. This inquiry will do so by giving special emphasis to some largely unexplored territory, as it considers how film and the film industry, or what we might term the cinematic imagination, impacted the development of the SF imagination as it sought to respond to the new world of science and technology and the changes they were rapidly bringing to modern culture. Adopting Casetti's terminology, we shall examine how the "script" of one modernist form was being absorbed into or unconsciously influencing that of the other, and how that relationship can help us to better understand the early development of SF, particularly in the United States, where a most distinctive venue for the new literature of SF had appeared in the specialized SF pulp magazines, as exemplified by such *wondrous* titles as *Wonder Stories, Amazing Stories, Astounding Stories of Super-Science* (hereafter *Astounding Stories*), and *Thrilling Wonder Stories*. In these and other publications, SF was throughout the late modernist period of the 1920s through the 1940s visibly working through its own development as a distinct genre—or at least as Carl Freedman would suggest that we more accurately describe it, constructing "a generic tendency" (20).[1] In the various ways they contributed to this "tendency," these magazines, reflecting the popular science enthusiasm of the era, afford a telling test case for the impact on SF of the even more popular modernist art of the movies.

While hardly the originators of this new SF literature, the pulp magazines—so-called because of the cheap pulpwood paper on which they were printed—were the primary purveyors of SF from the mid-1920s to approximately the mid-1950s. They provided attractive publishing platforms for this literature, their editors—and besides Gernsback, we might list such influential and often more hands-on figures as T. O'Conor Sloane, F. Orlin Tremaine, John W. Campbell, Jr., Raymond A. Palmer, David Lasser, and others—encouraged and helped to develop a group of writers who throughout this period would become major exponents and shapers of the genre, and they also assisted in building a dedicated fandom. As noted SF author and historian Adam Roberts observes, "the pulp idiom, and its huge popularity, remade SF" in this period by giving it wide distribution, making it easily affordable, and reaching out to a "socially diverse readership" (174)—one that included, as Lisa Yaszek and Patrick B. Sharp have shown, a frequently overlooked female audience that appreciated SF's "opportunities to engage science in both critical and creative ways" that women were not supposed to enjoy (xxi)—as well as the full audience of that other important late modernist development, the cinema. Just as significant, as this volume argues, the "pulp idiom" embraced and frequently depicted the world of the cinema, particularly its technologies, its artists, and its similarly dedicated fan base.

Coming of age in parallel, both SF and film, as they sought to establish themselves and develop an audience, similarly had to contend with a kind of modernist fallout, the blurring or, as Berman puts it, "melting" away of various prior distinctions—between high and low culture, between art and popular entertainment, and between traditional forms of representation and modern, machine-driven or machine-influenced ones. For Roberts, one of SF's most important struggles was not just against a realist tradition in literature, but also against the tide of what he describes as a "High Modernism" (157) that neither took SF very seriously nor viewed it as what Brooks Landon neatly terms "a clearly identified category of literature" (14). Making that struggle for identity and acceptance all the more difficult was the fact that many of those High Modernists demonstrated what Roberts suggests was a "hostility towards technology" (158), and thus to a popular culture literature such as SF—and, in some instances, to a technologically based form such as film—that trafficked in, even celebrated the work of science and technology. Such literature was often seen as symptomatic of a larger "drift of contemporary society towards technology" and technological products (Roberts 158), and thus away from traditional art, the natural world, and even the real—a drift that, many felt, would ultimately induce inauthentic, machine-like lives and machinic thinking, neither of which, it was suspected, would allow the individual to properly cope with the world of change that modern culture and its lack of what Berman might call *solidity* were already ringing in.

Of course, in its early development film was at times viewed in nearly the same light, in part because it, too, was born of technology and embodied what we might describe as a technological experience—the mechanical reproduction, re-experiencing, and even reshaping of reality. Because of that context film immediately raised the question that was at the heart of Walter Benjamin's famous discussion of this new technological culture, that is, what might constitute a "work of art in the age of mechanical reproduction," and, perhaps more to the point, whether a machine-connected, machine-created *art* was even a possibility. Moreover, film readily appealed to a popular culture audience, especially in its early identity as what film historian Tom Gunning has labeled a "cinema of attractions," ruled by an aesthetic of "astonishment" (63). Gunning's influential description of film's early form and appeal suggests that it primarily capitalized on what some might have seen as superficial effects, while addressing a "naïve" audience through its fantastic illusions, surprising juxtapositions of images, and the construction of a new spectatorial experience—one that trafficked in the psychological pleasures of the visual, or what is termed scopophilia. While film's emphasis on fashioning new and striking visual relationships was, in fact, far from superficial—indeed, its striking visual relationships were one reason it would be embraced by the era's avant-garde artists, such as Salvador Dali, Fernand Leger, and Marcel Duchamp—and the audience, as Gunning also observes, hardly naïve, elements of that original myth about the cinema took firm hold. We might even blame this lingering impact for a circumstance that Mark Bould has noted as he describes how, in contrast to the pulps, their editors, and readers, early SF cinema seems to have shown far less of a concern with or "self-awareness about its generic identity" (81), and as a result was usually relegated, even in filmic circles, to rather hazy categories of fantasy, horror, or as French film pioneer Georges Melies referred to his own work, "feerie films."

And yet that same master of "attractions," Melies, with Jules Verne serving as a kind of guiding spirit, or perhaps with an implicit understanding that there was indeed a shared nature, a kinship between Verne's pioneering SF work and the newcomer cinema, would repeatedly concoct unmistakably SF-like efforts. The result was a series of major landmarks in the development of the cinematic genre, represented by such film adaptations as his *A Trip to the Moon* (1902), *An Impossible Voyage* (1904), and *Under the Seas (Deux cent mille lieues sous les mers*, 1907). But since these works typically cast the work of SF in a fantastic and often even satiric light, they also helped justify a tendency even within SF circles to look past this early SF-film connection (Figure 1.1). Demonstrating that tendency is Edward James's influential history, *Science Fiction in the Twentieth Century*, which does not address Melies or any other of the film efforts at packaging SF or SF-like narratives for a broad public early in the century, while Roberts, even as he acknowledges the existence of these popular works, demonstrates a similar tendency to keep that cinematic imagination at arm's length from the work of SF as he dismisses such early productions as "whimsies" or, in a particularly deprecating description, as "short representations of pantomimic oddity designed as diversions" (186). But given their similar origins in a late modernist fascination with the impact of science and technology, their common concern with change, their taking breath from the same "science saturated atmosphere," as Gernsback put it ("Science Wonder Stories" 5), I want to argue that we should give further consideration to these "diversions" and to the linkage of SF and the cinema if we are to craft more comprehensive and nuanced histories of SF's development, even if only as "a generic tendency."

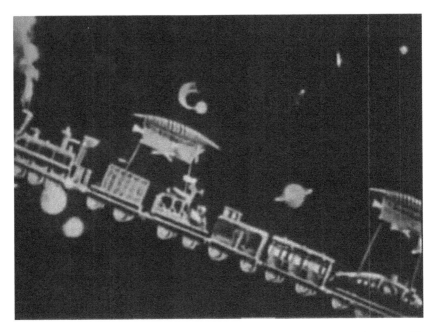

Figure 1.1. One of Melies's Verne-inspired "attractions": a space train in *An Impossible Voyage* (1904).

As a starting point for examining this early connection, I want to turn to the major pulp magazines, both the specialist ones previously noted and some, like *Weird Tales* and *Fantastic Adventures,* whose content overlapped several closely related genres. These publications were all a part of what John Rieder terms the developing "mass cultural system" (*Science Fiction* 1) that provided the foundation for modern SF's emergence, identity, and early definition, at least in the United States.[2] It is a foundation that practically every major history of the genre has acknowledged and addressed, since these pulps dominated SF publishing well into the 1950s. In support of his own emphasis on the critical role played by the "pulp idiom," Roberts in his history of the genre describes how the pulps managed to insert SF— and the broader SF imagination—into the popular consciousness, setting it alongside other elements of the modernist spirit, even sharing that spirit. Further emphasizing that shared attitude—as well as a possible link to film—Roberts also suggests that the pulps marked a significant "cultural shift" from an earlier SF (that which is usually bound to such mainstream and relatively conventional writers as Verne, Mary Shelley, Edgar Allen Poe, and H. G. Wells), because of the way those publications not only helped to shape SF's generic identity, but also to markedly shift it "from a verbal to a visual form of art" (186), thanks to their heavy reliance on elaborate cover art, internal story illustrations, and even a marked emphasis on visual description—all helping to craft what we might see as a rough correspondence to the early cinema of "attractions." In fact, we might even view this development as an early stage-setting for the great outpouring of SF film that would eventually follow, particularly in the post-war period. Thus, by considering the relationship between SF and the cinema, specifically as reflected in the great body of pre-World War II pulps, we might begin to see some of the reason for that "cultural shift" Roberts describes, and also better understand some of the ways in which the "script" of film intersected with pulp SF's own story, helping to reinforce its particular modernist vision and even introducing a new, combinatory term into both the SF pulps and the fanzines' discussions of the period—and one that has gone largely unremarked—the "scientifilm."[3] If, as Leo Charney and Vanessa R. Schwartz have argued in their study of early twentieth-century modernist culture, most "modern forms of experience relied . . . on the juncture of movement and vision: moving pictures" (6), then we would do well to consider how that same "juncture" surfaced in and supported the work of a developing SF literature, which was itself so obviously fascinated with movement, change, and visual dynamism, with basic characteristics of the modern age. In short, as Charney and Schwartz suggest, this work, like much of the rest of late modernist culture, might profitably be "best understood as inherently cinematic" (2).

At once both form and text, medium and message, pulp SF and film in this period actually functioned in a very similar manner, blurring conventional boundaries while prompting us to see the world in a new way, in part by framing it from the vantage provided by an ascendant science and technology. The pulps offered what some of the magazine editors commonly referred to as "thought experiments" or "thought variants," fictions that explored the trajectory or impact of various science-spurred developments or possibilities. How might we respond to some new technology or new discovery, such as robots, thinking machines, or the appearance of aliens, these SF stories wondered, while at times suggesting how such things could even, as Brooks Landon notes, "point toward the improvement of the world" (51). In similar fashion, film applied its technological apparatus not just to the recording of reality and helping us to see it in a new way, but also to producing its own quite fundamental "variants," even "improvements" on the real. For by its ability to reconstruct—or edit—our sense of time and space, film was able to afford entirely new perspectives on and experiences of (or experiments on) the world, as when Rene Clair's early SF film *Paris qui dort* (1924) introduces a machine that can make time—and all of Paris—stand still, while leaving the city open for intimate inspection and possibly better understanding by those who, by chance untouched by the machine's rays, wander the streets and examine its suddenly frozen reality (Figure 1.2). Such works demonstrate the possibility for other sorts of re-forming, even implicitly for a kind of utopian vision by implying that if film were able to real-ize some new circumstance, then its audiences might as well.

In the course of crafting such variants, both SF and film foregrounded their fundamental investment in what we might describe as a *visualizable world*. With that term I mean to suggest not just what Anne Friedberg terms "the predominance of the visible" that was taking hold in this period and that was demonstrated by the new emphasis on advertisements, visual entertainments of a great many sorts, and the practice of "window shopping" (*Window* 16), but its concomitant spirit, our ability to draw in a practical way on what Miriam Hansen allusively refers to as this age's "new visuality" (72): the common expectation that we *could visualize* much that had heretofore seemed beyond the powers of actual observation (lodged only hazily in the imagination), and thus that we could bring into focus and see those wonders that were SF's stock-in-trade as capable of being imported into our world, and as indeed *possible*.

Figure 1.2. Inspecting a pickpocket and a policeman, frozen in mid-chase in *Paris qui dort* (1924).

This expectation is at the heart of Casetti's description of what film generally offered to audiences in this late modernist period—how it had "developed a composite gaze, in which reality and fantasy merge, but in which the two planes are often carefully distinguished" (3). It is this same sense of a double or "composite gaze," of a realistic yet possible vision, that echoes in many of the comments of pulp editors like Gernsback, as they insisted that even the most fantastic contributions to their magazines should have a solid grounding in scientific fact and possibility, or as the masthead of *Amazing Stories* would put it, that "Extravagant Fiction" and "Cold Fact" are connected and could, profitably, function together. And while the former could draw from and build on the latter, it could also forecast the latter by inspiring the discovery of other "Cold Facts." By framing the pulps in terms of this shared or "composite" emphasis, by observing how in several ways SF and the cinema might during the pre-war period even be considered each other's shadow doubles, we might begin to build a broader foundation for SF history and start to see some reason not only in numerous commentators' description of film as in many ways science fictional, but also in the possibility for viewing SF as in many ways cinematic.

Indeed, even before Gernsback's nod in this direction, SF pioneer H. G. Wells was already pointing down this path, particularly as he became involved in another sort of "composite" project, one that promised to link both of these relatively new forms in an innovative kind of storytelling. In his study of the author, Keith Williams examines this linked interest, noting how, in both its style and subjects, Wells' early writing "yokes into a striking parallelism with cinema from the outset" (24)—a parallel that was quickly appreciated by British film pioneer Robert Paul[4] who, admiring Wells' work, contacted the author, and suggested a project through which they might collaboratively exploit this connection. The first extensive account of their contact shows up in Terry Ramsaye's pioneering history of film's early days, where he recounts how Paul approached Wells with an idea that would draw upon the strengths of both the author's SF and the filmmaker's new technology[5] through the creation of an elaborate device that would simulate time travel after the fashion described in Wells' *The Time Machine*. As outlined in the patent application (number 19984) filed on October 24, 1895, the mechanism Paul proposed would have audiences seated on a motorized, rocking platform, where they would feel wind currents blowing across their bodies to suggest forward or reverse motion, experience intermittent moments of light and dark to indicate rapidly passing time, and view projected film clips depicting different places and different times, providing them with the illusion of traveling in a Wellsian time machine. While Raymond Fielding suggests that the project's "excessive cost" most likely prompted Wells and Paul to abandon this plan for what he most fittingly describes as a "motion picture spacecraft" (117), the concept reminds us that even in the relative infancy of both forms, there was a recognition that they shared certain characteristics, particularly a potential for visualizing new ideas, that pioneers in these fields recognized and looked to explore this appeal, and that from this connection there might even emerge a new sort of narrative experience, or as Ramsaye sums up, "no less than a whole new art form" (158), drawing together the great possibilities afforded by SF literature and the cinema.

Another, closely related effort at such a "new art form"—and one that in fact took the shape of a spacecraft—would actually be constructed in this period and become a central attraction at the 1901 Pan American Exposition. This World's Fair had its own "composite" theme, as it aimed to celebrate the link between the new efforts at widespread electrification and the larger notion of technological progress, or as Kristen Whissel puts it, to demonstrate the intertwined "circuits of technological modernity" (121), after the fashion of the "circuit" of influences we are sketching here. One of the most popular attractions offered at the fair was Frederic Thompson and Elmer Dundy's SF experience, "A Trip to the Moon," a 40,000 square foot mixed-media show that featured a simulated flight to the moon via the winged airship *Luna*.[6] Riders boarded the *Luna*, felt it rock and sway as its massive mechanical wings began to flap, viewed projected images of the Earth as the ship seemed to lift off and gain altitude, and experienced the same air currents that the Wells/Paul project planned to use, as the riders then "flew" to the moon (Figure 1.3). Once there, they encountered Selenites, toured the Man in the Moon's palace, watched moon maidens dance, and, like the riders of so many theme park attractions today, had an opportunity to purchase souvenirs of their "trip." By various accounts the most successful attraction at the Exposition, "A Trip to the Moon" would be filmed by Thomas Edison later in 1901 and the film—now apparently lost—was distributed by his company, reportedly enjoying "tremendous sales" (Musser 33). After the Exposition's close, the show was recreated as a traveling attraction, the original ride was moved to Coney Island where it would give the name to the famous Luna Park entertainment area, and it would inspire a variety of early SF films, probably including, as Richard Abel and others have argued, Melies' *A Trip to the Moon*, easily the most famous work of the early SF cinema (135).

A number of other such new, SF-like, and quasi-cinematic narrative experiences would also emerge in the late nineteenth and early twentieth centuries, all building on this intersection of SF narrative and early film technology. Echoing Casetti's terminology, Thierry Lefebvre terms them

Figure 1.3. The "Trip to the Moon" attraction at the 1901 Pan American Exposition.

"composite" presentations, as he describes a number of such entertainments that appeared in Europe during this period—fairground demonstrations, illustrated lectures, and World's Fair exhibits, including astronomer and SF pioneer Camille Flammarion's "Panorama of Different Worlds," a presentation planned for the 1900 Paris Exposition or Exposition Universelle (50–51). Mining this same vein, Abel has catalogued a variety of traveling cycloramas, dioramas, plays, and carnival rides—including different versions of the 1901 "A Trip to the Moon" attraction—that toured the United States at the same time, all of them capitalizing on that "new visuality" of the age by using film or projected images in concert with the science fictional experiences they offered (134–35). And Lauren Rabinovitz, in the course of examining the amusement park's emergence in this period, has similarly chronicled the development of a number of fairground attractions that "fused motion pictures and the amusement park mechanical ride" (20). Among the most popular of these were the disaster and apocalypse shows (like the Galveston Flood attraction presented at the 1904 World's Fair) that, in the best tradition of SF wonder, physically placed viewers at the brink of some great calamity—an experience that was evoked by pyrotechnics, moving cars, blasts of air, and film projections. New but symptomatic entertainments, all of these "composite" or "fused" productions created their impact by linking SF or fantasy concepts with what Casetti describes as "the gaze that film claimed for the twentieth century" (2).

It is within this broad cultural context that we might begin to situate the more common sort of SF experience provided by the specialized SF pulps, and typically offered in the United States by titles like *Amazing Stories, Astounding Stories, Wonder Stories* (later *Thrilling Wonder Stories*), *Planet Stories*, and *Fantastic Adventures*, and in Britain by *Tales of Wonder, Fantasy*, and somewhat later by *New Worlds*. These and other publications offered their own sort of "composite" vision, one that we might link to pulp historian Mike Ashley's description of such specialized magazines as "the next logical step in the progression of science fiction" (1). Of course, the SF story itself, as we have already noted, was hardly new, and pulp-like magazines had been around long before Hugo Gernsback gave them a specifically SF focus with the introduction of *Amazing Stories* in 1926. In France Pierre Hetzel had begun publishing his *Magasin d'education et de recreation* in 1864, featuring the work of Jules Verne. Germany, Sweden, and Russia all produced magazines or serial fiction containing some SF and fantasy in the late nineteenth and early twentieth centuries—with titles like *Der Luftpirat* (Germany), *Stella* (Sweden), and *Mir Prikliuchenii/World of Adventures* (Russia). In England popular magazines throughout the nineteenth century published a variety of proto-SF stories, a trend that notably increased late in the century as periodicals took up the practice of liberally spicing their pages with illustrations and photographs, an approach that especially favored SF, Ashley argues, because "the genre particularly lent itself to clever ideas for new inventions which could now be comically illustrated rather than laboriously described" (7).

In America both magazines and dime novels had flourished during the nineteenth century, each offering a ready home to a nascent SF literature, in part because America was such a technologically enthusiastic culture. That enthusiasm, as Ashley suggests, meant that "any fiction that explored social or scientific advance" tended to be "not only welcomed but encouraged" (18), gaining a ready readership. Thus by the 1890s one could find a variety of serialized novels, such as those published by the *Frank Reade Library*, as well as pulp magazine antecedents like *Munsey's Magazine* and *The Argosy*, all regularly mixing in a few SF-type stories among their other literary offerings, while they also, symptomatic of their modern flavor, as Jess Nevins points out, "actively incorporated the material of science fiction" within other genre stories as well (94). Moreover, these general pulp publications, with their "preponderance of science-fictional tropes, motifs, and plots" (Nevins 94), increasingly assumed a highly visual character, illustrating their pieces with dynamic line drawings or photographs, such as the *Frank Reade Library*'s action-oriented cover images for stories like "Frank Reade, Jr. and His New Steam Man" (1892, 1.1), "Frank Reade, Jr.'s New Electric Submarine Boat" (1893, 1.17), and "Frank Reade, Jr. and His Electric Prairie Schooner" (1894, 3.70). These fanciful and dynamic images of new technologies dramatically at work gave the stories' SF imaginings added resonance, while anticipating the visual turn that would become a hallmark of so much modern popular culture.

Also helping to construct this context of a visualized science and technology were the various electric and radio-oriented magazines that began appearing in the 1900s to 1910s, publications such as *Modern Electrics* (1908–14), *Wireless Age* (1913–25), *The Electrical Experimenter* (1913–20), and *Radio News* (1919–59), among others.[7] Their often artistic covers, internal photographs (both *Electrical Experimenter* and *Science and Invention* requested that any submissions be accompanied by "good photographs"), schematic drawings, and illustrated advertisements for radio and electrical parts readily suggest the impact of that new visuality of the age, while their focus on the science surrounding the new technology of radio anticipates the scientific emphasis—and appeal—that would help drive the specialized SF pulps that emerged just a few years later (Figure 1.4). In fact, Gernsback would found several of these hobby-type magazines, in part as a way of selling radio kits and components to enthusiasts of the new technology, but also, as his lead editorial in the first issue of *Radio News* proudly proclaims, as an effort at promoting the "astounding growth of the art" of radio ("Why" 4). While suggesting another dimension of that "composite" character we have been noting, this overt effort to link the radio with "art," technology with aesthetics, seems particularly noteworthy, since it explicitly points to the more than technical appeal that Gernsback and others ascribed to the work of science, to the stories these scientific publications often included, and to the general nature of these magazines—as something much more than hobbyist entertainment.

It is an appeal that gives reason to two important developments in these early radio/science/invention magazines that look toward the later, specialized SF pulps. The first of these is the introduction of a science-laced fiction—even full-fledged SF—into some of these publications, with Gernsback again proving a key figure in this development. In 1911 he began the serialization of his pioneering SF novel *Ralph 124C 41+* in his *Modern Electrics*, a practice he would continue in this magazine, and one that he carried over to his *Electrical Experimenter*, where, alongside articles on "Ball

Figure 1.4. Radio and hobby magazines offer an SF-like vision of the latest in science and technology (*Electrical Experimenter*, Aug. 1918).

Lightning" and "The Transmission of Photographs Telegraphically," he serialized his second novel *Baron Munchausen's New Scientific Adventures* and published short stories by other authors. Attesting to its success, this pattern would continue in that publication's successor *Science and Invention*, which regularly included SF stories. Most often the fiction appearing in these magazines was of a sort that Mike Ashley and Robert Lowndes term the "scientific problem story" (49), usually serious but sometimes comic explorations of a scientific principle, at times illustrated, and with many of them highlighting the primary and highly popular technology that was most prominently featured and, as noted previously, actively sold by these magazines, the radio.

The second development is their special treatment of the emerging medium of the radio, as it inspired a new vein of SF stories. We might situate these various radio/science/invention pulps as part of what Jeffrey Sconce describes as the "enthusiastic celebration" of the emerging medium of radio during the first decades of the twentieth century. Assessing that enthusiasm, Sconce observes how popular culture of the time attached an almost "abstract wonder" to the phenomenon of "electronic communication through the open air" or the "ocean of ether," evoking a nearly magical sense that was both "fascinating" and "disturbing" (62), and suggesting the sort of technology that easily tapped into SF's "wonder" appeal. In fact, that appeal helps explain why much of the SF of the 1920s, appearing in the Gernsback magazines, other wireless periodicals, as well as the emerging specialized pulps, was awash with references to radio sets, radio transmitters, and radio frequencies. Plots involved a wide variety of radio applications, such as the use of the radio as a mysterious remote control device, seen in Robert Francis Smith's "The Strong Arm Circuit" (*Radio News*, May 1925); the discovery of puzzling, seemingly deadly radio signals, as in C. Sterling Gleason's scientific mystery "The Voice of the People" (*Radio News*, Nov. 1927); and the reception of warning messages from other planets in Ray Cummings' serialized space opera *Tarrano the Conqueror* (*Science and Invention*, July 1925–Aug. 1926). Resonating with the magazines' many ads for radio components, radio training, and books about radio, as well as readers' letters detailing their problems and accomplishments with this technology, these stories suggest an educated, enthusiastic, and highly media-conscious audience, interested in how the latest science and technology were impacting their lives. But more to the point, these magazines, their media-focused fiction, and various other features also anticipate how another, even more popular technology, film, would similarly become integrated into the new SF pulps that would soon appear.

Of course, the specialized SF magazines that show up in the later 1920s would take a focus somewhat different from the radio and invention magazines. The radio would still figure significantly in the plots of many of their early stories, as evidence: Charles S. Wolfe's "Whispering Ether" (*Amazing Stories*, June 1926), in which the radio becomes a model for mental telepathy and an advanced receiver capable of capturing—or intercepting—thoughts; Leslie F. Stone's space exploration tale "Out of the Void" (*Amazing Stories*, Aug.–Sept. 1929), which revolves around the construction of powerful interplanetary transmitters; or Edsel Newton's "The Torpedo Terror" (*Wonder Stories* Sept. 1930), which describes how radio becomes a device for conducting remote control warfare. But increasingly film would take the radio's place of prominence—and fascination—as the latter technology underwent a major shift in cultural valence. William Boddy has chronicled this shift, recounting how once the radio assumed a significant role in "the new consumer economy" of the 1920s, its appeal too changed (37). Thanks to a variety of developments, including the growth of commercial stations and networks, government regulation of the airwaves, changes in radio design, and especially a shift in audience, the original concerns of radio users became "increasingly marginalized" (41) and the medium began to lose its original SF appeal—or in a few cases to take on more menacing roles, such as a force for mind control or a device for remote combat. Echoing the notion that the SF pulps were largely a masculine form, Boddy also argues that the building and use of radios, once "an activity of adolescent male hobbyists," gave way to a new characterization, thanks to the "US industry's construction of the radio listener as distracted housewife" (41), along with the radio's new position as a familiar domestic appliance, even a decorative piece of furniture. In light of this shift, the SF pulps' increasing emphasis on film with its more fundamental visual or scopophilic appeal—one that could easily draw in that "adolescent male" audience while also drawing its audience out of the home—seems a rather natural development.

But cinematic resonances were just a small part of the different sort of narrative experience that the new specialized SF pulps would provide. Where detective and western stories largely dominated the pulp market early in the decade, where SF-type stories appeared just intermittently in those earlier pulp magazines like *The Argosy* or in near-kin such as *Weird Tales*, and where serious science-oriented publications like *Modern Electrics, Electrical Experimenter*, or *Science and Mechanics* irregularly included fictional contributions, magazines such as *Amazing Stories, Astounding Stories*, and *Wonder Stories* had a singular and avowedly serious focus. They gathered together a variety of SF story types—ones about strange inventions, interplanetary travel, biological transformations, etc.—that typically had their roots in scientific fact and with an announced aim not just to entertain but also, as Gernsback with an eye to both scientific and artistic possibilities claimed, to open readers' minds to the new possibilities afforded by science and technology, "offer 'inspiration' to inventors" or young scientists who might be interested in pursuing "new ideas" (qtd. in Westfahl 20), and take readers, or fans as they became known, along a trajectory leading from fantasy to the "Cold Facts" of the modern—and future—world.

More precisely, these publications offered a new amalgam of elements found in the varied predecessors we have described, truly "composite" experiences themselves that, in addition to their SF stories, included a similarly focused bill of fare. Thus their tables of contents typically listed discussion columns that aimed to bring readers together in sharing their enthusiasm for this new literature and, as in the radio/invention magazines, the scientific ideas it offered; contests of various sorts, sometimes with promised (if not always paid) cash prizes; different kinds of quizzes, most often testing basic scientific knowledge; short, factual pieces, such as the "Scientifacts" column of *Thrilling Wonder Stories* or *Amazing*'s "This Amazing Universe"; advertisements, frequently illustrated, some of them aimed at those with an interest in what we might term hobby science but others marketing a wide gamut of nostrums, novelties, and educational opportunities; and reviews of new SF novels and, later on, of pertinent films. Another and indeed a key part of this diverse package was the lively color covers and interior illustrations that pleasurably visualized the strange places, figures, and contraptions described in the stories. The product was a self-reinforcing composite—one we might well liken to an amusement ride—that attracted a large following and resulted in a number of imitators and offshoots, all focused on the general fascination with science and technology that marked the late modernist era, while giving that fascination an additional dimension through an emphatic emphasis on what I have termed the visualizable nature of these attractions.

As suggested previously, though, a largely overlooked part of that emphasis—and an important component of the pulps' own composite gaze—was that analogous agent and near double, the cinema. Ultimately, even more than radio, the movies—and the movie industry—filtered into the pulp experience not just in spirit, but also in a variety of quite substantial ways during this formative era. As I began this study, armed with some background on late modernist culture, I simply assumed as much. I also expected to find one primary and substantial manifestation of this relationship, that of the film advertising which, I was sure, Hollywood would have undertaken to promote its early SF-like efforts—films such as *The Mysterious Island* (1929), *Just Imagine* (1930), *Frankenstein* (1931), and *The Invisible Man* (1933)—to a specialized and rapidly growing readership of the sort associated with the SF pulps. However, after searching through the primary pre-war pulps, I was surprised to find that there were practically no film ads of the sort that the newspapers and non-specialist magazines of the era boasted in plenty. Yet at the same time, and in their place, I discovered a great many other and hardly subtle traces of the cinema that cropped up throughout the pages—and covers—of *Amazing Stories, Astounding*

Stories, Wonder Stories, Startling Stories, Thrilling Wonder Stories, and their ilk. So while ads for specific films proved disappointingly elusive, I repeatedly glimpsed the instantly recognizable shadow of a cinematic presence throughout the pre-war pulps—a presence that not only attested to the deep imprint of film on the popular consciousness of the time, one that seemed to go much deeper than the "wonder" of radio, but also suggested another way in which modernism's new visuality was being translated into the new world and new language of SF.

We can track this cinematic presence across the whole pulp landscape in a variety of ways. Most obviously, and as in the radio/invention magazines, there are stories that involve the movies, their technology, or the movie industry; there is a noticeable tendency to advertise film-related jobs and film products of various sorts; there are recurrent editorial and reader discussions about how films—or as they were often termed, in an apparent effort to claim a kinship to the literature, scientifilms—fit within the larger context of SF and its fandom; there are reviews of many of the major SF films produced in the pre-war period; and then there are the celebrated—although at times also criticized—illustrations, both within the stories and, more significantly, on the covers of the pulps, that visually, arrestingly, and unmistakably contribute to this composite identity I have described, binding the cinema to the work of the SF imagination while adding an emphatic scopophilic stamp (Figure 1.5). All these traces suggest that film, like the SF genre itself, was generally seen not just as one more product of the Machine Age, but, after the fashion that Casetti describes, as a fundamental element of the modernist climate, a "constant point of reference" (1), a sign of the era's decidedly visual thrust, and an important component of its imagination. In short, film was obviously influencing how audiences "read" this scientifically and technologically inflected era, including, as I am suggesting, how SF itself presented this new climate—as a world that could, and indeed *should*, be *seen* in a new way, as a realm of visualizable possibilities.

With the exception of John Cheng's analysis of the complex fandom that the pulps helped to develop, however, most histories and discussions of SF's emergence and development in the late modernist period have largely looked past this character in order to concentrate on what Gernsback termed the pulps' "charming" stories. That is, the very understandable tendency of most commentary has been to focus primarily on modern SF's noteworthy literary roots, a pattern that Gernsback demonstrated when, in trying to outline the genre's scope, he pointed rather broadly to "the Jules Verne, H. G. Wells, and Edgar Allan Poe type of story" as a model, and when, to fill out the very first issue of *Amazing Stories*—and others

Figure 1.5. Pulp covers exploit the new visuality of the modern age, linking their appeal to the cinema experience (*Amazing*, Dec. 1936).

thereafter—he reprinted what he referred to as the "prophetic" fiction that had been produced by each of these genre fathers ("A New Sort of Magazine" 3). Logically, most genre histories have generally followed this lead, framing SF as a particular sort of literature that, inspired by these early figures, incorporates a great range of narrative—and sometimes dramatic—efforts. But most of those accounts, as I would suggest, are typically characterized by a kind of media exclusivity, as they have emphasized the genre's literary lineage—and nature—while largely neglecting some other shaping influences on this "art," such as film (or, for that matter, radio).

Of course, other media were drawing on the same scientific and technological source material, even adapting—and, in the process, leaving their own imprint on—key SF texts. We can readily see this activity, this similar response to the period, at work in the cinema with the appearance of Melies' 1907 trick film *Under the Seas*, the 1916 live-action feature *Twenty Thousand Leagues under the Sea*, and the 1917 animated burlesque *20,000 Feats under the Sea*, all of them based on the famous Jules Verne novel, and all "telling" the Verne story in different ways and with very different aims. But other films, both earlier and later, were spurred as much by the very spirit of the Machine Age as by an antecedent SF literature, as they worked independently of such source material to explore subject matter similar to that which would surface in the pulps during the genre's early development. Pioneering films like *A Trip to Mars* (1910), *The Inventor's Secret* (1911), *The Conquest of the Pole* (1912), and *The Mechanical Man* (1921) offer stories about, respectively, space exploration, mad scientists, fantastic inventions, and menacing robots—that is, about the same subjects that were inspiring the new body of pulp fiction. What is also noteworthy about these early films is that they present their science fictional material with less of an emphasis on narratizing their subjects than on producing compelling visual spectacles or, to return to Gunning's term, "attractions." In their deployment of these spectacular images, though, we can see how the cinema was, from a very early moment, already staking out a place in the larger SF imagination, already setting up camp within its boundaries, already underscoring the extent to which SF was a very fluid, indeed "composite" form, as film drew upon its own very visual and highly "attractive" ability to do what the best SF sought to accomplish, that is, as Joseph Corn and Brian Horrigan simply put it, to "make a dazzling futuristic dream come true" (14).

That sense of making a "dream come true," of bringing it to life or visualizing the work of the broader SF imagination, is, in fact, one of the most consistent notes struck in the pulps, with their stories and features on current and future technology working, as Corn and Horrigan argue, practically as "exhortations to the readers to project themselves into the future, literally to remake themselves" (8). It is the sort of assessment that is very much in tune with Gernsback's approach to the larger "art" of which SF was a part. He consistently claimed a highly serious, even "prophetic" purpose for the work of his magazines, whether it was the pulp fiction of an *Amazing Stories* or the popular science articles to be found in a sister publication like *Science and Invention*. Such material, he believed, was valuable because it could "interest young readers in science and channel them into scientific or technological careers" (Bleiler xxi), in effect, changing their lives by making their personal and cultural dreams for the future a reality. It is an ideal, I would suggest, that also becomes quite literally visible when we begin to survey those various ways in which film surfaced in this early literature.

By examining a few of the most common pulp features where that media influence becomes especially visible, then, the following chapters will help us to better understand some of the specific ways in which these cinematic imaginings resonated in and with SF's early development. As we shall see, advertising, offering to sell films, film images, and film equipment to readers, but also suggesting opportunities for work within the film industry, is one of those areas that readily shows traces of the genre's composite form (Figure 1.6). A second is the fiction, the primary attraction of the pulps. Just as the radio magazines included stories centered around the radio's pervasive presence, in the SF pulps we frequently encounter stories that are about the world of film or that explore film's cultural impact. But also—and significantly—we find ones that speak the rhetoric of the cinema, drawing images, metaphors, even characters from the audience's shared film experience, and in the process reminding us that new experiences produce new words to address those experiences and, in turn, produce a new sense of what our world is like. A third area, and one just as telling as the fiction, is the extensive dialogue between editors, writers, and fans that took place largely in the various readers' columns sported by all of the SF pulps. In these "backyard" type conversations, as John Cheng styles them (52), as well as in the reviews that would increasingly appear through the pre-war years, we get a clear sense of just how much literature and film were seen as mutually engaged with the serious function of SF, mutually reinforcing the work of the SF imagination, and mutually appealing. In one of the pulps' most obvious exploitations of modernism's new visuality, their colorful covers and interior illustrations, we can observe a fourth major link to the world of the movies, with images that repeatedly draw on film-like activities—photographing, projecting, even watching motion pictures—while also underscoring the implicitly shared project of SF and

Figure 1.6. The pulps offer training to enter the movie business, putting readers "behind the camera" (*Amazing*, Jan. 1930).

the movies. As a postscript, as well as a reminder of how the modernist climate changed in character with the coming of World War II and its Cold War aftermath—as well as how much the genre was itself still evolving— we shall also look at how these same categories help to measure out a shift in both SF literature and film during this later period, marking a kind of cleavage in that composite activity as the pulps recede from their place of prominence, as SF becomes recognized as akin to "serious" literature, and as the SF film itself gains a new cultural popularity—even notoriety.

I want to emphasize that the tracing out of this shift and describing the various forms of that pulp/film linkage do not radically alter the trajectory of SF that has already been chronicled in most major histories of the genre, particularly those by James, Landon, and Roberts.[8] But by emphasizing this modernist linkage—or what I have described for convenience as a composite character—of film and the pulp literature, we might, as John Reider has suggested, begin to gain a better sense "of the capaciousness and complexity that a narrative of the formation and maintenance of SF would entail" ("On Defining" 206). All history has texture but SF in part because of what Mark Bould and Sherryl Vint describe as its rather "fluid and tenuous" character (48), both challenges and invites ongoing efforts to examine and describe its generic texture, how it proceeds in its "generic tendency," and how its emphases subtly change over time. By considering SF in the context of what Reider terms "a shared territory" ("On Defining" 204), in this case one "shared" with the cinema, we might better appreciate its early history and especially its ties to that heady late-modernist "atmosphere" that, as Gernsback hazily offered, gave it such life and breath.

CHAPTER 2
The Pulps in the Consumer's Republic

In trying to assess the broad appeal of pulp magazines, Erin A. Smith notes that it "is easy to overlook" the pulps' "significant participation in consumer culture," in part because of a commonly made "distinction between the pulps and the advertising-supported slicks" (50). "Slick" magazines were so-called because they were printed on higher-quality, glossy paper, while they also usually catered to a wide audience, or as John Rieder puts it, one of "calculated variety or hybridity," that allowed them to publish fiction that "was as popular and risk-free as possible" (*Science Fiction* 51). In contrast, the pulps published for a narrower or niche readership were generally not as dependent on national advertising as the more expensively produced slicks, and consequently they contained fewer ads—and of different sorts—than did more elaborate, high-brow publications such as *Harper's*, *Saturday Evening Post*, and *Collier's*. Yet it would be a mistake to overlook this element of the pulps' composite package, as many have, for in the ways they address their readership, the pulps' ads tell us a good deal about both the magazines and their audience, or as Smith in her discussion of other sorts of pulps puts it, their "patterns in the advertising . . . offer a rough indication of the readers' concerns" (9). In the specific case of the SF pulps, the ads often literally visualize how the readers' concerns and those of the magazines themselves intersected with the modern world of the movies.

While the pulp audience may indeed have differed from that of the slicks, it was *not* the case, as some commentators have claimed, that the pulps did not market with that audience in mind or that they "carried little consumer advertising" (Cheng 23). As Rieder argues, in the 1920s and 1930s the "new genre" of SF was responding "not just to changing social conditions but also to the new commercial opportunities being opened up by a new mode of publicity—mass cultural distribution—and the new business model that organizes mass cultural publicity around advertising" (*Science Fiction* 163). That model was already informing Hugo Gernsback's early magazine efforts, such as *Electrical Experimenter, Radio News*, and *Science and Invention*, wherein we see their editor's obvious efforts to market his own and others' electrical products, with each magazine liberally interspersing its technical articles, how-to pieces, and even fiction with many pages of ads, hawking radio parts, books, novelties, and various sorts of professional instruction. Trying to differentiate the thrust of the SF pulps from these predecessors, Rieder notes that when Gernsback published the first issue of *Amazing Stories* in 1926 it contained only four pages of advertising in its one hundred pages of text, from which he assumes that "advertisers were not abundant" (52). Yet that seems a problematic conclusion for a period of rapid—even too rapid—economic expansion in the United States and for a new magazine trying to reach a relatively new audience. While that pattern of scant advertising continued for a few issues, *Amazing* gradually grew its advertising base, just as it did its readership, so that by the ninth issue it included 14 pages containing advertising, a year later there were 24 pages of such promotions, and when Gernsback's *Wonder Stories* debuted in 1930—and with Gernsback calling upon many of the same advertisers who had appeared in his previous publications—it did so with 24 pages featuring advertisements, which translates to a rather considerable number of advertisers[1] helping to support SF's quickly developing place in the mass cultural genre system, while also signaling some of the interests shared by its growing fanbase.

We should also note that, like the earlier radio and invention magazines, the early SF pulps, along with Gernsback's *Air Wonder Stories* and *Science Wonder Stories*, followed a very similar pattern in their approach to advertising. Each publication featured the same sort of large-scale, even full-page notices, usually placed at the front or back of the issue, columns of smaller, often illustrated ads, typically in the later pages of the magazine, and what Gernsback termed "ad-lets," that is, classified columns of 25 to 50 word solicitations, advertising products, services, or offers to trade specific items. I want to emphasize this "consumer" dimension of the SF pulps not just because, apart from Rieder's brief discussion, it has received little notice in commentaries on SF's early development, but because a number of those ads directly implicate the cinema and a kind of cinematic mindset in ways that can help us begin to give more specificity to the film influence that the previous chapter only broadly described.

Before considering the focus of those ads and what they might tell us about the pulps and their readership, though, we should first give some attention to their very nature. Both the full-page ads and the column pieces—those that were typically arranged vertically three or four in a row along the outside and inside columns of a page where readers' eyes customarily go first—were usually in black and white, often were illustrated, and typically used multiple type sizes and fonts. In the larger of these and certainly in the case of the full-page pieces, they also commonly employed dynamic design principles that set them apart from those appearing in earlier generations of magazines and the small ad-lets. These principles involved the use of differing sizes of print and image, mixed boxes and circles enclosing print, diagonally arranged images, irregularly shaped coupons, and so on. With their prominent placement of images and dynamic design schemes (Figure 2.1), the ads were highly visual attractions in themselves and might remind us of a point made in the previous chapter, where we noted how film in its first decades was driven not by a narrative impulse but by what film historians have termed a principle of "attractions," or as Tom Gunning puts it, a kind of "exhibitionist" spirit, as the early cinema frequently "displays its visibility" ("Cinema" 64). It seems no great leap to see in this advertising something like that "exhibitionist" spirit at work in the pulps, for even though the magazines' primary purpose was to sell narratives—as short stories or serialized novels—to the growing body of SF consumers, they often did so by capitalizing on a similar principle of "attractions."

In his own effort at clarifying this somewhat allusive, even elusive description of early movies, film theorist Andre Gaudreault posed the natural question, "what exactly is an attraction?" and his explanation is one that resonates for both film and the sort of advertising that this chapter will consider. As he offers, we might think of the attraction as "a moment of pure 'visual display' characterized by an implicit acknowledgment of the viewer's presence, a viewer who is directly confronted with an exhibitionist display" (50) that seems to have been created expressly for his or her gaze. It is further, he suggests, a pointedly non-narrative moment, as when one of the "outlaws" in Edwin S. Porter's early film *The Great Train Robbery* (1903) stands against a blank backdrop and fires his gun at the camera (Figure 2.2), effectively providing an emblem of the exciting and Western character of the film, but without any particular placement in or link to its narrative.[2] However, as film would develop its more pointedly narrative thrust during the late 1910s and 1920s, such attractions would be transformed into a kind of common point of punctuation or accent, as in the case of a character's reaction shot or a sudden close-up of a telling,

Figure 2.1. One of Coyne's dynamic ads for opportunities in radio, television, and talking pictures (*Wonder Stories*, Nov. 1930).

perhaps ironic detail. Such "attractive" or compelling shots were folded into and became just one more component in the larger cinematic "infrastructure" (51), much as do the various ads, I want to suggest, that demonstrate a similar spirit at work in one typical element of the general pulp magazine infrastructure.

I want to emphasize this similarity in presence and function in order to introduce one of the ways in which the pulps participated in the same

Figure 2.2. A typical "attraction," a cowboy fires his pistol into the camera in *The Great Train Robbery* (1903).

modernist thrust as the cinema or, as Gernsback put it, breathed from the same atmosphere. Before, after, and even in the midst of turning the pages to read an SF narrative, the pulp reader, too, was "directly confronted" by "an exhibitionist display" designed to attract his or her attention. As examples we might consider such placements as the National Radio Institute ad in the very first issue of *Amazing Stories* wherein a well-dressed man points a finger at and fixes the viewer with his eyes to drum home his imperative message, "Be a Radio Expert!" (July 1926, 2); in *Wonder Stories* where a suggestively illustrated piece promises to reveal "At Last! Secrets of Sex and Marriage" (Aug. 1933, 100); or when any of the numerous body-building ads that appeared in most of the pulps challenged readers to remake their physiques after the strongman images of Charles Atlas, George F. Jowett, or Lionel Strongfort. We should see such ads, preceding, following, and in some cases enframing the other "products" here, that is, the SF narratives, as less an annoyance or distraction from the real work of SF and the SF pulps than as film-like attractions, punctuating or adding spice to the full bill of fare that was being served up by the magazines and contributing to the larger modernist atmosphere within which the science fictional elements were to be properly consumed.

Harold Brainerd Hersey, editor and founder of several chains of pulp magazines, including the short-lived SF pulp *Miracle Science and Fantasy Stories* (1931), offers precisely this sort of characterization in the course of his insider's account of the pulp industry. As he discusses the role of advertising, Hersey explains that the pulps were typically designed to offer their readers two allied "methods of escape from reality" (77). The first and most obvious was their fiction, a "magic carpet that carries the reader off to parts unknown," and the second was "their advertising of comparatively inexpensive means to keep the reader physically and mentally fit so that he can take the hero's part" in the various adventures he was reading—or dreaming—about (77). Even beyond that sense of mutually reinforcing elements, Hersey indicates that pulp editors and publishers alike saw the advertising as an important component of the magazine's larger strategy, with the pages dedicated to ads "as much a part of the magazine as those devoted to stories: parallel lines spoken . . . with but a single thought: to catch and hold the reader's attention," much like the various acts in the then-popular vaudeville programs (83), or the assorted offerings that might be found on a typical movie bill of fare throughout the pre-war and into the early post-war eras.

I want to suggest, then, that we need to consider the constant advertising boxes, columns, and pages in the SF pulps not as extraneous "noise" or distractions from the fiction contained therein, but as additional, even integral attractions that helped serve the aims commonly associated with SF in this emergent period. As Gernsback's editorial in the first issue of *Amazing* offered, good scientifiction stories "have the knack of imparting knowledge, and even inspiration" ("A New Sort" 3) to their readers, suggesting that they might, thanks to the SF experience, actually transform both the self and the world in which they live. And many advertisements of the sort cited earlier certainly smack of this modernist flavor of change or development, as they speak of personal improvement ("Correct Your Nose!" promised one common ad, "Enjoy Perfect Vision!" said another), of individual fulfillment ("'Cash in' on Your Unrealized Abilities," offered one), of having a stake in the future ("Is This Prize Yours?" wondered yet another). They appealed to an audience interested in altering or making a difference in their lives, and when viewed in this light, they help remind us of how SF, too, from its earliest development, was marked by a kind of utopian or at least hopeful thrust, as it explored various possibilities for *producing difference*—in the world or the self—and how much its readers were also invested in such hopes.

In the United States this sense of change and potential was, as we have already hinted, a prominent part of another cultural development of the pre-war years, the emergence of the new consumer culture or what noted historian Lizabeth Cohen has dubbed "the Consumers' Republic" (11) of modern America. As Cohen explains, this concept was an integral component of the new American economy that was taking shape in the early twentieth century—one that had at its base not the sort of socialist agenda that was playing out so violently in Europe, but a collaborative triad of government, business, and newly formed consumer groups that, particularly after the onset of the Depression, saw the development of the new "citizen consumer ideal" as one of the keys to combating that situation and achieving long-term prosperity and cultural development. This "ideal" thus emphasized the attractions of consumerism (28) as another kind of punctuation or spice for the budding narrative of modern America, as consumers, through the work of advertising, were encouraged to dream, to shop, and thereby to function as important participants in building—or rebuilding—a modern America. In effect, constructing this consumer identity became central to building the future, to creating hope, even in the face of the Depression, and to reaching for a certain kind of utopian or science-fictional ideal. This effort is one that we can see reflected in the variety of advertising that was a routine part of the pulp experience throughout this period.

To better sketch the relationship between pulp advertising and the model of cinematic attractions or, as Gunning also terms them, "astonishments," I want to consider the pulps' ads under a number of their most common categories, particularly as they related to film, filmmaking, and film consumption. One and probably the most frequent type of film-connected ad drew precisely on that notion of personal identity and fulfillment by offering instruction, especially in media technologies, and ultimately the promise of jobs that were connected in various ways to the film industry. A second type addressed individuals who might wish to be involved in the movies at a creative level, as writers, actors, and even "stars." A third sort of ad directly appeals to the SF pulp audience as also a movie audience: one that collects film-related materials, that regularly attends the movies, and that might even purchase home versions of popular movies. Taken together, these various kinds of advertising underscore not only the abiding consumerist attraction of the movies throughout the pre-war period—a point when their appeal was, like SF itself, rapidly growing, and when they were already being used to "sell" the public on many things—but also the way in which a cinematic imagination was already a part of, even a reinforcement for the SF imagination, with both (and here we might evoke Hersey's description of the typical pulp strategy as composed of "parallel lines . . . with but a single thought") drawing their energy from the larger modernist agenda.

As we have seen, an emphasis on personal improvement, on the training that could almost guarantee one a place in the new "Consumer's Republic," was a note commonly struck in the pulp advertising. Among the many different types of personal improvement ads were those offering weight gain tablets, weight loss appliances, skin cleansers like Fleischmann's Yeast Treatment, hair growth topicals, nose straighteners, and especially the seemingly ubiquitous body-building courses that were typified by Charles Atlas's long running ads, which at times took the form of a visuals-heavy comic and always promised, on a note of direct address, with a stripped-down Atlas looking right at the reader, to "make you a new man." Among the many other promised make-overs were various programs to learn to play a musical instrument, instruction in becoming "a master of magic," draftsmanship lessons, and even training as a "scientific detective." More clearly aimed at an SF audience were the many other ads describing personal opportunities in technological or scientific careers. These include notices promising "Big Money in Chemistry," showing an "Amazingly Easy Way to Get into Electricity," or—in a most obvious illustration of the rather dreamy dimension that characterized many such notices—the Aviation Institute of America's ad offering aircraft pilot training "at home." All of these opportunities for reshaping the self or finding a new future were readily available to anyone willing to send away for the usual booklets, training manuals, or mail-order lessons. However, to get a better sense of their presumed audience, we might note that such opportunities generally seem targeted at a male audience, a point underscored by Erin Smith, who fashions, extrapolating from the bulk of such advertising, a less-than-flattering portrait of the typical pulp reader, someone she describes as a young man largely "concerned with getting autonomous, well-paid work, practical education, and products to enhance his embattled manliness" (11).

While Smith's characterization may be somewhat exaggerated,[3] it finds some support in one of the most common types of advertising found in the first decades of the pulps, a sort that appears in all the major publications and suggests a direct link to the entertainment industries that might have seen SF fans as ready subjects for their appeals. Repeatedly, readers were promised "Good Jobs . . . in Radio-Television-Talking Pictures," jobs that involved not just the expected technological training, such as electronics expertise or radio repair—which would have been natural adjuncts to Gernsback's original fascination with and promotion of electronics and radios—but notably skill positions in various areas of the still young and growing film industry, such as projectionists, soundmen, or even camera operators. In fact, as early as the December 1926 issue of *Amazing*, the tellingly titled Movie Operators School of Detroit was advertising for

"Men . . . to Learn Motion Picture Projection," while promising them "short hours, big pay" (870). Similarly guaranteeing "Big Pay" as well as "Fascinating Work," the New York Institute of Photography offered to train not just projectionists but "movie cameramen" for jobs directly in the film industry (*Amazing*, Jan. 1931, 959), which at this point still had a significant studio presence in the New York area, credibly allowing the Institute to claim quick placements for its trainees. The well-established Coyne Electrical School of Chicago, which had first begun business at approximately the same time that the film industry appeared on the scene, was one of the more frequent advertisers in all of the pulps. Its typically full-page ads, such as the "Good Jobs" notice cited earlier, touted the school's record for "placing men" in well-paying jobs and described its completely equipped film facilities, which could provide training not only in camera operation, but also in the use of "both 'sound on film' and 'sound on disk'" recording technologies (*Wonder Stories*, Oct. 1931, 579)—a description that, while promising to prepare its graduates to work with whatever sound recording format would eventually rule the film industry as it continued to transition from silent to "talking pictures," clearly implied that its nationwide pulp audience had a fairly sophisticated understanding of early film technology, of how both the aural and visual gaze of the movies was constructed.

Perhaps the most interesting advertisement in this area, though, was one that not only offered training in various film technologies, but also sought to capitalize on the way in which film had become such a common part of modern life and of everyone's experience. Appearing in multiple issues of *Amazing Stories*, a half-page ad for the tellingly titled "National School of Visual Education" offered the usual training in a number of electrical and mechanical fields, including various areas of "talking movies" (Figure 2.3). However, it differentiated itself from the many other such schools and educational opportunities we have noted through its unique mode of instruction, foregrounded in its ads. It promised "easier, quicker, better" results for its students "through Motion Pictures right in your own home," even offering to provide a DeVry motion picture projector for use with its training films "at no extra cost." Obviously trying to appeal to a clientele thoroughly familiar with the movies, fascinated by their technology, and receptive to the latest "scientific" developments in education, the National School headlined its offering with a motto that combines several of the educational lures we have already noted: "Take the Film Way to Bigger Pay" (Aug. 1929, 475).

Another common category of advertising played upon a very different appeal and sought to reach another sort of reader, although again one largely conceived as male. Besides providing the limited technical training

Figure 2.3. The National School of Visual Education offers a "Film Way to Bigger Pay" (*Amazing*, Aug. 1929).

that might qualify someone for what might only turn out to be fringe film industry jobs—if jobs there were at all in the deepest Depression years— many ads solicited readers who dreamed of being more directly involved in the film world by participating creatively. Thus a series of offers in *Amazing Stories*, linked to one of the ubiquitous body-building courses, promised to "Put You in the Movies," while offering a "Free Trip to Hollywood" to those judged to have particularly "athletic" bodies or striking appearances. Going a step further, while extrapolating from the appeal of Charles Atlas's promise to build a "new man," Joe Bonomo's physical culture ads in *Astounding Stories* underscored their promise to help clients attain a movie-star-like body with an arresting headline, "Movie Contract Guaranteed."

But the most visible—and spectacular—of such offers appeared in multiple issues of *Astounding*, as part of a joint promotion with *Picture Play Magazine* and Warner Bros. Pictures. Obviously trying to appeal to female readers as well as male in this instance, the full-page advertisement headlined "Hollywood Wants You" depicted a woman's head with her facial features covered by a question mark and accompanied by the legend, *"Picture Play Magazine* Offers You a Lifetime Opportunity" (Aug. 1938, 156). To qualify for one of three promised Warner Bros. screen tests, along with a free trip to Hollywood, readers were asked to "make your own screen test in your own home with your own, borrowed or rented movie camera." The entries were then to be submitted to *Picture Play* where, it was promised, they would be judged by the magazine's editor, two Warner Bros. executives, as well as Warners' top male and female stars of the period, Errol Flynn and Bette Davis (156). Certainly a rather far-fetched promise in many ways, the promotion seems more attuned to the typical film fan readership of *Picture Play* or other movie fanzines than to what many SF historians like to think of as the more sober pulp readership. And yet, the ad's large size and deliberate placement facing *Astounding*'s "Brass Tacks" readers' column each time it ran not only assured that it would be highly visible, but also suggested that the contest sponsors assumed the pulp readers were both male and female, and just as fascinated by the world of the movies as were those who read the fan magazines (Figure 2.4).

For readers interested in a different way of becoming creatively involved in the film industry, George Paquin, Jr. in his *Amazing* notices offered instruction in "How to Write Moving Picture Plays" (Apr. 1928, 95). Similarly, a series of ads run in the 1930 and 1931 issues of *Amazing*—and repeated in various forms in other pulps—appealed to those interested in "movie writing." Soliciting readers to submit their story ideas, the Daniel O'Malley Company of New York offered to help "shape and sell" stories to various "talkie and movie producers" who, readers were assured, were "clamoring" for new material (April 1931, 94). And following in this vein, a group of ads from the alluringly titled Universal Scenario Co. of Hollywood, appearing throughout the 1934 run of *Astounding*, promised "rich rewards" to anyone interested in writing "stories for talking pictures." Presumably these and many other such ads hoped to attract SF readers who imagined that, with just a bit of professional guidance or stylistic polish, they might be able to translate their own enthusiasm for and familiarity with SF literature and its ideas into just the sort of scenarios that Hollywood film companies, such as the real Universal Studios, would be interested in purchasing. The very existence of such advertising, appearing across most of the key pulps, indicates more than just an eagerness for any sort of job during the

HOLLYWOOD ❓ WANTS YOU

THE WARNER BROS.—UNIVEX
"HOME SCREEN TEST" CONTEST

=== SPONSORED BY ===

PICTURE PLAY MAGAZINE

OFFERS YOU A LIFETIME OPPORTUNITY

★　　　★　　　★

This new exciting contest offers you a chance to win one of three WARNER BROS. SCREEN TESTS with FREE trips to HOLLYWOOD as guests of the fashionable BEVERLY HILLS HOTEL or any one of 75 other valuable prizes.

All you have to do is make your own screen test in your own home with your own, borrowed or rented movie camera. Anybody can enter. All you need is a face and a movie camera. There's no age limit! Films will be judged by Bette Davis, Errol Flynn, the editor of PICTURE PLAY MAGAZINE and two WARNER BROS. executives to be announced at a later date.

Be sure and read all contest rules, instructions and suggestions for HOME SCREEN TEST contestants in the current issue of PICTURE PLAY.

A completely informative booklet has been prepared especially for you. It tells you how to act before a camera, how to use and apply stage cosmetics, the art of dress and camera technique, etc. This booklet is yours for the asking. Fill in the entry blank below and send it with a self-addressed, stamped envelope to PICTURE PLAY MAGAZINE, 79 Seventh Avenue, New York, N. Y., and this booklet will be sent to you immediately, absolutely free.

Don't delay! Reserve your issue of PICTURE PLAY MAGAZINE at your newsstand now. Enter the greatest of all contests today—the WARNER BROS.-UNIVEX "HOME SCREEN TEST". It offers you fame, fortune and fun!

HURRY! Mail this Entrance Blank to-day to PICTURE PLAY, Box S-7, 79 Seventh Avenue, New York, N. Y. Enclose a stamped, self-addressed envelope and our special booklet giving valuable instructions will be mailed to you immediately.

NAME ....

ADDRESS ....

CITY.................................... STATE.................................

AGE.................... HEIGHT...................... WEIGHT.................

COLOR OF EYES.............. COLOR OF HAIR.............. COMPLEXION............

Figure 2.4. *Astounding* partners with *Picture Play Magazine* to sponsor a screen test contest (Aug. 1938).

Depression years. It also suggests that film already occupied a place in what John Cheng terms the "participatory culture" or mindset that had quickly become one hallmark of a growing SF fandom (77), as that desire for participation, which also repeatedly surfaced in the various readers' columns of the magazines, promised to hurdle any media boundaries, transporting SF readers into the world of the movies, helping them to step right into the picture—or pictures—of the modern age, even to write their own scripts for such pictures.

Another sort of ad addressed a different dimension of that participatory culture, speaking to the film fan who sought a more tangible and clearly consumerist connection to the movie industry. These were readers, male or female, who were interested in collecting its artifacts, including movie star portraits, film-based novels, and even home versions of theatrical films. One ad in this category, typified by the offering of the Star and Studio Picture Corporation, is fairly common to a wide range of magazines and newspapers of the 1920s and early 1930s, which had quickly identified and sought to capitalize on the growing base of film fans. Offering a "Movie Star Portrait Album," along with twenty "autographed" photos of "famous movie stars" (*Amazing*, July 1930, 381), the Star and Studio ad additionally noted that other star photos could be purchased for placement in the album, thereby encouraging readers/film enthusiasts to become active collectors of these images. This and similar ads would also, and most appropriately, appear in more specialized movie magazines such as *Photoplay*, *Picture Play*, and *Screenland*. While such star appeals would not last long in the SF pulps, they did pave the way for a later, even more specialized sort of advertisement, as several companies would eventually offer products specifically targeted at an SF readership—stills from famous fantasy or SF films. In fact, in one *Thrilling Wonder Stories* report on the activities of the Science Fiction League fan club there is an account of Forrest J. Ackerman displaying "a great variety" of such stills to appreciative members at a Los Angeles chapter meeting (Aug. 1936, 118).

A second ad in this category sought to appeal to a more traditional audience of readers who were also avid moviegoers or fans. While most issues of the SF pulps featured book ads, and in the late 1930s and early 1940s a number of those ads would, in a kind of joint publicity move, indicate that particular novels were also being issued as films, several companies clearly sought to reach an audience made up specifically of film enthusiasts. Among its other offerings, the Popular Book Corporation, a frequent pulp advertiser, marketed an extensive line of "Best Movie Sellers" that included novelizations of various recent films, including *Streets of Shanghai*, *The Sensation Seekers*, and the popular horror mystery *The Cat and the*

Canary (all 1927). Offering a similar product was a publishing concern founded by Hugo Gernsback, the Consrad Company. Previously known as Experimenter Publishing, Consrad had early on offered radio instruction books of various sorts, but in issues of *Amazing Stories* it began advertising its own novel adaptations of a number of popular movies, including Charlie Chaplin's first feature *Tillie's Punctured Romance* (1914) and Lon Chaney's biggest hit *Tell It to the Marines* (1926), while it also touted a special visual inducement to differentiate its product from competing book advertisers. The promotion promised that each volume would include "at least two color 'stills' of an actual scene from the photoplay" (June 1928, 284). But very much like the publishers of the various pulp magazines, Consrad seemed mindful that for some people the movies, rather like the pulps themselves, still had some lower-class associations, so a portion of the ad copy sought to counter that perception, emphasizing that these books were all quality products—"beautiful," "durable," and "a worthwhile addition to your home library," in effect, a visual attraction in themselves, an affirmation of the purchaser's "class," and thus another reminder of how one might, as a consumer of such materials, effect a degree of personal improvement.

A third sort of fan-directed advertisement obviously targeted a different part of this audience, one that was more knowledgeable, technically astute, and probably a bit more affluent. One of *Amazing*'s "ad-lets" in 1927 offered "movie supplies and films," and starting in 1929 the Home Movie Supply Co. announced that it had "standard gauge" entertainment films (most likely 8mm or 16mm, although no specific gauge is indicated) that were available for purchase. Since SF films were far from common at this time—with Fritz Lang's *Metropolis* (1927) and the special effects epic *The Lost World* (1925) among the few works frequently cited in readers' letters to the pulps in the 1920s—it is hardly surprising that the ad specified no SF titles but did offer examples of the two most common genres of the period, "Western or comedy," both of which had also been widely produced in easy-to-distribute, one- and two-reel formats throughout the first two decades of motion pictures. More important than the genre of these films, though, is the obvious sense that the SF audience was being recognized by companies throughout the United States as also being a movie audience, spectators, and even a body of potential collectors/consumers who would have invested money in the projection equipment needed to play these films at a time when that technology was not commonplace and hardly inexpensive. Like the rest of modern American culture, these consumers were explicitly seen as a ready market for what Charney and Schwartz describe as "modernity's simulations and distractions," most readily packaged and made available in the form of the movies (6).

And yet conspicuously missing from these various movie-related appeals is the sort of ad that one might most expect to find, especially in light of the many letters printed in the pulps' readers' columns (which will be discussed in chapter 4): ads that market specific scientifilms to an eager SF audience. That is, the movie industry itself, throughout almost the entire pre-war period, seems to have been reluctant to advertise its own films in the SF pulps, even such particularly appropriate and highly anticipated SF productions as Universal's *Frankenstein* (1931), the H. G. Wells adaptation *The Invisible Man* (1933), or the popular space opera serials such as *Flash Gordon* (1936, 1938, 1940) and *Buck Rogers* (1939). Certainly, the film industry heavily advertised in many of the slick magazines throughout the pre-war period, and film ads do show up somewhat irregularly in a few non-SF pulps, such as *Illustrated Detective Magazine*, *Crime Busters*, and *Startling Detective*, as well as in the many film fan magazines. But perhaps since SF was not yet recognized as a well-defined and even popular genre—and certainly one that had not been heavily exploited by Hollywood—the major film companies proved slow to address SF fandom directly and to recognize the full extent of that audience's investment in the world of film.

A sense of that difficulty in properly assessing and addressing the SF readership might at least be glimpsed in one of the few major film ads posted to the SF pulps by a major studio during the pre-war period. Included in the March 1935 issue of *Amazing Stories* was a full-page ad from 20th Century (soon to be 20th Century-Fox), announcing the studio's upcoming release of *Clive of India* (1935), a historical biopic that would be heavily covered in the popular press and described by the *New York Times* reviewer as "a sprawling screen biography of England's great soldier-politician" Robert Clive (Sennwald). An entry in Darryl F. Zanuck's new program of big-budget prestige films, which included such other works in this vein as *The House of Rothschild* (1934) and *Cardinal Richelieu* (1935), *Clive of India*, with its subject the early days of the British Raj, was questionably the sort of film that might be expected to easily cross over to an SF audience. However, *Amazing Stories* had been included as part of a massive publicity campaign for the movie that had as its announced goal reaching sixty million of the country's magazine readers. In fact, the scope of the campaign itself functioned as a kind of publicity ploy, with that targeted readership providing a numerical measure of the film's own vast scope and appeal.[4] As Zanuck's biographer George F. Custen observes, the producer wanted his new series of historical epics to place "a premium on the pure power of visual spectacle" (196). That emphasis is immediately obvious in the nature of the ad, a third of which depicts a giant fist (presumably Clive's) smashing down between two battling groups, one a herd of what the copy terms "armored battle elephants . . . the strangest warriors in history," and the other an army of European-dressed soldiers firing rifles and cannon (Figure 2.5). Given this content and its replication in many other period magazines and industry newspapers, we can safely assume that the ad did not directly target the SF audience or the SF imagination, although its highly dramatic visual

Figure 2.5. The first feature film advertisement in the SF pulps, for 20th Century's adventure epic *Clive of India* (*Amazing*, Mar. 1935).

presentation suggests that it was designed to tap into a mindset that was shared by multiple audiences of the period—viewers appreciative of exotic adventure and powerful figures, all in some way attuned to the era's new visuality and thus appreciative of the immense visual spectacle that the film promised to audiences.

Another, slightly later advertising campaign, however, merits more detailed examination, since it was the first marketing effort that seemed particularly appropriate for and directly addressed to the SF pulp readership/viewership. Paramount Pictures had demonstrated an early interest in SF when it acquired the rights to film H. G. Wells's *The War of the Worlds* in 1925 (Williams 138), produced *Dr. Jekyll and Mr. Hyde* in 1932, adapted Wells' *Island of Lost Souls* the following year, and started pre-production work on *The War of the Worlds* in 1935 (Idwal Jones). However, the studio would once more shelve *The War of the Worlds*, perhaps because of its declaration of bankruptcy in 1935, and it undertook little else in an SF vein until 1940 when Paramount released the first SF film to be shot in the still somewhat new—and expensive—three-strip Technicolor format, the mad scientist story *Dr. Cyclops* (1940). The film would be the subject of a large-scale publicity campaign, reminiscent of the one for *Clive of India*, that would not only reach into the world of the pulps, but would also involve *Thrilling Wonder Stories* in an ambitious novelization of its plot by popular SF author Henry Kuttner, known for his own fascination with the movies that had already been prominently shown with his popular "Hollywood on the Moon" stories for the magazine.

While *Dr. Cyclops* is clearly a legitimate work of SF, it would also seem like a difficult match for the usual SF readership. A pre-release article in *Motion Picture Daily*, for example, seemed to marginalize the film, describing it as a production intended for "the unsophisticates of all ages," and as "so bizarre that it inevitably will create much word of mouth" (King 4). While praising the film for its special effects work, as offering moviegoers "the latest and best in camera magic," a later review in *The Film Daily* still termed it "a decided novelty" ("Dr. Cyclops" 8). David Skal's more recent description of the movie as "a distillation of all the Depression decade's suspicions about experts and intellectuals and runaway science" (167) clarifies this difficulty, as it points to the film's explicit strike at science and scientific interests, an attitude that was obviously at odds with the usual promise—and appeal—of SF and the SF pulps. But the expensive Technicolor process, the film's elaborate special effects work, and its direction by famed *King Kong* (1933) director Ernest B. Schoedsack all underscore the ambitious nature of this project, which would prompt Paramount to mount an elaborate exploitation campaign. That campaign would involve special test runs of the film in six cities, the hiring of additional "exploiteers," as they were termed, to energize the film's promotion ("Para. Adds" 2), and the partnering with *Thrilling Wonder Stories*—among other magazines—to help build a large audience.

On the surface, an advertisement in *Thrilling Wonder Stories* might tell us very little about the film industry's SF consciousness. As David M. Earle has explained, much pulp advertising was supplied by an advertisement service that might have been "either an in-house or out-of-house advertisement agency that specialized in low cost and often low culture but mass-market products," and that typically placed ad packages with publishing groups rather than with individual magazines (202). One result was a sometimes jarring "continuity of ads across the spectrum of genres," as well as some "discontinuity" between a particular magazine's subject matter and the advertising it contained (202). We see some evidence of that sort of "discontinuity" with the *Dr. Cyclops* material, as at least one other pulp member of the Thrilling Publications (or Better Publications and later Standard Magazines) family of magazines, *Thrilling Ranch Stories*, also contained a notice for the film. Headlined as "The Sinister Dr. Cyclops!" the piece included a close-up of the title character and a note that the Paramount film would soon be playing in theaters (June 1940, 8). However, in another sort of "composite" thrust, the *Ranch Stories* announcement, while promoting the forthcoming film, seems more intent on urging readers to buy its sister publication *Thrilling Wonder Stories* in order to read its own version of the movie story.

More noteworthy, though, is the fact that *Thrilling Wonder Stories'* contribution to Paramount's campaign was far more than a simple movie ad. Framing the film's novelization as the featured attraction of its June 1940 issue, the pulp's cover reproduced a scene depicting the film's mad scientist, while an editorial piece by Mort Weisinger on "This Month's Cover" described—in what is termed a "confidential lowdown" (119)—how both the illustration and the story came into being. The editor there explains that artist Howard V. Brown painted the cover *after* seeing a special preview screening of the film.[5] And in what was probably a first for the pulps, the feature story had been adapted from the original Tom Kilpatrick screenplay by Henry Kuttner, who was also, we are told, invited to visit the studio during the film's shooting. Moreover, the piece was partly illustrated with Paramount-supplied production stills showing Albert Dekker as the mad scientist, along with one of the film's more striking special effects compositions, involving outsized props and a rear projection process shot. The payback to Paramount for this "exclusive" information, studio access, and the visual tease provided by the film's production stills was a two-page banner announcing that "This Sensational New Scientifiction Thriller is Soon to be Released by Paramount Pictures," and a headline urging the audience to "Read It Now—Then See It at Your Local Theatre!" (Figure 2.6).

Thrilling Wonder's access to the script, production, and publicity images, along with the cooperative approach to marketing, was hardly common for the period, and none of the other SF pulps would in this period undertake anything similar.[6] But it is a singular reminder of just how widespread

Read It Now—Then
See It at Your
Local Theatre!

Dr. Cyclops
glared balefully
at the little
people

Soon to be Released by PARAMOUNT PICTURES, INC.

Figure 2.6. *Thrilling Wonder Stories* partners with Paramount Pictures to promote *Dr. Cyclops* (June 1940).

the new concern with consumerism and with identifying specific groups of consumers was becoming at this time. In this instance we see both the publishing community and the film industry staking out some common ground between SF consumers and general film audiences, all seen as part of that "citizen consumer ideal" that Cohen describes and thus able to be reached across multiple media platforms. While the *Dr. Cyclops* case is more complex and dramatic than the other sorts of film-related advertising we have detailed in this chapter, all these examples demonstrate how the film industry, through both its peripheral representatives—trade schools, agents, producers of film-related products—and in the shape of the large Hollywood studios, was beginning to recognize SF readers as particularly appropriate consumers, invested in the future as well as the thoroughly modern medium of the movies, while the pulp editors and owners, in inviting these ads and even pursuing, as they did with Paramount, a more complex connection to the film industry, apparently sensed similar and mutually profitable possibilities—possibilities that would be more elaborately explored in the post-war period, especially when Paramount would, in a more ambitious fashion, partner with another pulp, *Astounding Stories*, on a series of significant publicity pieces that will be discussed in the final chapter.

Behind this consumerist relationship is, as I have suggested, a more fundamental link that had developed between the SF pulps and film throughout the pre-war era—a link in which film, largely because of its modernist sensibility, had come to seem a natural companion to this new sort of fiction, as if it constituted the necessary visualizing or realizing of the products of the SF imagination, as if the two might be composite voices, both speaking the exciting language of the modern age. Advertising, even of the intricate sort noted with *Dr. Cyclops*, was just one part of that complex film-SF relationship, although a part that reminds us of how SF was embedded in a culture that relished film's "attractions," that was already being shaped and sold by the film experience, and that was clearly on its way to becoming, as Paul Virilio has more recently described, "cinematized" or "mediatized" (59), with the genre's readers/ fans inhabiting a world that, as the *Dr. Cyclops* campaign hints, increasingly seemed to resemble an extended movie set. On this set many of our SF imaginings—and nightmares, including mad scientists, rockets, and fantastic conveyances—would soon be vividly realized by the looming war and further explored and exploited in the pulps.

But before that troubling wartime period, SF would itself have to be marketed, advertised, and sold to an audience that had already eagerly embraced the modernist message of film. Cinematically informed advertisements of various sorts, an attractive component of the full pulp SF experience, simply assisted in that selling of the genre by speaking the same modernist language as the SF readership. Of course, the sort of advertising described here was just a small sampling of the larger consumers' canvas that was spreading across the pages of the various pulps during the pre-war years and that would only increase in the post-war period. And admittedly, these film-related appeals were by no means the dominant figure in that canvas—as the various ads for rupture-relievers, itch creams, arthritis cures, and false teeth uncomfortably remind us. But the many different types of film-related ads we have noted were selling more than just cinematic dreams. They remind us that, much as was the case throughout popular culture of the era, the cinema had a pervasive presence in the pulps, that the pulp readership was often seen as moviegoers or film fans, and that the readership could be sold products, even attitudes by means of that film interest. Drawing on the common modernist emphases on visualization and change, such advertising helped conscript the SF readership into what Lizabeth Cohen terms the new Consumer Republic of modern America, while, in the process, it also allowed that citizenry to locate its own place, as SF fans and readers, in this thoroughly modern world.

CHAPTER 3

The Real Thing

The Pulps Imagine Film

The advertising described in the previous chapter was one part of an external discourse about the movies that was being imported into the SF pulps and was helping to shape the typical pulp experience. But another and more significant influence was taking shape in a corresponding and indeed primary internal discourse. The pulps' main—although by no means sole—attraction, the stories that they featured, just as clearly illustrate the impact that the world of the movies was having on a developing SF imagination. Because, as we have previously noted, both film and SF took breath from the same modernist atmosphere, were driven by similar impulses, and shared much the same audience, we should probably expect that the world of film would make its way into the new fiction in a variety of ways— as context, as principal subject matter, even as a kind of driving spirit, underscoring the extent to which the early story of "scientifilm" overlapped with and added resonance to the development of "scientifiction" during the pre-war years. This chapter considers a major portion of that internal discourse as it examines a variety of film-inflected pulp stories, tracing out how a general fascination with the movies gives way to a continuing debate about their illusionism and eventually an acceptance of their value as a way of "real"-izing the sort of wonders that were SF's stock in trade. While not always the best of pulp SF and hardly the worst, these short stories and novellas illustrate *how much* the movies were on the minds of both SF authors and fans, as well as how that movie consciousness mattered to the ongoing development of the SF imagination.

As a starting point—as well as an example—we might once more consider the work of SF pioneer, editor, and pulp icon Hugo Gernsback.[1] For in the serialization of his innovative SF novel *Ralph 124C 41+* in his own hobby magazine *Modern Electrics* (1911-12), Gernsback had already modeled an element of what we might today term a trans-media consciousness, as well as his own keen awareness of what, borrowing from Miriam Hansen, we have repeatedly referred to as modernism's new visuality. In the year 2660, his tale's protagonist Ralph lives a life surrounded—and constantly mediated—by cinema-like devices: on the walls of his home he has "telephot" screens (a combination of television and videophone), he reads the daily news by projecting it onto another large screen, and when he goes to sleep, he connects himself to a "hypnobioscope," a particularly allusive device that transforms his brain into a kind of "mindscreen" (Figure 3.1). The hypnobioscope transmits sounds and images directly to the brain, allowing Ralph not just to learn while asleep, but also to dream in a directed way, to visualize his own scripted adventures in a cinematic fashion, as when he loads a version of *The Odyssey* into his hypnobioscope so that he might personally experience that epic adventure. By rendering the products of the imagination *visualizable*—as was suggested in the previous chapters—the hypnobioscope was already suggesting the possibility of a kind of personal SF machine or cinematic device. But an even more fundamental point is worth noting: that Ralph seems continually connected to his world through a variety of such optical media, feeding him the images, information, and even the entertainment that, as a citizen of the future, he both needs and desires. In fact, he takes such connectedness for granted, as a natural feature of that future life. As we shall see, other writers would follow Gernsback's lead, finding in the basic cinematic idea inspiration for an array of technological wonders, as well as, in some cases, for technologically based nightmares, in the process reminding us that this cinematic impulse and a fully cinematized future also hold the potential to go wrong.

This fictional emphasis on optical technology's ability to give shape to our imaginings, to make the wonders of the SF imagination seem real, would drive many early pulp stories, practically pushing them in a cinematic direction, as if they were reflexively acting out the basic work of SF. Among these pre-war pulp offerings, I want to focus attention on three types of film-related stories that would prove especially prominent and illustrate the primary trajectory that this branch of the fiction would take. Some of these pieces I am singling out simply draw upon the world of the movies as an atmospheric backdrop for plots that turn on different scientific or technological developments, even for some that focus primarily on that other powerful modern medium, radio. In such stories a generic

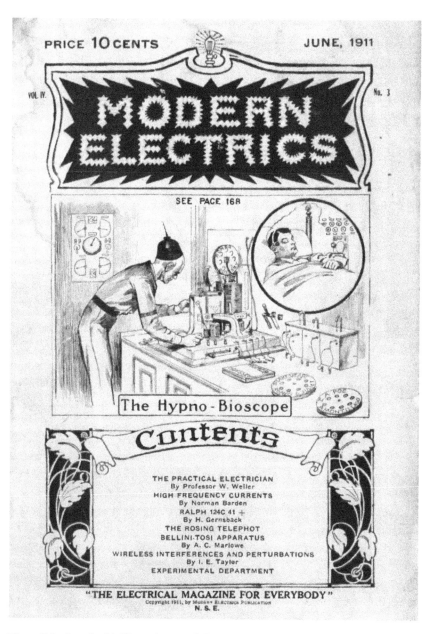

Figure 3.1. Gernsback's "Hypnobioscope" depicted on the cover of *Modern Electrics* magazine (June 1911). Note the film reels waiting to be loaded.

"Hollywood," symbolic of the modern, technologically driven world and of the wonders or "attractions" that early audiences typically associated with the realm of the movies, provides a fertile territory from which various sorts of imaginings readily arise. A second story type suggests a growing fascination with film technology itself, as if it were being received in much the way that many SF readers—and electrical hobbyists—had first reacted to radio, and as some were already beginning to respond to a growing discourse about the nascent technology of television. These tales, operating very much in the manner of other pulp SF thought experiments or thought variants, explore the possible implications of the various technologies that were involved in producing those "modern talking pictures," as Gernsback termed them. A third type finds its focus in what might be described as the driving spirit of the movies, as they foreground film's special gaze that, as Casetti offers, places us "in front of a world" and invites us to see it differently (152). In this sort of story, the movies become another SF meme— rather like the robot, rocket, or "hypnobioscope"—serving the impulse that infuses both film and SF for visual exploration and realistic representation. Although not the only story types that we might consider, these categories suggest the broad scope of the pulps' "cinematic" narratives, even as they point toward an interesting historical connection as both film and SF throughout the pre-World War II era meditate on their relationship to the real world, and on their audience's desire, even need for a more realistic vision of that world.

As we noted in chapter 1, William Boddy has described how radio in this same period followed a somewhat similar trajectory to that of film. He recounts how, over the first decades of the twentieth century, a variety of utopian predictions about radio coincided with just as many "fears" or "misgivings" (22) about the technology and its possible influences. Negotiating between these different possibilities, the public would eventually come to see radio not as some fantastic gadget or utopian device that could electronically unite the world, nor as something that would wield an irresistible and dangerous control over its listeners, but rather as part of the familiar cultural landscape, even a welcome fixture in what he terms the new "domestic technology" of the modern home (44). Pulp SF's treatment of the cinema reflects a fairly similar pattern of cultural familiarization and embrace, in fact, one wherein the cinema too seems by turns to hold out great promise, and at others to be fraught with "misgivings"—as when in Emil Petaja's story "Dinosaur Goes Hollywood," a real dinosaur, the accidental result of a breakthrough in time travel technology, is suddenly unleashed at a Hollywood movie premier (*Amazing Stories* 16.11), panicking some but prompting many of the attendees to assume that it is not real, but just another movie prop being used in an all too common in-dustry publicity stunt, in the process leaving the unsuspecting moviegoers vulnerable to unexpected dangers (Figure 3.2).

Among the earliest pulp efforts in this vein are a number of stories that, much like "Dinosaur Goes Hollywood," use Hollywood or the movie in-dustry as a kind of "wallpaper" or entertainment setting, and its trafficking in glamorous images as a simple reflection on the nature of modernist cul-ture. In such efforts film and the film industry usually function as little more than signs of wonders yet to come, the unreality of the movies pro-viding an appropriate context for evoking other fantasies and unrealities—even menaces as in the case of displaced dinosaurs. As film became a more obviously complex activity, with the technologies involved in producing sound, color, and three-dimensional imagery all entering into common cul-tural discussion and even becoming the subject of factual articles in the various hobby and science-oriented magazines,[2] pulp stories would in-creasingly focus on the nature of that technology with characters treating it as a tool of scientific experimentation and discovering in it both useful and threatening potentials. However, once that technological foundation became better understood—as some of the ads discussed in the previous chapter attest—and film's place within the culture firmly established, a third story type would come to prominence, with the movies, and movie-making, not quite domesticated, but providing a useful trope for how, in the modern, science-suffused climate, we might best see and interact with our world. In the course of the late 1920s and 1930s we see SF authors and audiences alike going through this familiarizing process, becoming not just more comfortable with the movies as a medium, but also with film technology's close relationship to the world of SF, as well as its ability, in the best modernist fashion, to provide them a greater access to and under-standing of reality.

It is a process that should not be surprising, not just because of the his-torical experience of radio—which was similarly reflected in the fiction—but because it also tracks along with the larger cultural experience of the movies. In fact, in its earliest days, the budding film industry made much capital from reflexively foregrounding the strange new world that it represented, and particularly the relatively new activities of film going and film making, while playing upon the naiveté that was often a part of audiences' first experiences with the movies. To establish this context, we might consider a pair of such pioneer efforts, the English film pioneer Robert Paul's *The Countryman's First Sight of the Animated Pictures* (1901) and its better-known American remake, Edwin S. Porter's *Uncle Josh at the Moving Picture Show* (1902). The narratives are approximately the same,

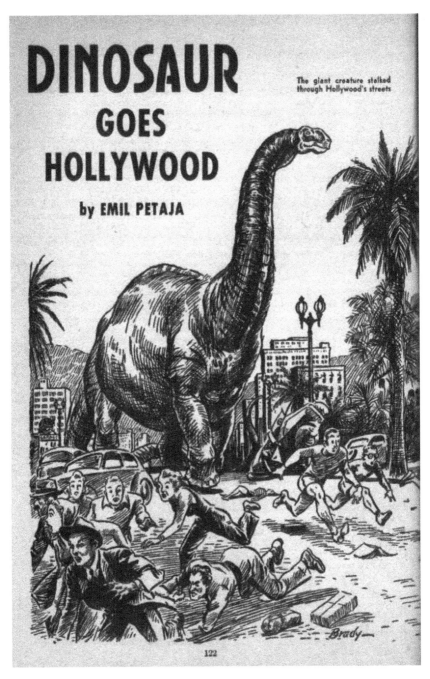

The giant creature stalked through Hollywood's streets

DINOSAUR
GOES
HOLLYWOOD

by EMIL PETAJA

Brady—

122

Figure 3.2. Time travel comes to the movies: *Amazing*'s "Dinosaur Goes Hollywood" (Nov. 1942).

with both detailing the difficulties a country bumpkin or "rube" (the "Uncle Josh" character, we might note, was a familiar American film version of the bumpkin) has when he first encounters the new technology of the movies. In his initial experience with going to the movies, he has to figure out how to account for and react to the attractive images that are being projected onto a screen and that he repeatedly mistakes for present, substantial, and even seductive realities. These include an attractive dancing girl whose image he tries to embrace, only to grasp at air, disrupting the show with his enthusiasm, eventually bringing down the screen and, eventually, drawing the wrath of the projectionist who then beats him. These and a number of similar films turn on an ongoing blurring of the line between reality and its representations, or what, as Miriam Hansen observes, is a frequently deployed gimmick of such early movies, one that involves showing a "cultural disparity between the spectator-in-the-film and the spectator-of-the-film" (*Babel* 28). Such narratives comically illustrate the difference between those who are inexperienced with technology and the ways of the modern world and those, the spectators-of-the-film—or in another context, the readers of the SF pulps—who are by implication more knowing, more attuned to the real, and, implicitly, more modern.

A slightly later effort, Charlie Chaplin's first film, *Kid Auto Races at Venice* (1914), suggests how quickly such attitudes changed, and also how quickly audiences became accustomed to that blurring of distinctions (Figure 3.3). In it we see the first version of Chaplin's little tramp character watching a film crew as they record a kids' soapbox derby race. More than curiously observing the crew at work, the tramp repeatedly inserts himself into the action, purposely walking into the frame, looking toward the camera, and interacting with the filmmakers who, in turn, constantly try to get this irritating character out of the picture. The little tramp, an iconic cultural outcast who would have been essentially invisible to much of society, obviously understands what is involved in the film process—the crew's concern with point of view, framing, and focus—and the comedy here derives from his constant efforts at hijacking that process in order to claim a few minutes of fame or, more precisely, to use film as a way of making himself visible to that heedless modern culture. But the narrative here obviously depends not on the simple disparity of knowledge Hansen describes, but rather on the new level of knowledge about movie technology that even society's outsiders, the littlest of tramps, at this early point already possessed and sought to exploit for their own benefit.

By the time of late silent-era feature films like Josef von Sternberg's *The Last Command* and Buster Keaton's *The Cameraman* (both 1928), both concerned with the nature of the film industry and the at times crippling

Figure 3.3. The movie-conscious little tramp hijacks the scene in *Kid Auto Races at Venice* (1914).

dreams it could foster, film had become not just a primary entertainment and familiar element of popular culture, but a significant part of the cultural discourse. In fact, it is this very familiarity with the movies, by both the characters within the films—the former depicts a Russian general-turned-actor and the latter an inept newsreel cameraman—and the film audience that was seeing these films at the very end of the silent era when film had achieved a high level of narrative sophistication, that allows these works to frame their medium in a more complex manner. Both movies are fundamentally about the film industry and the filmmaking process, which they subject to analysis and criticism in the course of dramatizing how the cinema affects human motivations and human psychology, in these instances to both tragic (*The Last Command*) and comic (*The Cameraman*) ends.

We can trace out a similar pattern in the familiarization process and overall trajectory by looking at how the fiction of the SF pulps treated the movies throughout the pre-World War II era. However, before looking at specific ways in which the world of film was actually presented in the pulps, we need to acknowledge that there was already a very basic level of familiarity, perhaps a largely unconscious one, that contributed to this effect, making such presentations all the easier, or at least seeming all the more natural. As we have previously noted, many of the pulp stories seem to speak the language of the cinema, as they draw on images or metaphors that were already part of the common experience of the audience. For example, Murray Leinster in an early contribution to *Amazing Stories*, "The Runaway Skyscraper," describes how one of his time-traveling characters watches, from within a "time bubble," as an urban landscape undergoes seemingly rapid changes, observing that "the effect was the same as one of the old flickering motion-pictures" (253). Similarly, Harl Vincent in "Cat's Eye" has his space explorers communicate with other-world primitives by offering them what he terms "a swiftly changing panorama" of a modern city, projected "as if from the lens of a motion picture machine" (26). And the protagonist of Arthur J. Burks's "The Mind Master" recalls the hypnotic power another figure wields over him by noting that his "eyes seemed to leap at him growing large and glaring, just as the eyes of caricatured animals leap at the camera in trick motion pictures" (257). Such repeated appeals to the world of film—and to the readers' obvious familiarity with that world and its various "tricks"—are fairly common in the pre-war pulps, and they give substance to a point made by the contemporary filmmaker and editor of the early British film journal *Close Up*, Kenneth Macpherson. In a 1928 editorial he observed that "the cinema has become so much a habit of thought and word and deed as to make it impossible to visualize modern consciousness without it" (8).

But even before Macpherson's reflection, Hugo Gernsback was setting the precedent for a film-inflected consciousness and rhetoric in his second novel *Baron Munchhausen's New Scientific Adventures*, serialized in his electronics pulp *The Electrical Experimenter* from 1915 to 1917. In this tale Munchausen describes his first encounter with Martians and his sudden realization that they were "talking" to him "not in words and not in a strange language, but motion-picture wise. *We had experienced the first transference of thoughts*" ("Baron" 150) via shared visualizations. It is a kind of communication that prompts his character to suggest that something akin to the movies might eventually constitute a kind of universal language. These and other "motion-picture wise" communications simply remind us of how natural it had become, how much a "habit of thought" it was, even at the start of the pulp era, to think cinematically and to draw on that common language in order to evoke a thoroughly modern—or futuristic—world.

Given that sense of film as part of the common language of the day, we should only expect that film would also become a fairly frequent subject of pulp fiction. As a useful starting point we might consider the work of C. Sterling Gleason, who was himself a kind of transitional figure for the emerging genre of SF, as he had been a contributor of factual articles to the hobby and electrical magazines of the day (such as *Radio News*), before he began writing SF stories for those magazines and the early pulps. Frequently shifting between factual and fictional modes, and sometimes working with Joseph D. Mountain, Gleason authored a variety of stories that demonstrate some of the difficulty in doing early scientifiction, as well as the budding role of film and a film consciousness in that fiction. In fact, his stories tend to be less straightforward SF efforts than parodic tales that generally work in the vein of what Mike Ashley and Robert Lowndes characterize as the "scientific problem" or "scientific mystery" story (*Gernsback Days* 147), that is, as works that use science, scientific reasoning, or some esoteric technology, usually explained in elaborate detail, to untangle what seems to be an insoluble mystery or to cope with a dangerous dilemma. But what especially distinguishes these rather modest fictional efforts is Gleason's recurrent use of the world of film— even when the piece is concerned with radio technology—to provide the backdrop for his stories, as well as to link them into the sort of character-driven series that would soon become a staple and key attraction of the early SF pulps.

As a case in point, we might consider Gleason's 1929 story "The Radiation of the Chinese Vegetable" (*Science Wonder Stories* 1.7). This tale, like many of his others, is set in Hollywood, a place that Gleason, in intentionally inflated fashion, describes as "that distant metropolis of millionaires, movies and Mammon, that capital of sin and the cinema" (619). As a central feature of this pointedly fantastic setting, Gleason has much of his action take place in the fictional "Flicker Film Studio" where his series protagonist, Harold Dare, along with several other recurring characters, works. Dare is Gleason's central creation—a melodramatic cardboard figure. He is an improbable mixture of actor, detective, scientist, and philanthropist who is characterized in the story "The Port of Missing Airplanes" as "the most famous of conceivable film stars" (1322), and in "Silent Dynamite" as the "idol of the film-fans of the world," as well as the source of "the unrivaled entertainment and uplift disseminated through WROT," his own radio station (*Radio News* 9.3, 214). In keeping with the exaggerated descriptions of Hollywood, the artificial world of the studio, and especially the overheated characterization of Dare—who is also credited in "The Radiation of the Chinese Vegetable" with founding "the great Dare research laboratories, maintained by the celebrated screen star in the interests of the public welfare" (619)—Gleason's stories are less conventional (and even less realistic) narratives than they are parodies of a common sort of over-the-top film melodrama of the period. As such, they use film and the film industry in a curiously double way, in part as an appealing context because of the many modern associations they brought, yet also as a tool for criticizing the at times hyperbolic and highly unrealistic forms that the cinema's products often took in this early period.

What is gained from that sort of double take on film, the film industry, and their role in modern culture? We might note that an author's informational box attached to the publication of "The Radiation of the Chinese Vegetable" emphasizes Gleason's own scientific credentials, noting the many technical articles he had published in other magazines and describing him as "a radio authority of considerable reputation" (619). The point is to assure readers that the science involved in this piece of scientifiction will be reliable, even technically fascinating, in keeping with what, it was supposed, the early SF fandom most prized. Certainly, the detailed application of an oscilloscope to discover that an unconscious Dare is not dead but has simply been put into a coma in "The Voice of the People" (*Radio News*, Nov. 1927), the scientific deduction that local radio signals are being disrupted by a secret electrolysis process in "Silent Dynamite," and Dare's use of high-frequency electric current to turn his body into a human radio transmitter in "The Radiation of the Chinese Vegetable" all deliver the sort of entertaining—yet highly speculative—technological discourse readers might have desired, while also showing off the author's knowledge of various electrical principles and devices. And by framing this material in the exaggerated manner Gleason associates with the movies—including breathless last-minute rescues, saving damsels in distress, and constant physical and verbal sparring between Dare and a self-acknowledged villain, the "vile Dandy Diavolo" ("Silent Dynamite" 264)—the author could both draw on and distance his work from the movies, repeatedly reminding readers that the "real" work of science is not to be found in the cinema, despite its technological base, but rather in the work of the scientists and engineers who make it possible, and who have already made radio such an important adjunct to modern life. This point is particularly reinforced in "The Voice of the People" when Dare is himself saved from a deadly hypnotic signal by an observant radio engineer at WROT who is dutifully reading his gauges and detects the unseen threat. But the easily satirized body of early movie conventions also provides these stories with a humorous twist, usually at the conclusion when Gleason underscores the artificial and ephemeral cinematic world in which his hero operates. As an example, we might note the conclusion of "The Port of Missing Airplanes" when Dare once more disrupts a plot by Diavolo, while also reminding him, in a typically exaggerated monologue, that, "as in a scenario, you must be foiled in the last reel, and this is The End" (1374)—with those final capital letters collapsing the finish of Diavolo's "fiendish" plot with the story's parodic one.

While usually lacking this sort of parodic thrust, a number of other stories would follow Gleason's early lead, suggesting an ongoing tension between the real world of science and technology and the over-wrought visions that the movies often seemed to draw out of their own technological base. Bob Olsen, for example, better known for his "Four-Dimensional" stories, also authored a group of scientific detective tales known as the "Master of Mystery" series. One of these, "The Pool of Death" (*Amazing Stories*, Jan. 1933), uses Hollywood as the backdrop for its own highly exaggerated narrative about the investigation of filmmaker George Raymond's mysterious death. Olsen's recurrent detective character, Justin Pryor, headquartered in Hollywood and known as the "Master of Mystery," discovers that the death was caused by a jealous rival director, using a giant amoeba that the scientifically astute murderer had developed and hidden in his swimming pool. As in the various Gleason pieces, movie people, simply because of their connection to the industry, are here presented as being highly interested, even well versed in various aspects of science, although the larger world of the movies, in this case the fictional Ajax Motion Picture Studio, becomes an object of criticism as Pryor, throughout his investigation of the case, is confronted with a variety of characters who clearly dwell in a world of exaggerated behavior and illusion linked to general cultural impressions of Hollywood.

A story like "The Pool of Death" also begins to signal a key shift in attitude toward the movies, a recognition that they are more than a simple set of attractions for the masses, but actually symptomatic of an attitude that SF, because its own province was the world of science and technology, was especially well placed to address. While the optical medium of the movies was seen by many as part of the public taste for reality in late nineteenth and early twentieth-century popular culture, or by others in a rather more significant light, as Jeannene Przyblyski puts it, as part of a new political "will toward making visible" the truths of everyday life (254), there was also some skepticism about the products of what we have termed this new visuality, about whether they were simply fragments of reality *made* visible, or images of a world that had been *constructed by* the cinematic apparatus and that reflected its own exaggerated form. Thus Przyblyski describes how the optical product of the movies was, in fact, "a matrix of representational structures, already existing and only dreamt of, which photography appropriates, compresses, displaces, and occludes," with that compression, displacement, and occlusion challenging audiences to engage in a kind of "unmasking" (274) process or recognition if they are to better understand their world, its dynamics, and its trajectory. It is this process that a story like "The Pool of Death" hints of, but which we can better see at work in a number of works that focus more specifically on the illusory nature of the Hollywood product—stories that represent a growing level of familiarity with the technology of the movies, but that also undertake a more critical appraisal of how that technology was being used, that is, with the increasingly familiar cinematic product.

Several examples of this more complex exploration of cinematic illusionism can be found in the work of W. Varick Nevins, III, a frequent contributor to Gernsback's *Wonder Stories*. Nevins' "The Mystery of the -/-" (*Wonder Stories*, June 1935) describes a startling discovery made by two college professors and their wives while on a camping trip. In the desert just beyond Los Angeles these intellectual, and obviously science-minded types come upon a strange metal cylinder, partially buried in sand and marked with the enigmatic symbols "-/-." Their scientific curiosity prompts them to uncover much of the object, and judging by the mysterious writing, unusually shaped seats and control panel inside, and what looks to be a strange sort of engine, they conclude that the cylinder is actually a crashed spaceship (Figure 3.4). However, further investigation of the area eventually troubles that conclusion, as the group also finds various everyday objects in and around the cylinder, indicating that other humans had recently been there. The group then encounters a "property man" from the N.L.N. Motion Picture Company, who explains that the "ship" is actually an abandoned—yet quite convincing—movie prop, left behind after N.L.N. had finished shooting its latest opus *The Moon Avengers*. It was so convincing because, as the property man explains, N.L.N. always strives for realism: "We do not like to resort to trick photography and fake scenery" (47). Yet the impact of that "realism" on an unsuspecting group, especially outside of the framing effect of the theatrical experience, is precisely the problem that Nevins' story proceeds to examine, as it weighs the movies' common claims for realistic depiction against the impact their illusionism might have even on scientifically inclined viewers.

Nevins's "Cosmic Calamity" (*Wonder Stories*, June 1934) works a slight variation on this theme of cinema's convincing illusionism, as its protagonist, who had fallen asleep on a park bench, meets famed scientist Charles Farmell and is invited to witness his upcoming experiment in interplanetary communication by reflecting cosmic rays to Mars. But instead of being a witness to history—to the first communication with other beings on another world—he observes what he believes to be a "cosmic calamity" when the experiment goes wrong, producing "something sinister and supernatural" that shakes the room and creates a blinding white light, then total darkness (63). However, when the protagonist awakes, he discovers that he has actually been asleep in a theater, watching a highly realistic SF film,

(Illustration by Paul)

Figure 3.4. Scientists uncover not a spaceship but a movie prop in "-/-" (*Wonder Stories*, June 1935).

its images and special effects apparently powerful enough to convince him that he was viewing a real calamity about to unfold. Affording a kind of editorial comment on the nature and impact of those images is the overheard voice of the movie projectionist, as he complains to a co-worker about the quality of the films he has been getting lately, offers his judgment about how "far-fetched" "these science-fiction films" have become (63), and, on a final ironic note, wonders why anyone would even watch such things. Here again Nevins foregrounds the "reality" illusion of the movies to remind us not only of the great appeal that they have—as well as a frequently cited validation for their illusions—but also of the adverse power of that mobilized gaze, which might easily extend its influence, fooling us through its own potent dreams, in this case controlling how the protagonist interprets everyday experiences, much as Gernsback's hypnobioscope could supposedly "script" one's sleep experiences.

In fact, a collaboration by Laurence Manning and Fletcher Pratt, "The City of the Living Dead" (*Science Wonder Stories*, May 1930), even more directly pursues and cautions against the power of illusion that devices like the hypnobioscope—or the movies—might mobilize for our pleasure, as well as to our detriment. Echoing E. M. Forster's "The Machine Stops," the story describes a remote city where the citizens became so fascinated by the artificial world of the movies and television that they began to spend more and more of their time hooked up to sensory machines that allowed them to more directly and pleasurably view a variety of programmed adventures, or as the narrator tellingly offers, "experience them as natural" (1107). So that the machines could work still more powerfully, many of the people eventually had their major sensory organs removed in favor of direct technological interfaces with certain nerves and pleasure centers. In the course of time, the lure of those electronic illusions, the power of their realistic dreams, became so strong that all but a handful of scientists "readily abandoned the outside world in which everything was rapidly becoming dead" (1136). As the story's title suggests, the eventual result was an entire city of half-alive "dreamers" or what we might today term media zombies who live only through their plugged-in technology and can no longer even care for themselves, as the irresistible illusion of reality effectively snuffs out reality itself.

These stories, and others like them, illustrate what Jeffrey Sconce has described as some of the pre-war period's more "fantastic conceptions of media presence" (7)—conceptions that would find in the new media of radio and the movies a powerful potential for reshaping our sense of reality by opening us up all the more directly to the shocks and sensations that were commonly associated with the experience of modernity, here channeled through its latest technological extensions.[3] In fact, these stories would increasingly bring into focus the complex technology of the movie industry, which had recently been transformed from its original, largely mechanical form into an electrically driven one, putting it squarely within

Gernsback's (and his *Experimenters'*) electrical orbit and casting a new light on the dual work—technical and fictional—of writers such as Gleason. The new technologies for sound reproduction, for image projection, and for three-dimensional imagery would, consequently, all come into more critical examination, as various pulp stories sounded warnings against that constantly developing film technology, as if the films themselves—and in more ways than just their tendency to distract us from reality with their pleasant illusions—might well prove dangerous.

As an example of this warning note, we might consider a tale such as Rice Ray's (aka Russell Blaiklock) *Wonder Stories* contribution "To-Day's Yesterday" (Jan. 1934). It relates how, during the filming of a key scene in Criterion Film Company's "great mine epic" *Hard Rock Jones* the main microphone suddenly and mysteriously disappears from the set (609), prompting lead sound technician Earl Cavanaugh—another of that recurring pulp type, a movie employee who also happens to be an amateur scientist—to investigate the strange loss. Cavanaugh, we learn, "had been a pioneer in the field with one of the largest electrical companies from the earliest experiments in sound recording" (611), and his explanation to his roommate George about the "photophone" version of talking pictures, the "variable area system" of sound recording that it used, and the miles of wire that had been employed on this particular film set both attest to his expertise and provide the sort of "hard" science grounding for the story that was favored by the early pulp editors and applauded by many readers.[4] Cavanaugh theorizes that a short probably caused the wiring that had been wound around a portion of the set to become "charged" and to form "an immense radio frequency coil" (613). Drawing on the theory that time itself is simply a series of electrical waves, he determines that the short-circuited film sound system must have produced a brief temporal shift, thereby thrusting the microphone into another time period or other dimension— a theory he confirms when he examines the soundtrack portion of the exposed film and finds recorded there an image of the microphone situated in what seems to be a primitive landscape. The wondrous possibility for time travel—or "wave shifting" (613)—is undercut, though, when his friend recklessly experiments with the process on his own, sending himself back in time without forethought about the supplies he might need or resources for his return. When Cavanaugh tunes in the same primitive location where the microphone had previously been observed, hoping to contact George, he sees just a "shattered, twisted" microphone, "as though some giant hand had seized, crushed and cast it down," as well as a broken camera slate bearing a partial message "I can't . . ." (617), apparently indicating that his friend has been done in by this strange, wild world to which he had recklessly consigned himself. The story ends on that note of help-lessness, as it sounds a warning about the dangerous potential of the new sound technology, and implicitly about the seductive nature of the movies as well.

A later novella published in *Thrilling Wonder Stories* (Aug. 1940), Henry Kuttner's "No Man's World," takes a similar tack as it describes the real-world impact of a newly developed 3-D film technology. Offered in the form of a historical account of the most notable events from the previous century, "No Man's World" opens on what hardly seems a historical occasion—the premiere of a new film, *Men of Tomorrow*, billed as demonstrating "an en-tirely new technique in movie-making, superior to magnafilm, multiplane, or any of the attempts to make the screen three-dimensional" (43), and as having been filmed "with all the technical tricks at Hollywood's command" (44). With an eye to the technical interests of the pulp audience, Kuttner even inserts a detailed explanation of some of the techniques involved in 3-D films, describing the new, multilayered sort of screen that had been de-veloped, as well as a novel projection beam that was used, one combining "the unseen ultra-violet and infra-red with visible light of normal vibration" (43). While unimportant in themselves, these developments help explain the film's historical status, because the combined technologies accidentally open a dimensional portal for two races of alien invaders, the Silicates and the Titans, who quite literally take on three-dimensional form, emerging from the movie screen as if it were a giant door, and turning Earth into "an ant-hill in No Man's Land" (48), as they continue a long-standing war between their races with little concern for the devastation they are causing to Earth and its people. With references to the Maginot Line and the then ongoing "European conflict," as well as his historian/narrator's remark about how quickly "governments forget imperialism and trade to fight the common enemy" (46), Kuttner manages to use this conflation of cinematic and SF elements to frame the current real-world conflict,[5] using the two alien groups to suggest the warring factions in Europe and the devastating impact that their struggle was having on the rest of the world, while also pointing accusingly at America's current policy of neutrality, here linked to a tendency to look the other way, to seek out entertainment instead of engaging with such momentous events. Even given the story's strained concept, with film technology opening the door to alien invasion and world catastrophe, to potentially making the only "Men of Tomorrow" which-ever group of aliens, or non-men, manages to survive this conflict, "No Man's World" stands as not only an effective thought experiment based on movie technology that was indeed being developed at the time and that Kuttner had quite probably seen demonstrated,[6] but also as a thoughtful commentary on the World War that was just beginning to reveal its full dimensions to American audiences of both literature and film (Figure 3.5).

The Ray and Kuttner stories present film, much as radio had initially been viewed, as a highly complex technology, able to function as a source

Figure 3.5. New 3-D film technology becomes a portal for alien invaders in Kuttner's "No Man's World" (*Thrilling Wonder Stories*, Aug. 1940).

of entertainment, as well as a new tool for scientific inquiry or discovery. And both use this technology as the basis for the sort of thought experiment that was a commonplace pulp strategy, depicting film sound equipment, projection technology, and even the movie screen itself as if they were potential doorways into another dimension or into the flow of time, and in the process critiquing a careless use of the technology that was then being developed. But these stories, the first by a reported member of the Hollywood film industry (see Bleiler 333) and the second by the author of the "Hollywood on the Moon" series, a group of stories about a space-traveling cameraman, are probably most important for the way they investigate that mobile gaze of the movies, finding in it the same potential for fantastic imaginings that powered the larger SF imagination.

In fact, to suggest the further development of pulp fiction's attitude towards film, we might turn to some of Kuttner's other stories in this vein, especially those about his space cameraman, Tony Quade, all of which make great capital from suggesting the very naturalness of the links between film, its special gaze, and the SF genre. Often writing with his wife, C. L. Moore, and sometimes using the pseudonym Lewis Padgett (among various others), Kuttner is perhaps better known today for some of his comic SF stories, such as those about the drunken inventor Galloway Gallegher who often, after sobering up, cannot remember the purpose of his latest "invention," or the Pete Manx series, co-authored with Arthur K. Barnes, about a time-traveling con-man. However, a significant element of his pulp work is set in the world of Hollywood, including a number of his non-SF efforts. For example, one of many "weird" stories Kuttner authored, "The Shadow on the Screen" (*Weird Tales*, Mar. 1938), recounts how the reclusive director Arnold Keene has developed a reputation for making over-the-top horror films. Drawing on that reputation, he invites a curious and admiring fellow director to his home to view the rough cut of his latest work, *The Nameless*, while challenging him to figure out how he managed to create this "living masterpiece of sheer weirdness," as he terms it (325). While he projects the film about a series of grisly murders, he boasts to his guest that "there's no substitute for realism" (327). And indeed, there is no trick here, no disparity between the real and the usual Hollywood-style illusions, for as we learn, Keene has used automated lights, cameras, and mechanized shifting sets, along with a deadly creature he discovered in Central America, to film the real murders of those who have accidentally stumbled upon his home or who, like his latest guest, have been invited there. Highly passionate about the impact of a realist cinema and "keen" on exploring the "ultimate" boundaries to such art, he has become insane and taken to producing what we would today describe as "snuff porn." But the director's end, when he is killed by his captive creature, once again serves as a warning about becoming too zealous in the pursuit of such a techno-logical realism.

Yet even as Kuttner was taking this "weird" approach on a trend in the film industry, he was also authoring a memorable and well-received series of pieces[7] for *Thrilling Wonder Stories* that foreground and find a special value in the very visuality of the movies. Noted SF editor and historian Sam Moskowitz has suggested that Kuttner was actually recruited to write "a series of novelettes based on the motion picture industry of the future" by *Thrilling*'s editor, Mort Weisinger (324–25). The resulting stories, described by pulp historian Mike Ashley as Kuttner's "big break" in SF publishing (*Time Machines* 102), would take what I want to suggest is a particularly modernist slant on that subject by filtering their futuristic vision through the actions of Tony Quade, the ace cinematographer for Nine Planets Films, Inc. Quade would provide the central focus for the well-received stories "Hollywood on the Moon" (April 1938), "Doom World" (Aug. 1938), "The Star Parade" (Dec. 1938), "The Energy Eaters" (Oct. 1939), "The Seven Sleepers" (May 1940)—the last two co-authored with Arthur K. Barnes—and "Trouble on Titan" (Feb. 1947). Of course, fashioning a series around a cinematographer (and sometimes director) might seem a curious move, and it is probably more so than Barnes' parallel development of Gerry Carlyle, the lead of his "Interplanetary Huntress" stories about a female Frank Buck-type, who searches the solar system for strange life forms as an acquisitions agent for the London Interplanetary Zoo.[8] But both characters, who are often in the jointly authored stories set in competition with each other, represent an effort to revamp what was, by this time, an already hackneyed space opera formula by fashioning thoroughly modern and unconventional SF heroes and action.

Quade particularly seems a kind of cosmic *flaneur*, someone whose driving desire is for new and exciting sights and for using the latest technology—such as rockets, surface skimmers, robots, and gravity neutralizers—to en-able him to explore alien, often inhospitable worlds, and to see in ways that others might only dream of. In fact, the first story in the series announces that "films were the breath of life to Quade" ("Hollywood" 15). And both Quade and Barnes's Gerry Carlyle are presented as natural products of that modernist spirit, with its impulse to explore and exploit the new visuality of the age, as they illustrate two parallel thrusts that Miriam Hansen sees as characteristic of the modernist spirit: Quade in his movie work suggesting what she terms the "restructuration of human perception and interac-tion effected by industrial-capitalist modes of production" such as film, and Carlyle with her capture-and-show demonstrating the new "culture of consumption and spectacular display" ("America" 362–63), typified by her exotic zoo exhibits.

While both characters are commonly involved with the film industry of the future, I want to focus mainly on Quade, who is especially resonant for this modernist intersection, since he almost literally embodies the mobile gaze that SF was beginning to exploit, while repeatedly surfacing a commentary on how film might give us special access to the real. Employed by Nine Planets Films and its Hollywood mogul-like boss Ludwig Von Zorn, Quade works out of the massive moon-based film studio dubbed Hollywood on the Moon, using a special glass-nosed rocket, fitted with 3-D cameras, telephoto lenses, and powerful lights, with which he regularly flies between different solar system locations. And while he regularly handles assignments that involve difficult location photography or the creation of camera-based "special effects that entailed plenty of risk" ("Hollywood" 14), his real desire, as he notes, is to make realistic documentaries in the vein of such famous twentieth century efforts as *Grass* (1925) and *Chang* (1927) ("Trouble" 41).[9] In his first appearance in "Hollywood on the Moon" he faces an especially difficult challenge, when the asteroid location for *Space Bandit*, "the biggest picture on Nine Planets' schedule" ("Hollywood" 14), runs afoul of what is termed an "ether eddy" that, scientists predict, will soon obliterate it. But Nine Planets cannot afford to shut down or cancel the dangerous project because of the competition its adventure films have been facing from Carlyle whose ability to bring back "the real thing" for popular consumption is making headlines and overshadowing the studio's extravagant illusions. Caught in what Hansen describes as "the spiral of shock, stimuli protection, and ever greater sensations" ("America" 363) common to late modernist audiences, Quade must either confront this challenging new reality or "fake it," as the Nine Planets' movies are often rumored to do, using robots and visual trickery.

In this case, Quade manages to save *Space Bandit* in a telling way, by merging the latest cinematic technology with his own documentary leanings. From his eyeball-like ship he films the ether eddy with a new ultra-violet lens that reveals something more about this event, that the eddy is actually a dimensional rift, a "hole in space . . . created by a planet in another universe" ("Hollywood" 28). This cinematic revelation draws out of the unstable nature of the universe—the suddenly obliterated asteroid—a compensatory vision of other, previously unknown worlds, with that "hole" yielding images of what are termed "incredible things." The resulting view through the dimensional rift also allows Nine Planets, striking an unusual note of authenticity, to herald its latest release as a new achievement in film realism, the first "fourth-dimensional flicker" ("Hollywood" 28). This combination of the "incredible" and the "real" would repeatedly surface in the subsequent Tony Quade stories, with the cinematographer's consistent ability to capitalize on his movie ship's mobile gaze constantly satisfying that modernist promise, as Hansen offers, to open up "hitherto unperceived modes of sensory perception and experience" ("Mass Production" 72).

For a further development of that impulse we might consider a longer and perhaps the most cinematically resonant entry in the Quade series, "The Star Parade." This novella begins by establishing the same proven context as the first story: starting each chapter with script-like shot directions; describing Quade's "speedy, powerful ship with the usual transparent nose of camera-craft" ("Star" 32) (Figure 3.6); offering a paean to Quade's headquarters, the artificial city of Hollywood on the Moon, described as "a place where science reaches out to new frontiers" ("Star" 28); and noting that "spiral of . . . ever greater sensations" embodied in the public's demand for new and more realistic attractions of the sort being offered by Gerry Carlyle and her interplanetary zoo. In fact, Von Zorn reprises the same complaint found in "Hollywood on the Moon," as he tells Quade, "We've filmed so much interplanetary stuff that the public won't pay to see our pics any more when Carlyle brings back the real thing" ("Star" 29). Of course, the notion that the public might become jaded by what Von Zorn terms the "interplanetary stuff" of his films seems a bit forced, especially for an SF audience that, as commentators have repeatedly noted, thrives on the sense of "wonder" that always seems the product of Quade's skilled mobile gaze. But it is a commentary that we might see as a continuation of those double visions we noted in some of the earlier pulp stories, which repeatedly juxtaposed the illusory world of film with the increasingly amazing one of real science, acknowledging and capitalizing on the appeal of both thrusts.

But "The Star Parade" more pointedly interrogates contemporary Hollywood's penchant for artifice and exaggeration, here mainly embodied in the human film "stars" and the problems their behavior has caused, disrupting Nine Planets' latest effort. After the director of the movie *The Star Parade* is hurt early in the shoot, the cast of conventionally temperamental actors refuses to "work with the assistant director" ("Star" 30): one throws a temper tantrum, another goes on an alcoholic bender, and a husband and wife team notorious for their bickering fall into yet another quarrel and declare they can no longer work together. With the director hospitalized and the cast playing out this familiar story of high-strung and difficult actors, Quade is promoted to director and must figure out how to bring these different—and difficult—elements of his cast together, while also dealing with a strange and threatening reality discovered on the film's Martian location.

Figure 3.6. The mobile gaze of Tony Quade's camera ship in "The Star Parade" (*Thrilling Wonder Stories*, Dec. 1938).

But that figuring out process is not the real focus of this story; rather, it is the parallels between the fragmented production and this deadly creature. While unlike anything ever brought back to the international zoo— in fact, like nothing in conventional reality—the creature functions as a kind of metaphor for the equally spectacular film's more familiar problems, while also dramatizing the formal tension at work here between order and chaos that we might read as symptomatic of Kuttner's own modernist mindset. After photographing parts of the creature and studying its strange and unpredictable appearances, Quade dubs it "jigsaw," likening it to a jigsaw puzzle because of its ability to separate itself into component parts: claws, a stomach, tentacles, eyes, with each part able to move independently but all linked by a separate and central brain that "sends out electrical impulses that order its various extensions around" (Star" 39). In effect, the creature is a horrific version of the temperamental film cast, a monster as cinematic metaphor and a puzzle to be solved. Quade's task is to bring under control—or edit together—all of these "piecemeal monsters" of Mars ("Star" 40), while using both sets of puzzle pieces (cast and monster) to help him film a never-before-captured phenomenon known as the Inferno—a massive cavern that runs to the center of Mars and that spews heat and destructive "rays . . . stronger than radioactivity" ("Star" 29). In effect, Quade has to go almost literally through (or to) hell in order to shape both monsters into a working group, as he uses the fragmentary creature to carry cameras into the center of the planet, with its mobile eyes literally becoming the camera's mobile gaze. The resulting footage, when cobbled together with scenes made with the forced cooperation of his other "monster"—the fragmented cast—helps produce a satisfactory narrative, overcome any rumors of fakery, and make "a smash hit out of the corniest flicker ever made" ("Star" 44). It also suggests that it is indeed possible to work around and through film's various "modes of production" in order to gain a unique vantage on "the real thing"—or in this case, a Martian "thing."

The stories done in conjunction with Arthur K. Barnes, "The Energy Eaters" and "The Seven Sleepers," both of which bring together the characters of Quade and Gerry Carlyle, further develop this emphasis on the possibilities of a cinematic realism by framing the seeming tension between film and reality as a literal feud between these two figures. While Quade continues to find ways to "get the pix of a lifetime" in support of his boss Von Zorn's adventure films, Carlyle repeatedly rails against the film industry and especially the filmmakers of Nine Planets, whom she terms "the biggest bunch of crooked fakers in the [Solar] System" ("Seven" 96). When in "The Energy Eaters" it is suggested that she work with the film company on its latest project, she quickly refuses, announces that she will not "see the public hoaxed by such fake spectacles" ("Seven" 96–97), and once more asserts that "the name Gerry Carlyle means the real thing" (31). When in both stories Quade and Carlyle are forced by circumstances to combine their resources and skills, each schemes to trick the other, although their tricks amount to little more than neat plot twists that ultimately lead them to work together, in the process demonstrating what might be accomplished when a passion for film and a passion for "the real thing" are combined. In both cases Carlyle winds up acquiring a new creature for her interplanetary zoo, while Quade not only manages to get just the sort of exciting footage needed for his company's next "super epic of cosmic adventure" ("Seven" 97), but also to capture documentary footage of Carlyle in action, thereby allowing the studio to bill her as actually the "star" of its films *The Energy Eaters* and *Call of the Comet*. Brought together by film, the Carlyle and Quade pairings dramatize how the former's collecting activities and "attractions" might indeed mesh with the latter's conventional cinematic work, allowing the movies to achieve the sort of realist—and revealing—vision of which, Kuttner implies, they are ultimately capable.

The Quade/Carlyle pairing was well received, with several letters to *Thrilling Wonder Stories'* "The Reader Speaks" column labeling each one the "best story" of its respective issue, and a letter in the July 1940 number demanding "more of Quade and Carlyle" (121). That highly positive response may be partly due to the unusual sexual dynamic they embodied, one that matched the equally adventurous and capable male and female characters—even capitalizing at times on Carlyle, because of her name and dangerous activities, being mistaken for a man—without resolving their competition in the sort of easy romantic relationship commonly found in such stories or, more often, in movies of the period. But beyond that appeal there is the other dramatic connection that we have noted at work here, that embodied in the wondrous images of the Solar System that Quade captures and the equally wondrous samples of planetary life that Quade and Carlyle consistently refer to as "the real thing." In fact, both "The Energy Eaters" and "The Seven Sleepers" underscore the extent to which the filmmakers—for all of their dependence on advanced technology such as robotics, special suits, and a 3-D camera Carlyle dismissively describes as "an over-sized gadget composed chiefly of revolving mirrors and vari-colored lightbulbs" ("Seven" 99)—do indeed manage to capture the real. The surprise revelation at the end of the latter story is that the creatures Carlyle has discovered on a comet, Proteans as they are termed, actually communicate visually, "by projecting pictures of thought-images on their membranous surfaces"; ironically, what she has acquired for the London zoo in this case is described as a living "super motion-picture projector" ("Seven" 106), a creature that not only literalizes modernism's new visuality, but also suggests the combination of impulses that drive the Quade and Carlyle stories. It is an ironic but fitting cap to the series, as found creature and captured footage are presented as functioning similarly and equally contributing to a science fictional sense of wonder.

In light of the ongoing discussion throughout the pre-war period about the function of film, especially as outlined in Walter Benjamin's key essay "The Work of Art in the Age of Mechanical Reproduction," this ironic turn seems especially suggestive. Carlyle's attitude certainly echoes Benjamin's famous complaint about the commercial cinema wherein, he offers, the vaunted "equipment-free aspect of reality" that film supposedly delivers has too often "become the height of artifice," leaving the real a kind of "orchid in the land of technology" ("Work" 233). And yet, as "The Seven Sleepers" suggests, even nature might at times mimic film and its techniques. So while all these stories consistently acknowledge the film industry's reputation for artifice, outlandish "sensation," or "spectacles" ("Seven" 97)—a reputation they link to the bottom-line attitude of producers such as Von Zorn or the personalities of various self-centered actors and film executives—they also ultimately present film, thanks to its very "mechanical" or scientific nature, as a useful tool for piercing through what Benjamin termed the "aura" of things ("Work" 221), providing audiences with a new way of seeing and, in the process, giving them fresh access to the real. In the hands of figures like Quade, they might even furnish viewers with what could be described as a new and equally authentic sort of "zoo"—a series of attractions attesting to what might yet be seen in the outer and largely unknown spaces of the universe. With that turn, and despite the stories' repeated send-up of the personalities and superficial concerns of the movie industry, Kuttner was effectively endorsing what the cinema has to offer, especially its ability to function much like SF itself, providing audiences with an art well suited to their needs and desires, and inspiring them every bit as much as the latest developments in science and technology were then inspiring SF literature during the late pre-war period.

While both Kuttner and Barnes would return to these characters for a few other stories in the 1940s—Barnes with two *Thrilling Wonder Stories* entries, "Trouble on Titan" (Feb. 1941) and "Siren Satellite" (Winter 1946); and Kuttner with his own "Trouble on Titan" story done for the same magazine (Feb. 1947)—their key characters, Quade and Carlyle, would not be fictional partners again. There would be some interaction between Carlyle and Nine Planets Films in Barnes's "Trouble on Titan," wherein she would once again have to deal with the double-crossing of Von Zorn, "the Little Napoleon of the film industry" ("Trouble" 50), and Carlyle would continue to tout her reputation for bringing back "the real thing" for zoo exhibit. Similarly, the last of the Quade stories would mention that Von Zorn, as part of his ongoing feud with Carlyle, had created a series of "Gerri Murri" cartoons lampooning the hunter and her fantastic creatures, for which he was being sued for libel. But these references are largely to establish context and to provide links to the earlier pieces by both writers. The productive dynamic of the Quade and Carlyle figures, and especially the use of that combination to foreground, debate, and finally demonstrate film's own realistic possibilities, including its ability to provide audiences with the sort of visuality that was a signature effect of both the modernist agenda and a maturing SF genre, would be explored no further. Perhaps there was simply no further need. For in these last stories both Kuttner and Barnes describe a world that is already defined by its investment in the visual—with offices and space ships all equipped with tele-visors, visual newsfeeds, and televisions, and with "Hollywood" expanding throughout the solar system. The impact and importance of visual media like the movies seems taken for granted, a fact of life for both real post-war audiences, who were already encountering the new visual regime of television, and those fictional inhabitants of the future who remained avid fans of Hollywood on the Moon's products.

However, that development of an optically attuned world—or solar system—was already apparent in the larger body of pulp SF. Starting in the early 1930s a great many stories would present film and the visual record it embodies as a common element of future or advanced alien civilizations, in the process underscoring Gernsback's description of the movies as, like SF itself, symptomatic of a truly modern world. Contributions like Walter Kateley's "The World of a Hundred Men" (*Science Wonder Stories*, Mar. 1930), P. Schuyler Miller's "Through the Vibrations" (*Amazing Stories*, May 1931), Aladra Septama's "The Terrors of Arelli" (*Amazing Stories Quarterly*, Fall 1930), and Raymond Z. Gallun's "The Weapon" (*Amazing Stories*, May 1936) all describe modern-day humans stumbling upon—or being shown—motion picture records of ancient civilizations, dinosaurs or similarly strange creatures, and alien visitors, among other wondrous things. This repeated discovery of cultures that use film or its cognates as a kind of historical marker or testament begs further consideration. On the one hand, it serves as a kind of narrative shorthand, that is, a convenient way of allowing characters to access some historical context that might be important background for a particular story. But on the other hand, this use of film suggests that such optical media might also function as a kind of scientific authority, a reliable record of the real world. In these stories and others the movies form a useful, even necessary instrument for framing or understanding things: as a witness to events, a record of the past, or an important message—through an obviously valorized medium—that has been left by other, pointedly more advanced civilizations and other times.

Of course, that valorizing of film, whether as historical record, cultural communication, or alien artifact, presumes the sort of status that the Quade/Carlyle series had repeatedly argued for. It is a presumption we can see strongly demonstrated at the beginning of a slightly later story, Richard S. Shaver's *Amazing Stories* piece "We Dance for the Dom" (Jan. 1950). Here, to help Earth visitors understand the source of a conflict within a nearby solar system, the ruler Vanue offers a disc on which has been recorded the violent history of those planets. The effect of watching that visual history is such that, as one character notes, "the augmented record reached out and seized us with the greater-than-reality illusion that is the value of record" (10). Not just "the real thing," this "greater-than-reality illusion" is received by that audience as "recorded wisdom" (10), as providing access to truth itself, and its power, as the story then illustrates, serves a significant end, helping to ward off a contemporary cultural drift toward war—a drift that, we might assume, seemed already at work in the world of the Cold War. This DVD-like cognate for the cinema's own illusion of reality reminds us not only of how much the visuality of the movies mattered to the development of the SF imagination, but also of film's metaphoric role as part of an ongoing, yet increasingly self-assured discourse to be found in the pulps about how an imaginative form like SF, especially when delivered through a film-like medium, might itself be able to present "the real thing," that is, an accurate, forceful, and perhaps even *helpful* vision of other worlds, other times, and other beings.

CHAPTER 4

Convergence and the Rhetoric of Scientifilm

The extent to which film had become incorporated into pulp fiction's narratives—as context, subject matter, and visual inspiration— becomes especially apparent when we consider another sort of internal discourse in which the magazines' readers and editors were commonly engaged. Throughout the pre-war years, readers' letters to the magazines, editors' responses and editorial commentaries, and the introduction of formal movie reviews all highlight ongoing discussions—in the culture as well as in the SF magazines—about the potential of the scientifilm for doing the sort of work that was typically associated with SF and its modernist thrust, that is, for suggesting ways of revisioning and reshaping the world and the self. But Francesco Casetti reminds us that this sort of discourse should hardly be surprising, since in this period "the filmic image" afforded a common "field of convergence for different dimensions" of the modern imagination (75)—a "convergence" that we might see embodied in the way that readers and editors typically introduced the cinema into their discussions about science and technology, treating it not as a totally separate subject, but as another, and especially attractive way of thinking about, depicting, and arguing for the importance of science and technology to the shape of things to come. This chapter examines that particular internal discourse in the context of this modernist sense of convergence— or what John Rieder has more precisely termed "multiple communities of practice" (*Science Fiction* 11)—by way of demonstrating how envisioning the work of science and technology seemed almost inevitably to draw on an already widespread, culturally integrated cinematic imagination.

That such "communities"—of readers, writers, and editors—often thought cinematically, using it as a common source of description, reference, or metaphor, in a sense, as a common language, should hardly be surprising. As Laura Marcus has chronicled, in the early twentieth century the cinema had been rapidly assimilated into the common "habit of thought," as a "modernist and modernized consciousness" increasingly seemed to be "inflected by, and perhaps inseparable from, cinematic consciousness" (47). While we have already seen how pulp SF easily incorporated the cinema as subject, it is worth underscoring this point about a new "consciousness," already made in the previous chapter, by noting a few examples from fiction appearing in *Amazing Stories*. Recalling that emphasis on "the real thing" discussed in chapter 3, L. B. Rosborough's "Hastings—1066" has its central character excitedly tell a visiting friend about a new sort of time machine he has crafted. Faced with some skepticism and anticipating his friend's line of thinking, he offers a telling, even derisive comparison, promising the visitor that he will gaze "not at a motion picture with mere puppet players, but at the actual deeds of flesh-and-blood characters" (June 1934, 58), that is, at something more than just movies. In similar fashion, the narrator of Joe W. Skidmore's "The Velocity of Escape" observes that a character seems to be moving at a highly unnatural pace, "like a figure on a slow motion picture screen" (Aug. 1934, 74). And when an explorer of an advanced civilization describes a device holding the history of the people in Henry J. Kostkos' "North God's Temple," he employs an obvious simile, describing it as "a strip of metal tape, wound on a metal reel, like a motion picture film" (Aug., 1934, 109). Perhaps unconsciously, but more likely searching for an image that would immediately evoke the scene, character, or object in their readers' minds, these authors, like many others, naturally gravitated to cinematic examples or tropes, in the process demonstrating the sort of imaginative convergence of which Casetti speaks, as the familiar world of the filmic image not only provides their readers a common touchstone, but also reminds us how much the movies, even in this early period, had already colonized the cultural consciousness, linking subjective and objective realms and becoming, as Ian Christie puts it, a kind of "mirror of modern life" (39).

But as we have also noted, Hugo Gernsback in an early editorial had pointed the readers of his *Science Wonder Stories* in this very direction when he described the scientifilm as part of the same climate that had produced scientifiction and suggested that both were part of the same modern way of thinking—and talking—about our world. It should be no surprise that his suggestion would be taken up by the authors of the stories he published, or that they hoped to have him publish, as well as by the readers of the pulps and the work of subsequent magazine editors, all of whom in the publications' pages frequently alluded to the movies, the flickers, the talking pictures—or scientifilms. One result of this mindfulness would be an ongoing discourse throughout the pre-war period that not only assumed it was appropriate to talk about film and SF together, but also increasingly emphasized the kinship, in much the way that the fiction was tending to do. In that ongoing dialogue, one that, as we shall see, often inspired fans' calls for the film industry to increase its production of scientifilms, we can begin to sense how the modernity of SF might easily be translated into this context or, to borrow a line from Leo Charney and Vanessa Schwartz, might be "best understood as inherently cinematic" (2).

One of the most obvious instances of this sort of convergence or coming together occurs in the pulps' various letters columns, where readers, editors, and even the fiction writers themselves often engaged in conversations about science, technology, SF stories, and even the movies. All of the SF magazines encouraged their readers' comments, even interaction among those readers, as is evidenced by their printing the addresses of some letter writers and inviting others to weigh in on points that various correspondents had raised. The result was a kind of readers' culture that was a hallmark of the SF pulps, and one that found its special place in the department that each magazine devoted to this commentary. These included *Amazing Stories*' "Discussions" and later "Correspondence Corner," *Astounding*'s "Brass Tacks," *Wonder Stories*' and *Thrilling Wonder Stories*' "The Reader Speaks," *Startling Stories*' "The Ether Vibrates," *Captain Future*'s "Under Observation," and *Planet Stories*' "The Vizigraph"—its title perhaps most suggestively linking writing and new visual media. But this near-universal feature of the various pulps was more than just part of their common and freely imitated formula. While inviting such correspondence was certainly good business for the editors, providing them with free columns of print, unsolicited endorsements of their product, and emotional, as well as intellectual engagement for their readership, it was also an attraction in itself. In fact, pulp historian Everett F. Bleiler forthrightly styles this constant feature of the pulps as "entertainment" (xxvi), a description borne out by many correspondents who remarked that the letters department was one of the first things that they turned to in each issue. And when *Thrilling Wonder Stories* began to downsize its letters department in the early 1940s (as the magazine moved from a bimonthly to a monthly publication, and thus initially would have had fewer letters to draw from for each issue), readers quickly took note and complained that "The Reader Speaks" had become "much too small" (Aug. 1940, 118). Another correspondent to *Amazing Stories* not only praised its "Discussions" section, but also offered a keen insight into what the readers felt they derived from the various letters: "It is almost like a story, showing us who can read between the lines, the psychology of the people who write therein" (Apr. 1934, 135).

But more than just another sort of "story" to help fill out an issue, this popular feature contributed much to the character of the magazines. In his reader-focused history of the pulps, John Cheng describes how these columns formed a kind of gossipy "backyard" fence across which passed a wide range of comments about both the contents of the magazines and the larger culture of their readers. And what any survey of those readers' letters quickly reveals is the variety of responses to the magazines and their fictional offerings that the correspondence represented. Besides the expected commentaries both praising and pillorying the SF authors and almost invariably ranking their favorite stories, readers debated about the need for more—or less—science in the stories, challenged the presentation or accuracy of the fiction's science, commented on the cover illustrations and the talents of the artists responsible for them, suggested subjects for future stories or ideas for additional features, while they also responded—in varying tones—to other readers' comments as well as to recent cultural developments. In many cases the letters elicited editorial responses and extended commentary, and in some instances the SF authors would themselves join in these ongoing discussions, by responding to criticisms of their work, pointing to sources or inspirations for their pieces, or expanding on comments about the science and technology they had incorporated into the stories. As Cheng offers, this diversity of concerns and purposes made the readers feel, as was often expressed in the letters, as if their "opinions mattered" (58), while also helping to build the character of this new and constantly developing genre. The letters portrayed SF as an important gateway to "a participatory, democratic science" (Cheng 60), a science that was not only important to the future but was also something in which everyone—or at least everyone with an interest in science and technology—seemed able to play a role.

More to the point for this study, one of the ways those readers' opinions and editorial responses ranged beyond the stories and their correct or incorrect depiction of science and technology was in the way they tapped into what Marcus terms that "modernized consciousness," often drawing film into their discussions. Just as SF fans today take to the internet to spread word about forthcoming films, such as the latest installment in the *Star Wars*, *Guardians of the Galaxy*, or *Avengers* series, pulp letters often suggest a shared movie consciousness, as they offer opinions on those scientifilms that had recently been seen, list titles of works rumored to be in production, or suggest other stories that Hollywood, if only its moguls were really astute, should rush to produce. In short, they demonstrate an interest in and felt appetite for a cinematic companion to the literature of the pulps—and another way of binding together the rapidly coalescing SF community, which Gernsback, in announcing the formation of his fan group the Science Fiction League, and with his usual enthusiasm for the *idea* of SF, exaggeratedly referred to as "a vast movement" that reached across various media ("The Science Fiction League" 933).

Among the most vocal of those correspondents who helped rally an interest in SF cinema was Forrest J. Ackerman, who was also listed as an "Executive Director" of the Science Fiction League. Ackerman would later become a prolific writer, editor, and collector of SF film-related memorabilia, and was someone whom Mike Ashley and Robert Lowndes nicely describe as "the science-fiction voice of Hollywood" (*Gernsback Days* 182). Although barely a teenager when he first began writing letters to *Science Wonder Quarterly* (Fall 1929, 136), Ackerman, perhaps capitalizing on his Hollywood address and stressing his familiarity with what he—in an unfortunate although perhaps tongue-in-cheek coinage—labeled "Scientificinemaland" (*Wonder Stories*, Apr. 1936, 1020), grandiosely styled himself as a film industry insider and frequently contributed "news reports" to *Wonder Stories* and other pulps touting rumored SF film productions and initiating exchanges with fans who were likewise interested in discussing recent or forthcoming scientifilms. Later, after the formation of the Science Fiction League, which had its own department for letters and chapter news in *Wonder Stories* and later in *Thrilling Wonder Stories*, Ackerman would repeatedly feature in published reports from the Los Angeles chapter, usually describing his film-related contributions. For instance, in 1936, there was an account describing how he exhibited at a meeting "an exciting new selection of special stills from London of Wells's wonder film, 'Things to Come'" (*Wonder Stories*, Dec. 1936, 116). At a 1937 meeting "cinemauthority Ackerman audibly synopsized [the] scientifilm 'Man Who Lived Again'" (*Thrilling Wonder Stories*, Oct. 1937, 124). At the Christmas 1938 meeting he played a phonograph recording of *Things to Come* (*Thrilling Wonder Stories*, Apr. 1939, 115). And at various times he is noted as having organized outings to attend local SF or fantasy film screenings.[1]

But Ackerman's enthusiasm extended beyond local League activities. While Gernsback in another editorial piece announced that "the motion pictures have already been converted . . . to Science Fiction," resulting in the recent production of "a number of excellent films," he also reminded his readers that "much remains to be done" and exhorted them to join in the "great mission" of SF (*Wonder Stories*, May 1934, 1061–62). In one of his numerous letters to *Wonder Stories* we get a sense of Ackerman's enthusiasm and desire to play a leading role in that "mission," as he announces that he has initiated a personal "campaign for more science fiction motion pictures" and, as if it were linked to that personal campaign,[2] shares the information that RKO is currently preparing a film entitled *Creation*. Offering what must have seemed to many pulp readers a kind of privileged information, he explains that this effort will be in the vein of *The Lost World* (1925), a pioneering special effects film that was frequently cited—and praised—by other letter writers, and he notes that it will draw on the special effects talents of "the man who furnished the dinosaurs" for that movie—Willis O'Brien. Based on that pedigree, his judgment was that the film promised "to be an A-1 science fiction thriller" ("Another Science Fiction Movie," 806), as he urged other fans to watch for and support it (Figure 4.1).

In a slightly later letter to *Wonder Stories* Ackerman would suggest that his personal "campaign" was already meeting with some success, as was evidenced by a marked ramp up in SF production in Hollywood. In this piece he announced a bit precipitously that "there are twenty five scientifilms forthcoming" ("More Scientifilms," 286), and among that group he cited a number of titles that were sure to arouse interest because they were sourced in the work of the canonical SF author H. G. Wells. Probably drawing on accounts in such industry papers as *The Film Daily, Motion Picture Daily*, and *Variety*, he pointed specifically to Paramount's reported intention to film *The War of the Worlds*, Universal's to produce *The Invisible Man*, and another, unnamed studio's projected adaptation of *The Time Machine* (1286). While Ackerman's announcements obviously were more often enthusiastic than accurate—Paramount would eventually film *The War of the Worlds*, but not until 1953; MGM would produce *The Time Machine* but in 1960; and *Creation* would never advance beyond some very limited test footage, although it would become an interesting footnote in film history as a kind of trial run for *King Kong* (1933)[3]—his letters always radiated what Paul A. Carter refers to as a "hobbyist's enjoyment" (300), as he anticipated the possibility for SF's expansion throughout the film industry and sought to share that enthusiasm.

In fact, the final issue of *Wonder Stories* would print another Ackerman letter—longer than most—that would once again highlight his enthusiasm and demonstrate a further development of that cinematic consciousness. The point of this report was in part to update readers on several recent or soon-to-be-released SF films, including such titles as *The Invisible Ray, 100 Years to Come, The Man Who Could Work Miracles*, and *Unseen Death*, all of which, in a comment that speaks to a quickly forming sense of genre, he notes "will be recognized on sight as scientifilms" (Apr. 1936, 1011). But he also wanted to offer like-minded readers another source of such

Another Science Fiction Movie

Editor, WONDER STORIES:

Our campaign for more science fiction motion pictures is resulting in huge success. First Universal gave us "Frankenstein" and now—now R-K-O, I am happy to announce, is making "Creation"!

As you all know the plot of "Frankenstein," I will not retell it here. However, I am positive you would all be very interested in knowing a bit more about "Creation." It will be a modern story of weird adventure. A yacht is caught in a tropical storm. As it is driven near to a rocky shore, an earth shock dislodges the side of a cliff, revealing a subterranean passage. Helpless before the storm, the yacht is carried into the aperture to emerge finally in a world peopled by giant beast of another age. The man who furnished the dinosaurs for the silent film of "The Lost World" will supply the prehistoric monsters for this picture also. "Creation" ought to be an A-1 science fictional thriller!

Forrest J. Ackerman,
530 Staples Avenue,
San Francisco, Calif.

(There is no doubt but that motion picture companies will be willing, even eager to make science fiction movies if they can be assured that a public demand exists. The demand already exists in Germany and Russia. It is up to science fiction enthusiasts in America to create the demand here. WONDER STORIES is working on a plan now to organize that demand and make it effective.— *Editor.*)

Figure 4.1. One of Forrest J. Ackerman's early fan letters to *Wonder Stories* (Nov. 1931).

information. Directing them to *Fantasy* magazine (a fanzine better known as *Science Fiction Digest*), he notes that he has there begun authoring a new column "Scientifilm Snapshots" (eventually titled simply "The Scientifilms") that will provide "advance information on domestic *as well as* overseas' scientifilms" (1011). In this case, too, though, Ackerman would impulsively trumpet several films, as we can assume that *100 Years to Come* is the British production *Things to Come* (1936), already in release under its proper title by the time his letter was printed, and that *Unseen Death* probably refers to the American *Death from a Distance*.[4] Despite such errors and undeterred by past missteps, he promises that his regular reports will provide readers with "the facts" they want about the film industry's plans for scientifilm production (1011).

Yet in keeping with the backyard nature of the correspondence columns, Ackerman's letters almost always drew responses from both the editors and other, similarly enthusiastic film fans. One of those readers, for example, laments the seeming "indifference of movie producers to science fiction," particularly given the film industry's usual product, or what the writer terms, in contrast to European films, the general "deluge of hooey from Hollywood" (*Wonder Stories*, July 1931, 278). Another puts a more pointed cultural spin on that Hollywood neglect, observing that, based on the evidence of ambitious works like Fritz Lang's *Metropolis* (1927) and *Woman in the Moon* (1929), "Germany is way ahead of us in the production of science films," and urging like-minded readers to "start a deluge of letters traveling Hollywood-ward" to demand the production of our own "science fantasy pictures" (*Wonder Stories*, Aug. 1931, 426). Yet another would thank Ackerman for his frequent reports, while asking the logical question of why *Wonder Stories* did not itself provide such news as a regular feature. The writer would also take the editor (most likely David Lasser) to task for his seemingly skeptical attitude, as he had expressed doubt that American film companies were really interested in "scientifiction films," and were "merely sounding out the public" to determine if such films had any appeal ("Science Fiction Movies" 800). Pursuing a similar point, a reader in *Amazing Stories* requested that the editor consider creating a dedicated column that would provide the readers with "dope on some future scienti-films, viz: date of release, name of producing company, type of film, feature players, etc." (Apr. 1934, 137). And in the absence of such a column, yet another *Amazing* reader would write, asking how he might personally contact Ackerman, since he is obviously "an authority on scientifilms, and I would like some information concerning the new films" (Apr. 1937, 138).

Besides simply reflecting a burgeoning interest in seeing and learning more about scientifilms, such film-focused letters often seemed to converge on a particular vision of what the readers would most like to see in these movies. Specifically, they commonly pointed to the stories of the pulps as strangely neglected fodder for the movie industry, with several blaming the pulps' editors, suggesting that they should be doing more to promote the fiction they published, calling it to the attention of Hollywood producers, in effect, functioning like agents for the top SF writers or, more to the point, crusaders in the great cause of SF. A correspondent to *Wonder Stories*, for example, reported how, in his frustration at the lack of SF films, he had previously sent a letter to Carl Laemmle, President of Universal Pictures, suggesting "that a good talkie might be made from Mrs. Shelley's *Frankenstein*"—a film, he proudly noted, that was soon to be released—and he wondered why, with the pulps' demonstrably "popular" stories, "more of the same kind" of adaptations were not being suggested and made (July 1931, 280). Similarly, an English reader enthusiastically responded to *Thrilling Wonder Stories*' publication of the Henry Kuttner novella "Hollywood on the Moon" (one of the more popular pieces from this period) by suggesting that "Hollywood should film the story," and adding, "If they would take the risk, I'm sure that this stf. [scientifiction] film would be a box-office success owing to its originality" (Dec. 1938, 118). A slightly later issue of the same pulp would find a reader who, while praising the quality of recent publications, noted that Howard K. Barnes' Gerry Carlyle (the "Interplanetary Huntress") series also seemed unfairly neglected and "ideal for the movies," particularly since the stories usually had her involved with the film industry in some way, and he too wondered why these and other efforts were not being produced, once again blaming the pulps' editors for not advocating their fiction with the movie industry (Feb. 1941, 13). And suggesting an interesting variation on that convergence impulse, a *Thrilling Wonder Stories* reader, with little concern for issues of copyright, requested that the magazine consider introducing a "scientifilm series," that is, a string of stories adapted from "the many new futuristic films being released" and illustrated with "stills taken from the movies" (July 1940, 119). While all of these letters certainly paint a picture of a fan-ish fascination with and desire for more scientifilms, they also might suggest something more—that many SF readers connected to the magazines' fiction by visualizing it through imaginations that had been at least partially shaped by the film industry and its usual products, and they appreciated that fiction in part—and probably unconsciously—because of this connection; that is, because of film's ability to bring those popular imaginings so powerfully to life.

As a number of the cited letters further suggest, the editorial responses to this cinematic enthusiasm and the requests for more information about the world of scientifilm were far from uniform. In part that difference is probably traceable to the various editors of the pulps, each of whom may have had a different attitude toward film and its ability to effectively carry out the mission of SF, especially given the sort of "hooey" that, as we have seen, some associated with the movies—or at least with American movies, which were typically seen as less serious about the treatment of science and technology issues than their European counterparts. But part of that different attitude might also derive from, curiously enough, another sort of convergence that was at work in the world of SF and SF publishing. As Cheng observes, throughout the pre-war years the very term "science fiction" (or scientifiction) often shifted in reference and increasingly came to be marked by a certain convenient "ambiguity" in its use. Especially in the editorial columns, as he notes, it was freely used to refer, almost equally, to "fiction, magazines, cultural genre" (46); that is, not just to the sort of stories that were being marketed (the "fiction"), but also to the pulps as vehicles for new ideas, engaged in what many saw as the very serious work of SF (the "magazines"), as well as to the science-engaged sort of discourse that bulked beyond the boundaries of the purely literary medium (the "cultural genre"). This complex discourse, akin to what John Rieder refers to as the "mass cultural genre system" (*Science Fiction* 1), included film, radio, comic strips, and even the many world's fairs that appeared during the pre-war era and that almost always celebrated the latest developments in science and technology. That very convergence of references, I would suggest, allowed film to be excluded at times and to be drawn into the conversation at others, especially as editors—and in Gernsback's case, the publisher—sought to navigate the different and shifting interests of the readers by emphasizing one or another of those connotations that were built into the SF (or scientifiction) designation.

Where we can most easily notice this shifting (or shifty) valence is in the various editors' general comments on and direct responses to their readers' letters about the movies. In the pre-war years those editors, most well-known to the SF community, included Gernsback (*Amazing Stories, Wonder Stories*), David Lasser (*Wonder Stories*), Mort Weisinger (*Thrilling Wonder Stories*), T. O'Conor Sloane (*Amazing Stories*), Raymond A. Palmer (*Amazing Stories*), Harry Bates (*Astounding Stories*), F. Orlin Tremaine (*Astounding Stories*), John W. Campbell, Jr. (*Astounding Stories*), and Malcolm Reiss (*Planet Stories*), among others. Since in some cases they signed their editorial comments or replies to readers and in others did not, distinguishing individuals' attitudes toward the movies—perhaps with the exception of Gernsback, who, as we have already noted, argued for the inclusion of "talking pictures" under the big tent of SF—is a difficult and perhaps even unnecessary task. The key point here is that most of those commentators (or their assistants) were often drawn out about and given opportunities to address the issue of the scientifilm, usually in response to specific reader comments or queries, but in some cases in the form of general statements about the film industry's attitude toward SF and the SF community.

In a number of instances those editorial commentaries, as we previously noted, seem a bit skeptical if not totally dismissive of the possibilities for a true SF cinema, as when, in response to one of Ackerman's frequent reports of forthcoming scientifilms, the editor at *Wonder Stories* (probably Lasser) disdainfully observes that "film companies are in the habit of making announcements any time a bright young executive gets an idea" (Oct. 1933, 286)—a point perhaps underscored by the young Ackerman's eager announcement about seemingly every SF-related project whispered in the trade papers. More often, though, that skepticism seems to reflect a sense that such films might have difficulty matching the accomplishments of the literature in terms of scientific accuracy, challenging ideas, and especially a realistic treatment of science and technology. It is an attitude that at least hints of an element of media bias, based on both the popular conception of the Hollywood film industry—a conception given specific voice in Arthur K. Barnes's Gerry Carlyle stories wherein her character repeatedly derides the movies for not caring about "the real thing"—and the perceived limitations of movie technology, as a commentary in *Thrilling Wonder Stories*, most likely by editor Mort Weisinger, might illustrate. He begins by acknowledging a point noted in many readers' letters, as well as in printed reports from the various Science Fiction League chapters, that "scientifilms are popular in America today," but he then inserts a caution, describing what he sees as the prevailing industry climate, at least in America. It is, he claims, one in which "Hollywood producers are slow to satisfy the growing demand for them. For, while special photography can simulate almost any desired scene, the scope required by the scientifilm is something different to be reckoned with, something that bucks the ingenuity of the most expert cameramen and technicians" (Dec. 1939, 10). That emphasis on "scope" seems almost deliberately ambiguous, pointing as it does at both the ideas or subject matter of SF and the technological limits of the movies—either of which, in his eyes, might stand as a barrier to achieving the potential for a true SF cinema.

That comment echoes several earlier observations that appeared in the pages of *Wonder Stories*, probably offered by David Lasser and Charles Hornig, respectively (judging from the dates of publication), as they expressed an ongoing consternation with the American film industry's efforts in this area. Responding in the magazine's "The Reader Speaks" column, the former suggests, somewhat disdainfully, that "a great deal of what is projected in the minds of film executives, or in the releases of their publicity men, never materializes. They remain in the 4th dimension of desire and expectation" (Oct. 1933, 286). And the latter, in similar fashion, notes that "the film companies have bought stories that they have put on the shelf and have altogether abandoned other ideas for this kind of picture" (Feb. 1934, 800). Writing in much the same vein, C. A. Brandt of *Amazing* slightingly contrasts the national "intelligentsia" to what he terms "Hollywood 'Fillumgentsia,'" as he lambasts the American film industry's "reeling off sickly sweet idiocies and gangster adulations" while ignoring "what treasures are piled up in such stories as this Magazine [sic] has published" ("Notes" 135). Given Hollywood's frequent tendency throughout the pre-war years to relegate SF to the status of the B-film or serial, as is evidenced by works like *The Black Cat* (1934), *Murder by Television* (1935), *Undersea Kingdom* (1936), and *Buck Rogers* (1939); or bind it within a larger horror format, as in the cases of *Frankenstein* (1931), *Island of Lost Souls* (1933), and *The Invisible Ray* (1936), such attitudes certainly have some reason. However, the pulps were themselves far from pure in this regard, with writers—and we might single out such popular period authors as H. P. Lovecraft and Henry Kuttner—publishing very similar stories in avowedly SF magazines such as *Astounding Stories* and *Thrilling Wonder Stories*, as well as in pulps like *Weird Tales* that featured a variety of fantasy-oriented genres.

Yet there are also numerous occasions on which the various pulp editors express their genuine hopes for a more ambitious SF cinema—one that would support an SF and modernist agenda. For example, even while dismissing most of Hollywood's SF efforts, the editor of *Wonder Stories* also admits to having "fond memories of *Metropolis* and *The Lost World* of the silent days" ("Science Fiction Movies" 800). And in several other issues of *Wonder Stories* editorial commentaries pursue this more optimistic vein, arguing that "there is no reason why well-staged and thrilling stories of future science should not find a real place in the film schedules of all companies," and prophesying that there will soon be "an avalanche of such films" (*Wonder Stories*, July 1931, 280). Although that "avalanche," despite Forrest Ackerman's often premature announcements, would not appear until the 1950s, a later comment, probably by Hornig, attempts to reassure the readers that things are changing, as he declares that Hollywood is "becoming conscious of the increasing demand for scientifilms, and we are promised *A Trip to Mars, The Time Machine, The End of the World* and others" soon (*Wonder Stories*, Apr. 1934, 1049). And in response to an August 1936 letter from a British reader of *Thrilling Wonder Stories* who had recently seen—and wanted to highly recommend for American audiences—the H. G. Wells film *Things to Come* (1936), the editor acknowledges receiving many such letters of endorsement and expresses his hope that this much anticipated film—which, as we shall see later, had been heavily publicized and had already premiered in the United States in April—is "the forerunner of a great many more to come" (Aug. 1936, 124).

Of course, the existence of such reader-editor dialogue is noteworthy in itself, since it suggests both a widespread awareness of SF cinema, and a broad interest in discussing its place in or contribution to the serious work of SF. But it also reminds us of another way in which the pulp editors, as Mike Ashley discusses at great length in his history of the magazines, exercised a shaping hand on the genre and on SF attitudes in the pre-war era. Thus the ambiguous or shifting editorial positions that we find in these commentaries is hardly surprising, whether sourced in Gernsback, Lasser, Hornig, or others. They remind us that the pulp editors needed to walk a fine line regarding the genre's boundaries and possibilities. On the one hand, they wanted to encourage film-fan readers who hoped to see some of their favorite stories translated into film, as well as those who eagerly embraced the notion of SF not just as literature, but as a transformative *mode* or way of thinking with a potential for colonizing—and sharing the message of scientific and technological change with—other media such as film. Yet on the other hand, they also needed to remind their audience that the stories to be found in the pages of *Amazing, Astounding, Wonder Stories,* and their like were of primary importance, and that these magazines were, in effect, publishing the primary "script" for both visualizing the modern world and inspiring any "avalanche" of future scientifilms.

Perhaps we might see a better sense of this ambiguous attitude towards film in a noteworthy effort undertaken by *Wonder Stories* that in some ways seems to suggest the approach the editor accused Hollywood of taking, that is, at simply "sounding out the public" on its attitudes and preferences. That effort, which Mike Ashley and Robert Lowndes attribute to David Lasser (*Gernsback Days* 182), took the shape of a full-page notice with a petition requesting that the American film industry produce more films for the "rapidly growing" SF audience. Under the headline of "Do You Want Science Fiction Movies?" the editor invited "all lovers of science fiction," particularly "the rapidly growing reading public" represented by the pulps, to "make yourself heard" by signing a petition that was printed in the magazine. Each signee was also asked to sign and obtain four additional signatures of like-minded fans, and then to return the completed form to the editorial office of *Wonder Stories*, which pledged to "Make Your Demands Count" by collating all submissions into a "gigantic petition" and submitting it to the largest motion picture companies in Hollywood (Figure 4.2). The announced goal of this drive, which ran in full-page format for six straight issues (Dec. 1931 to May 1932), was

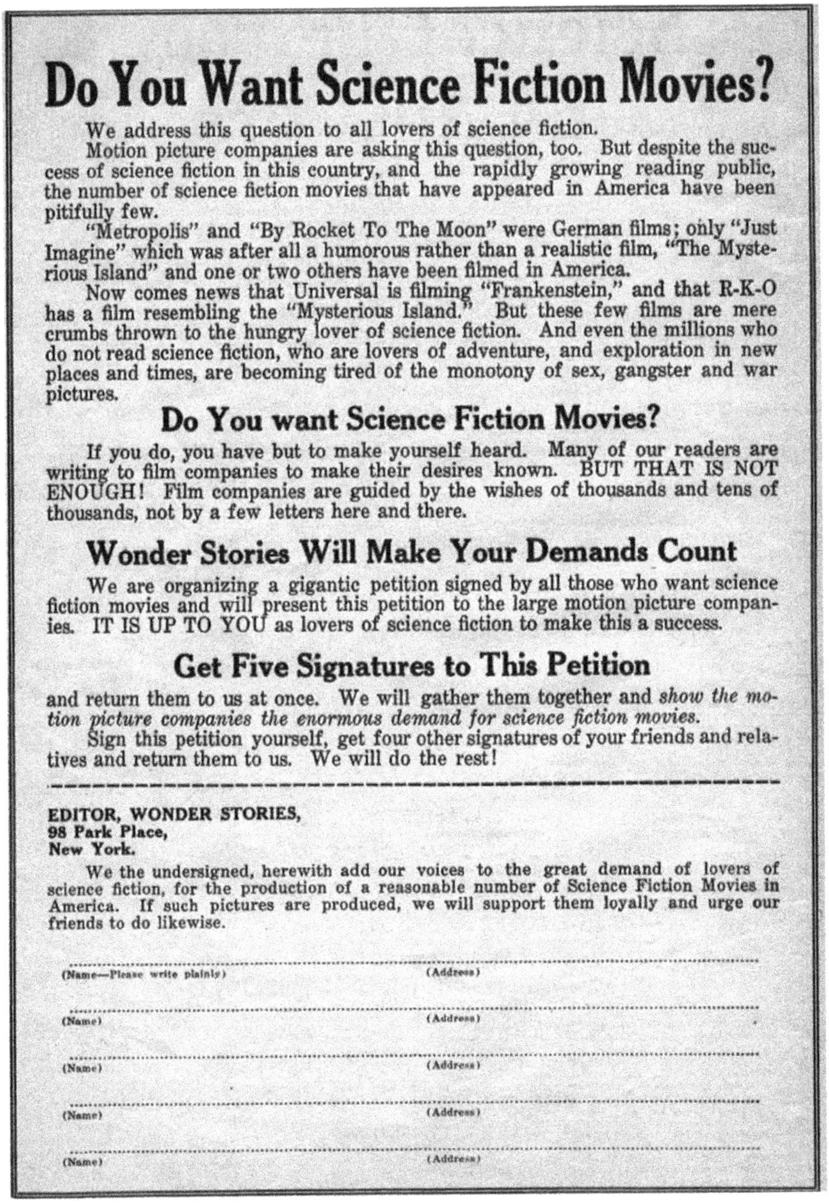

Do You Want Science Fiction Movies?

We address this question to all lovers of science fiction.

Motion picture companies are asking this question, too. But despite the success of science fiction in this country, and the rapidly growing reading public, the number of science fiction movies that have appeared in America have been pitifully few.

"Metropolis" and "By Rocket To The Moon" were German films; only "Just Imagine" which was after all a humorous rather than a realistic film, "The Mysterious Island" and one or two others have been filmed in America.

Now comes news that Universal is filming "Frankenstein," and that R-K-O has a film resembling the "Mysterious Island." But these few films are mere crumbs thrown to the hungry lover of science fiction. And even the millions who do not read science fiction, who are lovers of adventure, and exploration in new places and times, are becoming tired of the monotony of sex, gangster and war pictures.

Do You want Science Fiction Movies?

If you do, you have but to make yourself heard. Many of our readers are writing to film companies to make their desires known. BUT THAT IS NOT ENOUGH! Film companies are guided by the wishes of thousands and tens of thousands, not by a few letters here and there.

Wonder Stories Will Make Your Demands Count

We are organizing a gigantic petition signed by all those who want science fiction movies and will present this petition to the large motion picture companies. IT IS UP TO YOU as lovers of science fiction to make this a success.

Get Five Signatures to This Petition

and return them to us at once. We will gather them together and *show the motion picture companies the enormous demand for science fiction movies.*

Sign this petition yourself, get four other signatures of your friends and relatives and return them to us. We will do the rest!

EDITOR, WONDER STORIES,
98 Park Place,
New York.

We the undersigned, herewith add our voices to the great demand of lovers of science fiction, for the production of a reasonable number of Science Fiction Movies in America. If such pictures are produced, we will support them loyally and urge our friends to do likewise.

(Name—Please write plainly)   (Address)

(Name)   (Address)

(Name)   (Address)

(Name)   (Address)

(Name)   (Address)

Figure 4.2. *Wonder Stories* petitions Hollywood for more SF movies (Dec. 1931).

to "demand . . . the production of a reasonable number of Science Fiction Movies in America," while promising that "If such pictures are produced, we [the pulp readers] will support them loyally and urge our friends to do likewise." While *Wonder Stories* was in this period gradually growing its readership, which would reach nearly 50,000 by 1935,[5] it obviously did not represent a very large portion of the reading—or movie-going—public. However, this sort of initiative—much like Gernsback's formation of the Science Fiction League—had the effect of suggesting to readers that the magazine indeed represented a "leading" and influential voice within the SF community and that this community might well wield some power.

Of course, what a "reasonable number" of films might be was left to the imaginations of the readers who, through a fan involvement technique such as the petition, could readily see themselves as part of a larger movement, or what Cheng describes as the SF "collective whole" (72). Exploiting an obviously perceived interest in film, the petition suggested that respondents might be able to help shape the movie industry's offerings in much the way that many thought—and that editors like Gernsback had often implied—an SF literature was already doing with the explorations of contemporary science. While Ashley and Lowndes suggest that "many readers responded" (182) to the petition, there seems little evidence that the vaunted "gigantic petition" ever made its way out of the editorial offices of *Wonder Stories*, and it is possible that this drive might have been viewed from the start not just as a way of reinforcing SF fandom, but as another such fiction, what might even be described as a "thought experiment" or "thought variant" itself. In sum, regardless of its impact on Hollywood and like a number of other Gernsback initiatives, the petition served its purpose, tapping into what was perceived to be the magazine audience's film consciousness in order to reinforce their commitment to the *idea* of SF as a cross-genre and indeed a cultural movement.

It is against this backdrop of a rising fan and editorial discourse about scientifilms that we begin to see movie reviews joining the more common book notices as a feature of some of the pulps—a feature that formally acknowledged the pulp readers' interest in an SF cinema. In this part of that internal discourse *Wonder Stories* and *Amazing Stories* took the lead, offering reviews not of a great many, but certainly of the most famous (as well as some relatively obscure) SF films of the pre-war period. Among those featured we might note Fox's *Just Imagine* (1930), Universal's *The Invisible Man* (1933), RKO's *Deluge* (1933), MGM's *The Devil Doll* (1936), the German films *F. P. 1 Does Not Answer* (1933) and *Gold* (1934), the French *End of the World* (1931), the Soviet animated work *The New Gulliver* (1935), the Austrian-Swiss production *The Eternal Mask* (1935), the British film *Transatlantic Tunnel* (1935), and, after *Wonder Stories* was sold and became *Thrilling Wonder Stories*, several other famous British SF films of the period, including *Things to Come* (1936) and *The Man Who Could Work Miracles* (1937), two works bearing the pedigree of H. G. Wells adaptations. In fact, for a number of years *Thrilling* maintained a semi-regular "Scientifilm Review" column (usually alternating with the "Scientibook Review"), while *Amazing*, tellingly, usually embedded its film reviews in its "In the Realm of Books" column. The films discussed are certainly of varying quality, with many of them—such as *End of the World* and *The Eternal Mask*—often overlooked or forgotten in today's discussions of the period's SF movies. However, the commentaries are for the most part highly supportive and suggestive of another element of convergence. They seem to imply that the actual marriage of film and SF, that *being* an SF film, at least for a time was itself a noteworthy accomplishment.

And in a sense that status *was* noteworthy, since not until the 1950s would there finally be the sort of "deluge" of SF films that some readers and editors anticipated, although up to the early World War II years there would at least be a wide *variety* of scientifilms—big budget and small, foreign and domestic, literary adaptations and original conceptions. As an introduction to the reviews of these works, we might consider the unsigned *Wonder Stories* commentary on one of the earlier SF efforts, the strange generic hybrid *Just Imagine* (1930). While qualified in its response to this comedy/musical/scientifilm, the review was appreciative of its SF elements and pointed in directions that would most frequently be noted in assessments of other SF films throughout the pre-war period. While observing that *Just Imagine*, thanks to its musical and comic elements, would appeal primarily to "those who do not take their science fiction too seriously," the reviewer also "cordially recommended" it in light of several factors that speak to what film, with its visual emphasis, seemed to promise SF fans ("*Just Imagine*" 1054). Among those factors, the review notes how "the picture shows us many of the wonders that our science fiction writers have been writing about"—rockets, space travel, video phones, flying cars, even machines that can restore life; it describes "the sense of power and mystery" that "will delight the heart of every science fiction fan" (1054); and it emphasizes how the film maintains "a semblance of verisimilitude" (1055). Futuristic icons, a sense of wonder or mystery, an element of realism—these are some of the primary protocols that were repeatedly invoked in discussions of SF literature by fans and reviewers alike, and they largely provide similar touchstones for the various pulps' film reviews throughout this era. The movies' ability to realize those protocols, to follow—or complete—the SF imagination's "script," became the main point. Certainly, in the case of *Just Imagine*, and despite its musical-comedy trappings, it was point enough for the reviewer to laud Fox Studios as a "progressive enterprise" thanks simply to its undertaking such an unusual effort (1055).

While most of these early commentaries provide the usual—and usually fairly accurate—plot descriptions of the films under review, the most common assessment goes directly to the act of visualization, and eventually to the special effects—or "tricks"—that helped enable the visualizing capacity of the SF imagination and produce the genre's expected sense of wonder. As examples we might consider some of the reviews offered by C. A. Brandt, a former chemist, the Literary Editor at *Amazing Stories*, and someone whom Gernsback once dubbed "the greatest living expert on scientifiction" ("Experts" 380). Brandt regularly reviewed books as well as a number of films for *Amazing*, usually signed his reviews, and in several instances evaluated first the book and in a later issue its cinematic adaptation, as he did in the cases of *F. P. 1 Antwortet nicht/F. P. 1 Does Not Answer, The Shape of Things to Come/Things to Come*, and even the non-SF *Tarzan the Invincible/Tarzan the Fearless* (included, we can assume, because of their common origins in Edgar Rice Burroughs, a noted contributor to the field of SF with his Martian stories). In his reviews of *Deluge* (1933) and *The Invisible Man* (1933), published together, Brandt points in the direction of the books that were the sources of each film, but his aim, unlike many other reviewers of the time, is not to comment on either movie's faithfulness to its literary source. In fact, rather than belabor their plots, he simply notes that *Amazing*'s "readers are probably familiar with" these stories and even acknowledges that the S. Fowler Wright novel on which *Deluge* is based was, after all, "not so very interesting" ("Notes" 134). Instead, he centers his commentary in both cases on the films' visual accomplishments. Particularly, he focuses on the respective film creator's use of the latest special effects techniques to bring to the screen the more spectacular dimensions of the original Wright and H. G. Wells novels, effectively praising them for their own technical achievements, almost as if they were highly accomplished machines (Figure 4.3).

While neither of these reviews offers a detailed or particularly nuanced discussion of the nature of those cinematic techniques, Brandt is clearly trying to stake out some ways for his readers to appreciate the films on their own terms, to see them as separate accomplishments from their source novels and ultimately as independent SF texts. Consequently, his remarks emphasize each film's ability to use specifically cinematic effects to lend a sense of verisimilitude to its source's most fantastic elements, thereby realizing what the novels had largely left to their readers' imaginations. In fact, he recommends *Deluge* to his readers primarily because of its "visualization" of the many spectacular events described in the novel ("Notes" 134)—earthquakes, tsunamis, and flooding that all conspire to produce a global apocalypse which humanity must then struggle to survive. And in a

In the Realm of Books

"F.P.1 Does Not Reply," by Kurt Sodmak. Translated from the German by H. W. Farrel. Published by Little, Brown & Co., 290 pages, $2.00.

There seems to be a decided depression in science fiction also. Only one book really worth considering has come out, the English version of "F.P.1 Does Not Reply".

This is the book from which the film "F.P.1" was made which I reviewed in our February issue. The book is a very interesting technical romance, describing in great detail the construction of the first Floating Platform. Said Platform is to be anchored in mid-Atlantic between Bermuda and the Azores, and it is designed as a combination airport—hotel—restaurant—fuel station—repair shop, in other words, a floating "Tempelhofer Field." There is plenty of excitement in the story—sabotage—fights—gassing of the entire crew and the rescue in the usual nick of time. The Platform is also saved from sinking, by the finding of the missing valve-parts, so that the pumps can eject the thousands of tons of water, which the saboteurs hoped would sink the Platform. There is also a sort of sketchy romance appearing in the story—the love of Bernhard Droste, the designer and Gisela Lennartz, the beautiful—(naturally) daughter of the ship builder.

I have one serious fault to find with the book: The action jumps from Bremen to the Platform and other places with disconcerting rapidity and disturbing frequency. This is the usual fault with German publications.

Nevertheless, "F.P.1" is worth while reading.

C. A. Brandt.

"The Last of the Japs and the Jews," by Solomon Cruso. Published by Herman W. Lefkowitz, Inc., 1123 Broadway, New York City, N. Y. 333 pages, $2.50.

The jacket was headlined:

"The earth in flames, 16 million Jews exterminated, 60 million Japs annihilated, 100 million Americans killed in action, America again a wilderness," and other lurid phrases. I expected a sort of novel of the future, but I found an incredible accumulation of utter nonsense, badly written at that. The book is totally without rhyme or reason.

C. A. Brandt.

Notes on Moving and Talking Pictures

Several years ago S. Fowler Wright wrote a book called "The Deluge" depicting the swift destruction and slow rebuilding of civilization. In the book the chief action takes place in England and it was strongly reminiscent of "The People of the Ruins" by Shanks and "The Doomsmen", by Sutphen. The book itself was not so very interesting. It was written in the Wells manner—yet it drags along, an unending mass of detail and ending practically nowhere, the feeble plot lying on the wayside from lack of momentum. In the visualization the feebleness of the plot is well sustained, but the change of scene from England to America is much to the better, since it is far more impressive to see New York devoured by a tidal wave than even the rapid inundation of an English countryside.

The destruction of New York is exceedingly well done, quite realistic and plausible and well worth the price of admission. Aside from this, the story winds up in a gang-fight, from which the better element emerges triumphant.

C. A. Brandt.

"The Invisible Man," by Herbert George Wells —adapted for the screen by R. C. Sherriff and produced by Universal.

Congratulations "Universal!" You have done well! No fault can be found with any and all the changes made in the story since the "end justifies the means," and "The Invisible Man" is as perfect a film as could be wished for. Our readers are probably familiar with the story, but here is a short synopsis for those who are not.

A research chemist discovers a way of making himself invisible. Unable to discover ways and means of becoming visible again, he goes mad. He then decides to become Emperor of the World, institutes a reign of terror, but is finally killed by the authorities. The invisible man is depicted on the screen by Claude Rains, who plays a very difficult rôle, and whose face is visible only in the end as he is dying. The eerie atmosphere, which this film calls for, is excellently sustained throughout. The uncanniness of the various scenes is marvelously convincing, and the various humorous situations don't degenerate into slap-stick comedy. Mr. James Whale, who directed the picture, and his staff of technicians, who must have labored mightily to produce the "invisible" effects, have done a wonderful job.

C. A. Brandt.

Figure 4.3. Several of C. A. Brandt's film commentaries from *Amazing Stories* (May 1934).

hint of cultural commentary, he commends the film for shifting the original story's focus from England to America, noting that "it is far more impressive to see New York devoured by a tidal wave," while observing that the resulting vision of "destruction . . . is exceedingly well done, quite realistic and plausible, and well worth the price of admission" ("Notes" 134). In similar fashion, Brandt quickly shifts his review of *The Invisible Man* from a few comments on Wells's novel to the difficult task facing the filmmakers, that of visualizing the seemingly unvisualizeable, namely the film's treatment of the title character whose presence (or seeming absence) for much of the narrative can only be suggested by props, dialogue, and the reactions of other characters. Offering his "congratulations" to Universal Studios for its accomplishments in this vein, he underscores the film's consistently "eerie atmosphere" and the "uncanny" effect of the many scenes in which the unseen protagonist manipulates various stage props or taunts other characters, and he finally lauds director James Whale "and his staff of technicians who must have labored mightily to produce those 'invisible' effects" ("Notes" 134). Hardly in keeping with the sort of commentary that many readers might have expected from *Amazing's literary* editor, Brandt's remarks suggest something of his own cinematic awareness, as he conveys a keen appreciation of the visual supplement that the filmmakers, by skillfully exploiting their own technological art, brought to these literary narratives, enhancing both the weaker (*Deluge*) and the stronger (*The Invisible Man*) of their sources.

In contrast, some of the other film reviews found in the pulps seem driven mainly by what adaptation scholars refer to as *fidelity* issues, that is, by a primary consideration for the films' treatment of their literary sources, and perhaps by the sort of mindfulness of their readers' familiarity with and allegiance to those sources that Brandt's commentaries also acknowledged. This prioritizing of the literature is particularly evident in the unsigned *Thrilling Wonder Stories* review of MGM's *The Devil Doll* (1936), a revenge tale about a wrongly imprisoned banker who uses a shrinking formula to facilitate his reprisals on his accusers. The reviewer takes the film to task precisely for deviating from its source, the Abraham Merritt novel *Burn, Witch, Burn*, with that deviation resulting in "a run-of-the-mill thriller which does not attempt to capture the unique fantasy of Merritt's novel" (H. K. 119). After describing the plot of the original book, especially the climax which is "dear to the heart of the fantasy fan"—such as himself—the writer laments that the "story . . . is not Merritt's and . . . by no means novel" (H. K. 119).[6] While the more fantastic scenes involving shrunken people—the titular "dolls"—are, he suggests, somewhat interesting, the reviewer describes them as "merely further developments of the homunculus scenes" that can be found in the more valued *The Bride of Frankenstein* (1935) (H. K. 119). In a similar, albeit more appreciative vein, the *Wonder Stories* reviewer of the British film *Transatlantic Tunnel* (1935) spends most of his time outlining the film's fantastic plot, particularly the complications built into its narrative about an effort to build an under-ocean tunnel linking England and the United States. However, the unsigned reviewer confesses that his focus on the plot derives from the fact that he is writing "from a science-fictionist's view-point" ("*Transatlantic*" 894), that is, from a literary vantage that primarily prizes the science fictional conception at the heart of the film. Still, his appreciation clearly extends beyond this focus, as he also calls attention to *Transatlantic Tunnel*'s visualization of typical SF concerns and the sense of wonder it consistently conveys, while noting that there are "plenty of super-scientific scenes of the future" that allow audiences to "see, in real life, many of the things we have been reading about for so long—television, future cities, super-stream-lined automobiles, and a hundred-and-one other little details" (894). And, in an awkward conclusion that might suggest some discomfort with evaluating film, the reviewer, much like others previously cited, allows that "the technical effects are superb and an atmosphere of stupendous achievement is forever in our presence" (894).

The response to all these rather commonplace and for the most part unheralded films can provide us with a useful context for considering the pulps' reactions to the most anticipated scientifilm effort of the pre-war years, the previously mentioned *Things to Come* (1936). Scripted by H. G. Wells and adapted from his novel *Shape of Things to Come*, supposedly budgeted at over a million dollars ("$1,000,000") making it the most expensive British film to that date (Drazen 141), and advertised as having a cast of 20,000, the film was widely publicized and well-reviewed in England long before its American premiere in April 1936. When released in the United States, it was reviewed in all the major newspapers and given unprecedented multiple-page picture spreads in both *Time* and *Newsweek* magazines. More important, *Things to Come* was trumpeted as having precisely the sort of impact on current events and attitudes that Gernsback and others had long predicted for the best SF. Thus a report in *Motion Picture Daily* describes how it was "cited by speakers in both the British House of Commons and the French Chamber of Deputies," with Sir Philip Sassoon, Undersecretary of the Air Forces in Britain, addressing its "penetrative insight" into the "profound influence" of air power "over world relations," while the French Deputies made it part of "a spirited debate on the political situation across the border" ("Korda-Wells Film" 8), that is, in a newly remilitarized and clearly threatening Germany. In the United States the British ambassador Ronald Lindsay hosted a special preview for members of the Supreme Court, government cabinet members, and various Senators and Representatives, who were addressed by H. G. Wells himself via "transatlantic telephone" ("Hold Wells Preview" 2). With this high degree of visibility and anticipated impact on contemporary culture, the film seemed to represent a signal moment for SF—and we should only expect, for both the readers and editors of the specialized pulps (Figure 4.4).

In addition to mentions in the various readers' columns and in reports from several Science Fiction League chapters whose members were already anticipating its appearance and planning group excursions to see it, *Things to Come* would receive featured reviews in both *Amazing* and *Thrilling Wonder Stories*—although in a telling comment on *Astounding*'s largely literary focus, that magazine would not follow suit. But in evidence of the importance attached to the film, *Amazing* would offer two reviews, both by C. A. Brandt, the first of the film scenario that, in advance of the movie's release, had been published by Macmillan, and the second of the film itself. With a mindfulness of the fidelity issue previously noted (and which was obviously a concern of many readers), Brandt describes the Wells scenario as "a concentrated version of his book" *The Shape of Things to Come* (1933), and while noting some of the spectacular scenes that it seemed to promise for the film, he allows that he found the scenario somewhat disappointing since ultimately "it is left for the reader to visualize everything for himself" (Aug. 1936, 133). However, Brandt uses this occasion to criticize what he sees as the problematic position of an SF cinema in the United

Figure 4.4. The world of tomorrow in the most anticipated SF film of the 1930s, *Things to Come* (1936).

States. While he probably did not know that an American studio United Artists was already backing *Things to Come*, having provided a worldwide distribution deal and signing producer Alexander Korda to a ten-year production agreement,[7] Brandt argues that the Hollywood film industry had done little of value in this area and should acquire the rights to and adapt some of the other Wells stories that merited filming, especially *The War of the Worlds* and *The First Men in the Moon*, instead of continuing with its "wallowing in the pseudo-sentimental and sexy garbage" (Aug. 1936, 134) that he believed was typical of the US film industry.[8]

Brandt's review of the film itself several issues later softens this line of industry criticism somewhat, as he begins by observing that *Things to Come* differs from most Hollywood product in that the filmmakers did not try "to improve upon the original idea" or to rein in Wells's sense of wonder. Rather, he offers, this is an effort "lavishly produced in the Grand Manner" ("A Coming Prophesy [sic]" 135). And unlike other Brandt film reviews, this one concentrates on how the released film's ambitions align with what he perceived to be Wells's own attitudes, as it tries to carry out the visionary promise of SF itself. In illustration he describes how *Things to Come* "shows the life of the future, created, protected and governed by science. We are shown glimpses of a better and saner world," with Wells's ideas effectively translated to the screen and supported by impressive visual designs and model work, resulting in Brandt's judgment that the collaboration of Wells, Korda, and director William Cameron Menzies constitutes "Movie Magic at its best" (135).

While emphasizing many of these same characteristics, the *Thrilling Wonder Stories* review of *Things to Come* also hints at a different attitude towards the canonical Wells that was starting to emerge. In this period Wells's writing and public pronouncements had become much more polemical, or as Brian Stableford offers, he seemed intent on telling his audience "how desperate their contemporary historical situation really was" (51), how much western culture needed reform (51), and how painful that reform would probably be. *Things to Come* reflects much of these cautionary and polemical dimensions in Wells's work. It was the first instance in his career when Wells wrote the script for a film, and his contract had, as Keith Williams offers, "conferred virtually dictatorial rights over how the film would be made" (107)—a situation that resulted in some public disagreements with the producer and director over the production as Wells exercised an element of these rights, and comments about, as Christopher Frayling sums them up, "the preachiness of the piece" that suggested "perhaps Wells was on the wane" (76). However, in his signed review, editor Mort Weisinger would steer clear of much of this criticism. In fact, it seems telling that he never directly mentions Wells, his singular involvement in every step of the production, or the film's obvious "preachiness."

Instead, this review, like many of the others already cited, addresses *Things to Come*'s spectacular visual effects and their function in producing an SF sense of wonder. Weisinger compares the film directly to its peers with regard to the new visuality of the age, terming it "the most spectacular and fascinating of the various science fiction movies" of the era, as he describes in detail how the film paints "a vivid picture" of the future, envisioning the horrors of future warfare, cities of the future, "super machinery," and a climactic sequence in which "two people are shot to the moon through a giant 'Space Gun'" ("*Things*" 112). With the by now common nod to verisimilitude, he assures readers that, as visualized for the screen, these prophecies "are all realities" (112), and in a summary comment that suggests his appreciation of how central a visual appeal was to SF films, while also hinting at his own dissatisfaction with Wells's recent writings, Weisinger assures the readers that these "technical wonders of the picture should make up for any deficiencies the plot and underlying philosophies may have" (112). His elevation of the film's visual effects and "technical wonders" over the "underlying philosophies"—presumably sourced in Wells's polemical novel *The Shape of Things to Come*, but perhaps even in Wells's imagination or politics—signals a significant development in the period.[9] The mobilized "gaze" and resulting "astonishments" of the SF film seem to have, much as they had in the early days of film, taken on a new weight and value, thanks to their technical ability for bringing to life such a "vivid picture," for helping us see our world anew and making our dreams—at least seem to—come true in ways that Wells's fiction, despite its own often noted cinematic qualities, might not.[10]

While the pulps generally responded favorably to *Things to Come* and the film, at least in England, met with a strong critical if only moderate popular success, Weisinger's veiled comment on its "deficiencies" anticipated its tepid reception in the United States and elsewhere.[11] In the wake of its less than resounding success, which Keith Williams attributes to Wells's failure "to fuse popular entertainment with intelligent simulation" (121), the next film from this father of the genre was not only less heralded, but also framed—and received—quite differently. Released the following year (although largely shot before *Things to Come*), *The Man Who Could Work Miracles* is a story about a common man who, as a kind of sport of the gods, suddenly finds himself gifted with powers to alter his world (Figure 4.5). Like *Things to Come*, it was also based on a Wells story of the same title, with Alexander Korda once again producing, involving some of the same cast as the previous film, employing the same special effects director (Ned Mann)

Figure 4.5. Billed as a comedy, Wells's *The Man Who Could Work Miracles* (1937).

and effects cinematographer (Edward Cohen), and with Wells himself, assisted by his same co-writer Lajos Biro, working on the adaptation. Despite these many similarities in the production and its principles, there were few advance magazine articles or news releases in this case, and two-page advertising inserts into *The Film Daily* (Feb. 18, 1937, 6–7), *Motion Picture Herald* (Feb. 20, 1937, 62-63), and *Motion Picture Daily* (Mar. 1, 1937, 4–5) trade papers mentioned Wells just once and SF not at all, as the new film was in each case billed as "H. G. Wells's Comedy." Moreover, the industry notices suggested that distributors should use "cartoon ads" (of a sort illustrated in the insert) to "jolt . . . a sense of humor right into the box office," and described it as "the season's most unusual comedy with the year's loudest laughs." While prominently noting that *The Man Who Could Work Miracles* had been produced by Alexander Korda, none of the advertising spreads makes any mention of his connection to *Things to Come*. Rather, they note Korda's prior role as the creator of *The Ghost Goes West*, a successful 1935 comedy set in America. Following the lead of such advertising, the subsequent formal review of the film in *Film Daily* sums up its target appeal, describing it as a "delightful fantasy" and having "a fine whimsical sense" ("The Man" 6). While the fantasy narrative of *The Man Who Could Work Miracles* might not qualify it as SF, by framing it purely as comedy and emphasizing its sense of whimsy, the distributor, exhibitors, and even audiences little associated the film with the sort of seriousness of purpose that had previously been linked to Wells, SF, and *Things to Come*.

When it was reviewed in both *Thrilling Wonder Stories* and *Amazing Stories*, *The Man Who Could Work Miracles* received fairly similar treatment to that offered by the trade papers. Weisinger's review in *Thrilling Wonder Stories* offers just a passing, adjectival reference to Wells—calling the film "a typical Wellsian fantasy"—even as it praises producer Alexander Korda, whom it terms "probably the greatest and most adroit figure in films today" ("*The Man*" 127), and also notes the film's light tone. However, in an effort to claim an element of significance, the review does suggest that "the film achieves stature" precisely with the sort of scene for which *Things to Come* had been most criticized, that is, with the lengthy monologue by its every-man protagonist George Fotheringay wherein he catalogues the problems of the modern world—problems that he (with more than a hint of Wells's own felt frustrations) would, and despite all of his powers, prove unable to redress. Weisinger describes the scene as an "indictment of a bad old world by an average man who . . . has become suddenly powerful and articulate," and notes that, while "it is a long speech, trumpeting and scathing, . . . not once does it drag" (127). But Weisinger also tries to strike a balance for the pulp readers between such Wellsian polemic and more pointedly cinematic effects, as he suggests that the titular "miracles" achieved "are the meat of the picture" and a satisfying return "for all lovers of the fantastic and the startling" (127). C. A. Brandt's review for *Amazing* is revealing in its more concise nature. He simply notes that the film is from "the scenario of H. G. Wells," and allows that, given his assessment of the original story, it is a tale that he thought "we would never see . . . on the screen" (Dec. 1937, 135). While crediting the film with following that questionable source "with astounding fidelity," and while offering no comments on the film's tone or its ambitions, he gives primary attention, as in his other reviews cited here, to the film's special effects. Brandt especially lauds "the technicians who worked out the various productions of the miracles," as he suggests that the film's technical experts "themselves have produced a miracle" (135) with its visual effects. It is a commentary that, together with the review's lack of observations about the film's ideas, seems as much a dismissal of Wells's original as an endorsement of this new adaptation.

What we might especially note in both reviews of *The Man Who Could Work Miracles* is evidence of a kind of tension that marks many of the other film commentaries that appeared in the pulps, but especially those focused on Wells's film adaptations. In the first we see Weisinger speaking both to those who are invested in the *idea* of SF as a highly serious and purposeful literature, and to those who are interested in what we have termed the *visuality* of the modern age that was also playing such a significant role in the genre's formation. While emphasizing the seriousness of purpose that Gernsback had attached to genre SF—in this instance embodied in the polemic that the character Fotheringay addresses to the leaders of the major nations of the world—the review also lauds the atmosphere, look, and visual impact that, as Weisinger puts it, "all Hollywood could not achieve" (127). In the second Brandt offers what seems like little more than an obligatory nod in Wells's direction before turning to his real concern, the film's fantasy appeal and the difficulties involved in its creation—difficulties overcome through the manifest skills of the expert movie technicians. It is a dynamic that speaks to the growing sense reflected in these and other reviews that literary and cinematic SF were not quite the same thing after all, that they might not so easily be adapted from one medium to the other, and that, despite their shared sense of wonder, the literary and cinematic texts might actually appeal in quite distinct ways.

Despite that sense of a convergence of SF modes that we began by noting and that the pulps' internal discourse often seemed to forecast, the reviews begin to reflect, especially in the later 1930s, some of the problems involved in that element of convergence. As a literary form, SF seemed to find its greatest appeal in its ability to estrange readers from the real, to immerse them in a future or other world, full of the trappings of that otherness and—at least to some extent—ruled by what some writers refer to as the "cold logic" of science. Such visions effectively challenged the status quo of the readers while promising something different, wondrous, even better. And for many fans of the new genre, film seemed a natural complement to that agenda, since it could with some satisfaction render that otherness as a wondrous spectacle, make it seem real and thus *realizable*. Or as Francesco Casetti offers in his own effort at summing up film's modernist appeal, the imagery of the cinema "takes on such empirical weight that what we see automatically seems possible" (56). It is that sense of the possible, of *what might be*, as we earlier suggested, that constitutes one of those very fundamental and shared appeals that audiences were finding in both SF and the movies, and that many of the pulps' film reviews sought to address.

And yet throughout most of these formal film commentaries, what often filters back in is a kind of rift centered on that realistic insistence of film. Repeatedly and in a way that speaks well of the various pulp reviewers, the commentaries, especially those addressing the Wells films, emphasize an awareness and appreciation of cinema's different nature, while also recognizing that it is itself one of those rather amazing modern technologies, just like television, rockets, and robots, that were the frequent subject of SF. The wondrous images it produces are, readers were repeatedly reminded, "special" effects, "tricks," or "movie magic," the result—dutifully applauded in every review—of highly skilled technicians, enabled by a sophisticated, thoroughly modern entertainment technology, fashioned more impressively in some industrial contexts—such as England or Germany—than in others, and able to be appreciated, in C. A. Brandt's words, as "Movie Magic at its best." But in that core commentary, the reviews, despite their general appreciation, finally seem to find the period's scientifilms less satisfying than expected, both as SF and as part of the genre's exciting agenda of revisioning and remaking the world. It is as if the reviewers had foundered upon what Walter Benjamin in one of his best-known comments about the sophisticated commercial cinema of the period had described as "the height of artifice" that was at work in these films, even as they seemed to present an "equipment-free aspect of reality" (233). This confrontation suggests a level of frustration or dissatisfaction, or at least a sense that the convergence that many were anticipating and that had once seemed so natural, might be a long time in realization, at least not until the post-war period when SF literature and an SF cinema would, if informed by a rather different spirit, almost simultaneously begin to flourish.

CHAPTER 5

Cover Stories

With their visually arresting covers, practically all the pulp magazines brought with them another sort of discourse, the readers' commentary about those covers, as well as the magazines' interior illustrations. Their comments addressed a range of issues: the covers' scientific accuracy, the skill of the artists, the colors employed, their relationship to the stories inside the magazines, and, of course, the nature of their subject matter. For some of those readers the various illustrations that prompted their remarks were "striking," "swell," "eye-compelling," and "a work of art," while for others those same images registered quite differently, as simply "poor," "a little bit cockeyed," "sensational," and, in one of the more frequently used descriptions, even "lurid."[1] Of course, as readers' letters testify, a similar sort of disagreement commonly extended to many of the stories within the pulps. However, the brightly colored, strikingly designed, and usually highly dynamic illustrations, done by popular artists like Frank R. Paul, Howard V. Brown, Leo Morey, and Hans Wesso, seemed to strike a special chord, as they not only lured readers to those stories, allowing issues to stand out on newsstands that featured a wide variety of cheap competitors, but they also, as John Cheng observes, "expressed and reinforced, in visual terms, the representational logic" of the SF stories to be found between the covers (151). It is on the nature of that "representational logic"—often inflected, I would argue, by a note of *cinematic logic*—that this chapter will focus.

In his history of SF, Adam Roberts gives special attention to this dimension of the pulps, as he argues that their covers were "in many ways more important than the prose component" of the magazines (184). When we look at their highly saturated colors, use of strong diagonal lines, and iconic images we can readily see, as he says, "the creation of a wholly original mode of visual representation" (185) and the emergence of "a *distinctive* SF visual style" (186). While Roberts never specifies what constitutes this new "style" or how it differs from other visual styles of the period, such as that found on the covers of "slick" magazines or in near kin like the SF cartoons and comic strips of the era, he claims that because for the most part the pulp style corresponded to nothing in lived reality, it was ultimately "not representational," that is, not bound to a realistic regime, and that consequently its character was much nearer mainstream modern art, especially "abstract art" (185). If Roberts' seeming divorce of those cover images from their stories and elevation of them over the pulps' prose betrays his own skepticism about the value of much early pulp fiction, it also accurately underscores the difference of those images from most conventional magazine illustrations of the period and their felt power to sketch, in a quite distinct and appealing way, the possibilities that were being explored by the SF imagination. More than just a vivid packaging for the SF tales within— and as Mike Ashley reminds, "a major sales attraction" (*Time Machines* 49)—this artwork helped to codify the promise of the genre, especially its promise to let readers see their world, and perhaps other worlds as well, in a different, even exciting way.

Yet Roberts' suggestion that the covers and illustrations were not really "representational" seems an interesting assertion—and it merits some reconsideration as we continue to explore the cinematic character that, as we have seen, surged through the pre-war pulps in a variety of other ways. A few of those cover images readily support his assessment, since they function on a largely symbolic and even abstract level, practically calling attention to their "distinctive . . . style." A most obvious case in point is the giant eye with lightning bolts for lashes that adorned the April 1928 cover of *Amazing Stories* (Figure 5.1). This pointedly symbolic image resulted from Hugo Gernsback's announced project of creating an appropriate "emblem, or a trade-mark" for "scientifiction," in this case one that, he explains, "represents the mind's eye," with the various other components appearing within that eye image—gears, a turbine, an airplane, a planetarium, a submarine, and other SF icons—suggesting "everything that is represented by scientifiction" ("Wanted" 5). Frank R. Paul executed this unusual artwork, and it was offered as inspiration for a contest in which the magazine's readers were encouraged to submit their own, "better" ideas of a fitting "emblem" for the new field. Working in the same vein, and constituting what the editor would curiously describe as "an experiment" in creating "an ethical cover" in place of the many "gaudy" or "lurid" ones

Figure 5.1. Frank R. Paul's "abstract" representation of "scientifiction," done for *Amazing Stories* (Apr. 1928).

(Nov. 1928, 761) that had brought some complaints, the September 1928 issue of *Amazing* illustrated the supposed result of that contest.[2] The cover displayed a symbolic badge of scientifiction, showing "fact" and "theory," surrounded by steel girders with gears working like a machine to move an author's pen—writing, we can assume, scientifiction itself. It is an image that would be included on several other covers and, for a time, be featured on the magazine's table of contents. However, with the exception of a run of highly stylized illustrations for part of 1933, no similarly abstract or purely symbolic images followed onto *Amazing*'s covers throughout the pre-war years.[3]

In approximately the same period, *Wonder Stories* too would "experiment" with a number of abstract cover images. Its July, September, and November 1932 issues would move in a new visual direction as part of an effort, as the editor similarly explained, to address the same sort of comments that had first greeted *Amazing*, complaints that the pulp's covers were "too 'wild,' 'undignified' and lacking in aesthetic appeal" (July 1932, 180). The resulting abstract illustrations—of a field of multi-colored balls, of colored arcs, and of linked blue, red, and yellow splotches respectively, all in this case again attributed to Frank R. Paul—were designed as prompts in a science contest, with each representing a scientific principle that the readers were then challenged to explain, and with the editor suggesting that a key to puzzling out what the images represented might be to look at them differently, either at very close range or from a slight distance, in effect (and in the SF tradition of *estrangement*), to shift how one looks at things. This change in vantage was a fairly common piece of advice for better appreciating the abstract art of a period that had seen the introduction of Picasso and the appearance of Marcel Duchamp's groundbreaking *Nude Descending a Staircase, No. 2* with their explicit challenges to both realism and traditional perspective. But after those three puzzling cover efforts, such abstract patterns would, as in the case of *Amazing*, largely give way to the more familiar and "undignified" pulp images, colorfully illustrating key scenes from published stories, while mining the scopophilic pleasures to be found in powerful machines, large weapons, and suggestively dressed (or undressed) women.

While that same strategy aimed at inspiring or challenging readers would give rise to some other pulp covers, it was more commonly yoked to the depiction of a specific action or dramatic situation rather than a purely abstract concept. An early example is Paul's cover for the December 1926 issue of *Amazing Stories*, created as part of another prize contest, this one offering $500 for the best story submitted in response to its strange images. The cover shows a group of female nudes sitting on a rocky landscape, observing a metal satellite in the sky, while beneath it dangle lights, cables, and, incredibly, a suspended ocean liner. As Hugo Gernsback's editorial explains, the composition was meant to be "purely fanciful," and he admits that "we haven't the slightest idea what the picture is supposed to show" ("$500" 773). But having sundered image from any conventional meaning, he then challenged readers to produce a piece of fiction that would "take cognizance of even the smallest detail" in that illustration while also remaining true to "science" (773). A similar impulse was attributed to Howard V. Brown's *Thrilling Wonder Stories* illustration of June 1939. It shows two humans in a cage, apparently being photographed by red-skinned aliens—an image that corresponds to no story in that issue but one that was designed, as guest columnist and SF author Ray Cummings explains, to demonstrate how a single imagined scene "can inspire a number of widely varied stories" (37), which he then, in the spirit of so many other pulp contests, invited readers to imagine, write up, and submit to the magazine. And this sort of *imagined* story connection, with artwork often exaggerated or out of normal proportion and its subject matter wildly suggestive, would show up not only on other pulp covers during the pre-war era, but in interior artwork as well, as in the case of the February 1930 issue of *Air Wonder Stories*. A full-page image of angry-looking aliens in metal suits, rising from several domes on a rocky planet, was used to kick off another contest, this one offering "$300 for the Best Stories Written Around this Picture"—with that single image inspiring a number of contributions, including P. Schuyler Miller's "The Red Plague," which was subsequently published in the July *Wonder Stories*. Such pure *attractions* stimulated the imagination, motivated submissions, and suggested on several levels the sort of participatory role that readers were supposed to play in the SF pulp experience.

For the most part, though, the cover artwork for the pulps was actually rather conventionally representational, depicting what the editors typically described as a "dramatic scene" in a featured story, usually one involving human figures, picturing advanced but recognizable technology, and adhering to known—or explained—laws of science. In fact, readers frequently complemented the artists for their "accuracy," as when a letter to *Thrilling Wonder Stories* notes that a recent cover "was excellent. Almost photographic in its realism" (Apr. 1937, 114). For other readers, though, the covers seemed all too realistic or representational, largely because of their "undignified," or as others would suggest, "embarrassing" and even "lurid" imagery. Thus one correspondent—among quite a few—describes "furtively going up to the newsstand" and waiting "till no one is watching" before purchasing a copy of *Amazing Stories* (Apr. 1928, 83). And yet a few others would complain that the covers gave too much away, as is illustrated by a letter to *Amazing* asking if the covers could "be a little less explanatory," since they tend to "tell just what the story is about," which "takes the zest out of it" (Aug. 1929, 475).

Despite such conflicting accounts, the covers usually seem to have been designed to do both, to visualize a part of the story and to generate "zest," to accurately *represent* a particular event or situation, while employing an element of sensationalistic or exaggerated imagery—often sexual in nature, but at other times of a sort that might be described as *abstract* in an especially science fictional way, that is, imagery that extrapolates from known reality in order to project the sense of wonder typically linked to the genre. In keeping with this approach, *Amazing's* editor, in lieu of the usual cover description for the October 1929 issue, simply refers to the illustration that combines humans of starkly different sizes, a factory setting, and a number of placid, dinosaur-like creatures being fed as "an inexplicable phenomenon" (578). The aim of such covers was to allow readers who were attuned to what we have termed the *new visuality* of the modern world to anticipate the wonders—and pleasures—of the fiction within, while also prompting them to see differently, much as when the *Wonder Stories* editor literally prodded his cover contestants to view the images from a different distance or vantage. In fact, we can see a forecast of what was to come, of this combination of impulses, in the very first *Amazing Stories* cover, as it depicts happy ice skaters, gliding in front of several ice-bound sailing ships, while what appears to be the planet Saturn looms gigantically and incredibly close by—all in effectively impossible physical relationship, but taken *in essence* from Jules Verne's *Off on a Comet*, a story that was being serialized in the magazine's first two issues. It is an image that seems to ask the viewers to see things from different perspectives *at the same time*, as if it were trying to remake how we see—which indeed it is, just as is so much of SF, as Gernsback's abstract "eye" cover surely implied.

I have rather elaborately staked out this cover context to further frame the pulps' cinematic kinship, particularly by emphasizing two points about these covers and what I have suggested are their simultaneously representational and abstract—or simply wondrous—impulses. One is the way the covers function not just as illustrations for the stories inside the magazines or as broadly thematic statements, but how, thanks to their dynamic styling, suggestions of dramatic action, and suggestive, often sexually loaded imagery they seem rather like single action frames lifted from a film narrative or, perhaps more accurately, like another, equally powerful and multiply suggestive new graphic art form of the period, the lobby cards and posters that were commonly created for movie advertising. The other point of emphasis is the way in which this combination of representational and abstract thrusts recalls film's own double pull in its similarly formative period of the 1890s to 1920s—a dynamic that historians have often illustrated by referring to the *actualites* or everyday images that were produced in the 1890s by the Lumiere brothers and the *feeries* or fantastic films of Georges Melies made in the same period. But that dynamic is also inherent in, and perhaps better suggested by two broader thrusts that mark this early history: the previously noted early development of film as what Tom Gunning terms a "cinema of attractions" ("Cinema" 63) and its gradual growth into a convention-bound, narrative-driven form. Both these correspondences, though, should remind us how much SF and the cinema drew upon—and similarly reflected—a broader cultural emphasis on the visual that surged through western culture throughout the late modernist era and that, in a variety of fields, also seemed to draw together those realistic and more abstract impulses.

Probably the most obvious of these correspondences is that between the pulp covers and film advertising that was beginning to find its own style in the 1920s, the same period that saw the birth of the SF pulps. As Richard Koszarski has chronicled, posters, lobby cards, billboards, and publicity stills first started to become important to the film industry in the mid-1910s to1920s. At this point the industry was moving away from its original exhibition practice involving the frequent turnover of similar shows, an emphasis on the studio producing the films, and a playbill typically changing two or three times a week. In its place a new exhibition practice was to emphasize the movie as a unique, longer running, and narrative-focused event with films carefully differentiated by stars, writers, spectacles, and other noteworthy—and visualizable—characteristics.[4] The advertising that developed to support this different approach involved highly colorful, action-oriented, and dynamically designed artwork, mixed with images drawn from the films, and eventually designed to coordinate with trailers, press releases, publicity stills, and other sorts of promotional material. Together, these items all constitute what we today often designate as *paratexts*, that is, the great variety of material that surrounds a film, helps to constitute the larger film experience, and works at least partly in the way that decorative and allusive covers bind and help advertise a book—or a magazine on a newsstand.

Much like the pulp covers, such paratexts were typically created by highly skilled illustrators and effectively functioned, as Jonathan Gray explains, "as gateways into the text, establishing meanings and frames for decoding before the audience member has even encountered the film" that they are touting (18). In a single striking image, either drawn from a particular scene or crafted by lifting dynamic and iconic elements from several shots and then combining them in a kind of static montage, these illustrative texts would serve multiple purposes, such as announcing the film's genre, providing some access to its narrative—what Gray terms "an environmental sampling" (50)—and striking a note of visual pleasure, excitement, or anticipation. For example, a poster for the early SF film *Just*

Imagine (1930) offers in its lower right corner stylized clouds and a female character (the actress Maureen O'Sullivan), her arms thrown back in excitement as she, improbably, *stands* atop a streamlined monoplane in flight, while an upper left corner contains an unrelated and outsized image of one of the film's stars, the comedian El Brendel, who, thanks to his eyeline which points to the other image, seems to be reacting in amazement at the sight (Figure 5.2). The futuristic plane, dynamic, even precarious posture of the woman, and El Brendel's comic look all combine to promise an exciting as well as amusing SF excursion for moviegoers.

The typical pulp cover functions in a similar "gateway" manner, as it usually presents potential readers with signs that they have indeed entered into the new world of SF, offers them an environmental sampling or dramatic context, and evokes a sense of wonder, often through a similar emphasis on a character's gaze. A *Wonder Stories* cover from approximately the same period (July 1930) as *Just Imagine* works in much the same fashion as the film poster. Illustrating a scene from the story "Flight of the Mercury" and created by Frank R. Paul, it too shows a streamlined monoplane angled above an alien landscape and alien creatures, while a human pilot dangles precariously from the cockpit, shaking his fist—as his own

Figure 5.2. Movie poster as pulp model, the early Fox SF film *Just Imagine* (1930).

eyeline underscores—at the aliens angled far below. The SF icons, dynamic positioning of aircraft and pilot, and dramatic gesture all combine to offer readers exciting entry into the illustrated and obviously SF text. But we should add one other resemblance, a point omitted from Gray's discussion, since he is focused only on what lies outside of the movie experience, on the paratextual encounter. Cover images like that from *Wonder Stories* almost invariably *anticipate* motion, as they usually seem to freeze an ongoing or forecast a soon-to-occur action. In sum, the typical pulp cover, like the film poster or lobby card, provides readers/viewers with the necessary—and sometimes more than necessary—information not just for reading the corresponding story, but also for gaining entry to and even some visual pleasure from its world, a pleasure keyed to this very dynamic, about-to-unfold vision, as if from a movie that is already being screened "inside" the magazine.

Beyond the attractive and dynamic pleasure bound up in such images, the implicit—or frozen—motion of the covers can direct us to the other element of cinematic convergence that we previously noted. In its early form as what has come to be known as the cinema of attractions, film drew for much of its appeal not on the flow and seductive character of narrative, but rather on the power of its images, particularly their ability to present fantastic, surprising, or dream-like visions, or to let audiences see the real in a new way. As Gunning explains this effect, the cinematic image in its early days simply "astonished" viewers with its "sudden burst of presence . . . the pure present tense of its appearance" ("Now" 6–7)—what we might think of as its own about-to-unfold-ness. That ability to shock, thrill, or excite curiosity in the audience created a new relationship to the present that was very much in step with modernism's (and SF's) own efforts to come to grips with what had come to seem not just an unstable world, or as Marshall Berman describes it, "the maelstrom of modern life" (16), but also, because of the great sense of change that was part of the era, a constantly elusive present moment—a moment that we see subjected to exciting and revealing visual analysis in a work like *Nude Descending a Staircase*, as well as in the montage approach to action and emotion found in the films of pioneering filmmakers such as D. W. Griffith, Sergei Eisenstein, and Dziga Vertov.

But film could also effectively grab that unstable and elusive present, place viewers within it—or at least in front of its screened presence—and render it pleasurable or satisfying in another way. In his famed *A Trip to the Moon* (1902), Georges Melies packaged his typical bag of tricks and other "astonishments"—exploding Selenites, astrological signs come to life, instantly growing plants—within a loose version of Jules Verne's story, effectively narratizing his *feerie* world. Thus Casetti suggests of Melies that "only by becoming a bit of a storyteller was he able to be an effective witness" to the swiftly moving marvels of this modern world (75), binding them up in a package designed for the audience's consumption. By combining the "sudden burst of presence" with the representational world of narrative that would come to play a dominant role in film by the early 1920s, the cinema found an even wider popularity, as it was able to craft an experience that was itself both representational and zestful, its present tense astonishments ultimately story-bound, much as both the pulp covers and movie posters implied.

While this sort of impact might seem to claim a bit much for the typical SF pulp cover—or movie poster—it can help explain some of the dynamic power of those justly famous pulp images, while also reminding us how they are linked to their stories and, like film, to the larger modernist project. With this linkage in mind, I want to suggest that many of these covers seem shaped or "scripted" partly by film's influence, although one might argue that they are just as much so because of SF's and film's shared modernist fascination with visuality. As Leo Charney and Vanessa R. Schwartz offer, the modernist climate was effectively defined by movement, by change, and by an "atmosphere of visual and sensory excitement" (5) that accompanied—and helped compensate for—an attendant, and unsettling, sense of the "fleeting and ephemeral" that was also part of the modern human experience (6). Most popular and even high art of the period, they argue, sought to provide audiences a point of "interchange between mobility and stasis, between the ephemerality of modernity's sensations and the resulting desire to freeze those sensations in a fixed moment of representation" so that viewers might better comprehend, or, in a properly capitalist sense, *consume* them (6). And like film and all of its paratexts, along with playbills, product advertisements, billboards, even political posters of the era, the pulp covers manage effectively to serve up that "fixed moment," to bind their wonderful imagery to an at least implied narrative in a way that, if felt by some to be rather "undignified," "lurid," or "too flashy" (*Thrilling Wonder Stories*, Dec. 1938, 123), obviously appealed to a mass audience, many of whom in their letters to the magazines would inquire of the editors how they might acquire copies of those alluring cover paintings.

Given that the pulp covers "act" so much like films and their advertising, then, we should hardly be surprised to note additional resemblances, particularly in the way they address the reader/viewer and even incorporate cinematic elements into their subjects. Here too Casetti provides us with an important lead, and one that we have already noted in passing, as he talks about the nature of the "spectatorial experience" typical of early film. It is one in which the viewer, as he says, not only stands "in front of the events," but also "finds him or herself in the heart of them, in communion with the world," even though "the separation between observer and observed persists" (184). Binding the viewer up in that modernist sense of constant motion with its attendant astonishments, even giving him or her an avatar-like figuration in that visual field, is balanced by film's permitting the viewer to remain detached and observant so that "reality, more than simply visible, also becomes intelligible" or "fixed" (184), enabling the viewer to experience a combination of the representational and the abstract, or as Friedrich Kittler in his own account of early film's impact on viewers suggests, experience "the impossible real" (40).

Thus, in the case of the pulps' illustrations, we repeatedly see characters depicted as spectators, watching through windows, portholes, cockpits, or televisual devices of various sorts, while exciting, threatening, titillating, or simply wondrous events play out before them, promising to quickly involve and transform them from rapt viewers or screened-off onlookers to active participants, from a film-like audience to actors within some unfolding futuristic drama. Of course, for the cover viewer and potential magazine purchaser, just as for the moviegoer, the "separation" remains; what Anne Friedberg terms "the architecture of spectatorship" (*Virtual* 150), while inviting, is never quite a *habitable* architecture. However, such dramatic scenes were not only consistent with the modernist sense of the individual as a kind of *flaneur* or window shopper, but they also tapped into the larger promise of SF, suggesting in yet another way something of its "prophetic" or anticipatory character, as well as the participatory spirit that the pulps, in various other ways we have already noted—contests, letters to the editors, debates about scientific correctness, etc.—seemed to encourage. And that "screened" vision of marvelous events had to have resonated with an audience that was already used to what Mort Weisinger in his *Things to Come* review had termed the many "technical wonders" that were to be found in modern motion pictures ("Scientifilm Review— *Things*" 112)—"wonders" that were a part of the pulps' SF discourse and, indeed, part of the whole modern, even futuristic environment in which the readers/viewers were effectively acolytes.

In order to better understand how the pulps' own "spectatorial experience" functioned, I want to focus on several of the ways in which a film-like experience filtered into the magazines' artwork, surfacing on both the pulps' covers and their internal illustrations. While the covers are typically marked by a variety of what Jerome Winter terms "common iconological reference points" (196), or frequently repeated SF icons such as spaceships, robots, aliens, and other worlds, one of the more frequent and often overlooked of such reference points involves what we might term *staging*, that is, a design of a sort previously described that dramatically places characters in a version of the movie viewer's position, watching events unfold on a screen of some sort, through a window, or via a mediating technology such as a television or some other screen (Figure 5.3). A second way that film experience surfaces is in subject matter that includes the depiction of movie cameras, theaters, and even the movie-making process—on Earth, on alien worlds, and in outer space—as the trappings of film and the film industry iconically bind together the science fictional and cinematic experiences. A third such reference point might be seen in images alluding to or taken from the movies themselves, providing inspiration or straightforward illustrations for the covers and interior artwork, as we noted in the second chapter with the *Thrilling Wonder Stories* cover based on the film *Dr. Cyclops*. These are all "gateways" that do more than just introduce their respective stories—or afford a kind of "environmental sampling." While evoking the world of SF, they also attach a decidedly cinematic character to the experiences they forecast, suggesting that audiences might anticipate in their SF subjects the same sort of visual excitement and pleasure commonly associated with the movies.

In keeping with that new visuality of the age that we have often cited, pulp covers frequently locate their implied spectators in an imagined foreground, watching a scene in which characters, usually in mid-frame, stand before a screen, windshield, or viewing port, as they observe some even more wondrous scene or action in the deep background. Particularly effective examples of this staging-in-depth format appear on such *Amazing* covers as those of Sept. 1932, Dec. 1936, and May 1939; among *Astounding Stories'* variations on this type we might especially note the covers of July 1934, Mar. 1935, and Nov. 1939; *Wonder Stories* and *Thrilling Wonder Stories* offer similar depictions on many issues, but especially those for June 1931, Jan. 1934, and Aug. 1939, while additional examples can be found in numerous other pre-war pulp covers, including issues from *Future Fiction, Science Wonder Stories, Startling Stories*, and *Super Science Stories*. Internal story illustrations in the same vein, while typically far less detailed and in a less alluring black and white, can also be readily found, especially—and most logically—as accompaniment for those stories that involve space flight, technological surveillance, or dimensional travel. All tend to follow a similar pattern of placing a screen or portal between the audience and some newly discovered, wondrous vision, while characters drawn from the depicted story serve as our avatars or stand-ins, as they watch, react to the framed vision, and model how *we* should react—or, it is presumed, *will react* upon reading the story. But more to the point, that act of looking through

Figure 5.3. The architecture of spectatorship demonstrated on a cover of *Science Wonder Stories* (Aug. 1929).

a portal, viewer, or screen reflexively—or abstractly—models the film experience, suggesting that the same aesthetic pleasures, the same thrills, wonders, or astonishments generated by the technology of the movies are available through the technologies depicted in these illustrations, whether they be spaceships, televisors, hypnobioscopes, or great cloud-piercing, windowed structures that take us far beyond our everyday vantage.

A more obvious development of this same reflexive potential shows up in those illustrations that depict the various mechanisms of the movies—screens, cameras, theaters—images that quite literally *represent* the technology and the world of film. Images and covers in this vein are only natural accompaniments for the sorts of stories discussed in chapter 3, those that take for their subject the world of the movies and movie-making, stories such as Emil Petaja's time-travel tale "Dinosaur Goes Hollywood," Rice Ray's mystery about sound-recording gone wrong, "To-Day's Yesterday," Henry Kuttner's series about the futuristic cinematographer Tony Quade working for "Hollywood on the Moon," or many of Howard K. Barnes's Gerry Carlyle stories, since his heroine is modeled on the film celebrity Frank Buck and her adventures almost invariably intersect with the film projects of Nine Planets Studio. More than just visual links to a fashionable topic, though, these images attest to an ongoing fascination with the "science" of the movies, even a desire to look behind the curtain of cinematic representation to see how the film industry fashions its various productions, how, through the artful application of technology, it creates its own zestful experiences.

A particularly noteworthy example of such backstage imagery is the full-page interior illustration used to introduce Rice Ray's time-shift story "To-Day's Yesterday." It shows the protagonist Cavanaugh, a sound engineer for the Criterion Film Company, sitting in a projection booth as he watches the "rushes" from the company's latest project *Hard Rock Jones*, while trying to figure out what has become of his friend George and a new microphone, both mysteriously missing. In the dark foreground we see a shadowy camera tripod, film cans, and a director's chair in which Cavanaugh is seated, while light from a projector on one side slashes across the frame to produce a smaller bright background image of a primitive tree and landscape, along with a character in modern dress and the misplaced microphone, its power cord detached and hanging limply. The illustration is of much more than what is usually termed a "profilmic event," that is, the stuff in front of and intended to be recorded by the camera and sound technology. In fact, much of this illustration emphasizes what usually escapes that event—the behind-the-scenes technology and activity, including the work of the director, that the moviegoer is not supposed to observe. But it is that external context, in fact a context gone wrong, as the misplaced and disconnected microphone underscores, that is the real focus of Ray's story about the mysterious temporal disjunction produced by the latest film sound recording equipment. While employing the same staging-in-depth format we have previously described, the elaborate illustration by Lumen Winter seems just as concerned with allowing viewers to take in the various technological trappings of the filmmaking process, the technology behind its magic, or in this case, behind the fantastic production of time or dimensional travel, as it is with "projecting" the audience's attention toward the small background image. The result is that film itself becomes the key SF element here.

A cover we have previously described, the one for *Thrilling Wonder Stories*' June 1939 issue, more explicitly evokes that movie technology and its function. One of those images intended to inspire readers to suggest their own plots, the Howard V. Brown illustration shows several large-headed, green-eyed aliens on the left foreground side of the frame, a seemingly advanced yet still recognizable movie camera on a tripod in the center, and, in the right background, two humans in explorers' outfits locked in a cage (Figure 5.4). The accompanying Ray Cummings essay, "The Story of the Cover," offers a helpful gloss on this invitingly ambiguous image. It explains how illustrations can draw viewers in a great many directions, in this case how that cover image, unconnected to any of the issue's stories, could easily evoke multiple possible scenarios. One potential plot, he offers, could involve alien filmmakers, such as Martian cameramen, photographing captured humans "for the newsreel audiences of Mars"; another, Cummings suggests, could imagine the aliens inspecting the camera technology with which the imprisoned humans had been observing and recording them; while a third might, more ominously, describe alien scientists preparing to "examine man" and record their examinations (37). Whichever the case, the central image of the camera, whether a human or alien device, is both the main focus and the pivot point for this "thought variant" and the multiple story possibilities it might inspire. The image thus reminds us that how we see—and also how the Martians with their emphatically bulging green eyes might see us—is a central concern of many SF narratives, and that the movies can provide a useful metaphor for exploring that seeing, even for showing how different cultures might view each other.

Another Brown cover, this one for the August 1940 issue of the same magazine, returns to the staging-in-depth approach we have previously described, but it shifts focus to emphasize its background imagery of green-skinned aliens and a motion picture screen. Depicting a scene from Henry Kuttner's story "No Man's World," the image shows the demonstration of a new 3-D film technology, as it accidentally opens a dimensional portal for two groups of alien invaders.[5] On this cover we see a contemporary movie theater with images being projected onto a large screen, but the film is apparently interrupted by two gigantic aliens who, as if movie

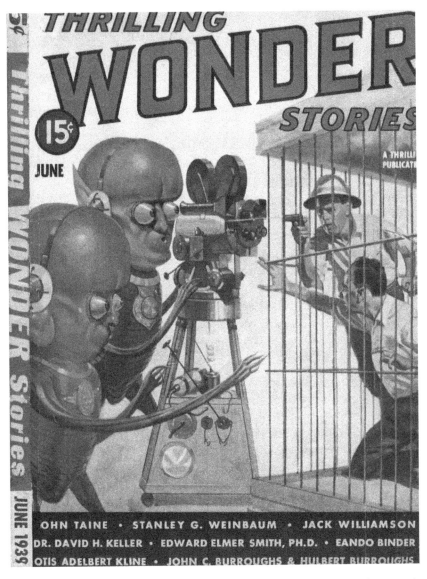

Figure 5.4. A camera forms the pivot point for several story lines in Howard V. Brown's *Thrilling Wonder Stories* cover (June 1939).

characters suddenly stepping into the real world—and we might recall how often this very gimmick surfaced in advertisements for 3-D films in the early 1950s—emerge from the screen and begin attacking the obviously panicked audience in the foreground. By presenting the movie screen as a kind of permeable membrane, with the theater as a site of unexpected alien contact, the illustration not only offers a reflexive commentary on the movies and the sort of unexpected access to reality that they might provide, but, much in the vein of "To-Day's Yesterday," it also sounds a warning about the nature of that access. In this case, it seems, film proves to be a dangerous technology, its possibilities not fully understood, and the pleasures it produces possibly coming at a great price for the unwitting moviegoers.

Striking a far less ominous note, while also emphasizing the attraction of the movies in this period, is another *Thrilling Wonder Stories* cover, this one illustrating a scene from what the magazine terms a "Novelette of Tomorrow's Movies" and one of the more favorably received stories of the era, Kuttner's "Hollywood on the Moon," discussed earlier. At first glance the Hans Wesso illustration—repeated with further details within the magazine—seems almost like a battle scene in outer space, with a dominant dark color scheme of reds and blues, and with characters scurrying about and aiming various devices at writhing space-suited figures in the deep background. The seemingly chaotic action, though, is simply that involved in a futuristic film shoot in the darkness of space, with space-suited cameramen and lighting assistants riding on dollies, trailing cables and wires that extend back to a massive movie "ship," its glass front displaying additional cameras, lighting equipment, and busy technicians, and all held in place by what the story, with an eye to scientific fact, tells us is a self-generated "neutralizing gravity field" (Kuttner, "Hollywood" 19). As an introductory piece within the issue further explains, the cover art is a vision of "technicians of a modern era" in the process of producing "de-luxe cinema presentations with marvelous three-dimensional effects" ("The Story Behind the Story" 6). Just as much to the point, it is a highly dynamic, indeed *cinematic* image in itself, composed on the diagonal, layered for depth effects, and containing much—at least implied—motion, as the real *action* of movie-making effectively displaces or renders irrelevant the fake action of the scene that is being photographed and which is here relegated to the deep and much darker background (Figure 5.5).

A nicely thematic conception for the larger SF-film intersection described in this chapter, the "Hollywood on the Moon" cover and story illustrations not only offer the expected speculative visions of space and encounters with strange figures, but like the other images we have just examined, they also frame their visions within the technical activities of film production and exhibition, linking that technological mode of seeing with SF's marvelous visions, as if one had produced the other. Of course, this impression of "production" is precisely the case in "No Man's World" with its film technology actually unlocking a dimensional portal into another world, just as it is as well with the sound technology that generates the time portal of

Figure 5.5. Henry Kuttner's "Hollywood on the Moon" story marries film production and the adventure of space exploration (*Thrilling Wonder Stories*, Apr. 1938).

"To-Day's Yesterday." But with the "Hollywood" cover especially we see not only a fascination with what a cinematic technology might produce, but practically a literalization of what Casetti describes as modernism's mobilized and "immersive gaze" (4). Here cameras and cameramen—Kuttner's protagonist Tony Quade is, in what I have suggested is one of the stranger castings of pulp SF, a space cinematographer—rocket about, their technological gaze "ready to grasp the totality of the world through movement" (Casetti 3), already and dramatically engaging the modernist world, or a universe of motion and change, on its own terms, as filmmaking itself becomes the ultimate SF adventure.

These and other images clearly remind us of the extent to which not just science and technology, but also the movies, had been installed at the center of modern—and conceivably future—life, with film rendered as science fictional, as an integral part of the genre's broadly utopian vision. The frontispiece illustration for another of Kuttner's *Thrilling Wonder* tales, "Doom World" (Aug. 1938, 12), makes this point even more dramatically, as it depicts a violent struggle between three humans and two monstrous figures, a metallic dragon and a gigantic white worm. It is a familiar-enough scene for most pulp readers and one rife with scopophilic pleasures, as an imperiled, scantily clad woman is being defended by two men who are firing their weapons at what are apparently attacking alien monsters—the seemingly ubiquitous BEMs or bug-eyed monsters of so many interplanetary stories—amid a jungle-like setting. But in the margins of this Alex Schomburg illustration we also see two partially camouflaged movie lights and at the bottom a concealed camera, apparently shooting this action scene. The story reveals not only that what we are seeing is a movie set, but that these monsters are, in fact, just robotic props—albeit props that have malfunctioned and, in another variant of the familiar technology-run-amok story, begun attacking their human "co-stars." Simply audioanimatronic creatures, they had been programmed to behave in conventionally threatening ways before being defeated as scripted. But this image captures the point at which these creatures have suddenly gone out of control and become in reality just the sort of monsters that, under proper programming and according to the script, they were only supposed to "play."

The bizarre shift that results, with filmic artifice turning into a kind of SF documentary as the camera continues to record this out-of-control moment—and all properly lit for dramatic effect—once again paints the movies in an adventurous, unpredictable, and strangely modernist light. Within Schomburg's image, "as a horde of radio-controlled robots menace the movie-makers of an ultra-modern era" (Kuttner, "Doom World" 13), we see story convention, film script, and real experience all suddenly collapse together, in the process frustrating any effort to sort out which is which, especially frustrating our ability to distinguish the real from the wondrous, actual science and technology from the fantastic movie about them, or even SF from the movies as a form. These suddenly combined elements not only paint the movies in an unpredictable, adventurous, and science fictional light, but they also afford a gloss on that "logic" of the pulp images, as the representational and abstract (or wondrous) characteristics become practically indistinguishable, become part of a single, complex, and pleasing SF vision. In the process they also remind us that what we think about real science and technology, and how the movies and our SF narratives prompt us to see the world might all occupy much the same territory.

Pulp historian Paul A. Carter has suggested yet another if perhaps not quite as obvious level of film's influence on these SF covers, as he argues that many of the illustrations are also generically indebted to Hollywood's customary imagery, as if that visual world were so familiar as to constitute part of a cultural imaginary or an insistent unconscious of the genre. He points especially to their depictions of the "glamorous Hollywood type of woman," placed in situations that recall various adventure films with which audiences of the era were well familiar (183). Perhaps overemphasizing the purely iconic nature of this sort of influence, Carter describes a *Planet Stories* cover showing metal-clad Amazons that, he says, reminds him of "a Busby Berkeley MGM song-and-dance spectacular" (183), as if such visual effects, because of their latent position in that cultural unconscious, might be expected to well up from time to time in unexpected situations.

More to the point is the usual configuration of such covers, which in their layouts remind readers/viewers of the sort of pleasurable, typically male gaze and objects of that gaze that were commonly encountered throughout the experience of conventional Hollywood cinema, evoking the dynamic of "visual pleasure" that Laura Mulvey describes in her famous essay "Visual Pleasure and Narrative Cinema."[6] For Mulvey—who also evokes Busby Berkeley's films as examples—the "conventional cinematic situation" not only "satisfies a primordial wish for pleasurable looking" (808), but also masculinizes that erotic looking, coding the spectator's position as fundamentally male, the object of the gaze as female, and its function as one of fetishistic pleasure. Translated into the typical pulp covers, this "cinematic situation" results in just the sort of heavily sexualized images that, as we have noted, readers repeatedly referred to as "undignified" or "lurid." Of course, since it occurs within a historically masculinized culture, this situation readily finds other visual cognates, and thus other possible correspondences and influences, such as in much advertising art of the period. Further complicating an all-too-easy judgment about this film linkage, Lisa Yaszek and Patrick B. Sharp have identified another, usually overlooked vein of pulp art created by women artists, trained in commercial art and fashion illustration. In this vein we might even see some resistance to this common pattern, as the artists that Yaszek and Sharp discuss often depict female figures in a different way, focusing more on their "reactions to the situations at hand" than their objectified status (333), showing them as more active characters than purely passive objects of "visual pleasure." However, the pervasive, even leading influence of the cinema across the entire range of modernist culture argues for its dominant, structuring impact on much of this featured pulp art, reinforcing the general characteristics of what Dean Conrad has effectively described as a "masculinized genre within an historically masculinized medium reflecting an undoubtedly masculinized society" (53).

Besides this sort of psychologically suggestive or for some simply iconic imagery, though, we should acknowledge some cover illustrations that do, almost literally, seem traceable to specific cinematic influences. One example is the December 1939 *Thrilling Wonder Stories* cover by Howard V. Brown, which offers an updated version of one of the most iconic movie images of the era—the climactic scene of King Kong atop the Empire State Building. In this instance, though, Brown replaces the giant ape with a huge insect attacking several people on that same building, while, as in the original film, futuristic planes swarm around and fire at the creature. Another instance is the *Thrilling Wonder Stories* cover of April 1939, also a Brown illustration, depicting a scene from the Ward Hawkins story "Men Must Die." It shows a number of diminutive figures—Lubians, as the story terms them—clambering over a tied-down and gigantic humanoid, a Jovian of Jupiter. The image obviously suggests an SF-take on *Gulliver's Travels*, the animated film of which, done by the Fleischer Studio, was to be released by Paramount that same year. With a massive advertising campaign for the film already under way and using similar imagery, it seems likely that the cover might well have been inspired by publicity stills that were widely circulated prior to the film's premier.[7] But although this instance of possible film inspiration is largely speculative, it helps frame another and previously noted Paramount collaboration with *Thrilling Wonder Stories* and Brown in the following year, that which was done to publicize the studio's live-action SF release *Dr. Cyclops* (1940), a story about a mad scientist who shrinks humans to "Lubian" size.

Intended to be part of a series of SF/horror movies that Paramount referred to as "Weird Chillers"—and that thus recall another highly popular pulp magazine, the genre-straddling *Weird Tales*—*Dr. Cyclops* is an example of the film industry's exploratory interest in fantasy and SF titles in the late pre-war period. In fact, to fully capitalize on the market for such titles, Paramount not only conducted numerous preview screenings in likely markets, but also, as a piece in *The Film Daily* notes, began "enlarging its exploitation staff to handle 'Dr. Cyclops' in key city engagements," hiring a great many "exploiteers," as they were termed, to exploit or help build interest in the film ("Para." 2). As part of that effort, a variety of visual gimmicks were created to attract attention to the film, such as the exhibit in one theater lobby of "a gigantic pair of black boots" weighing "approximately 400 pounds" that suggested some of the outsized props that had been created for the film's special effects scenes ("Huge" 8). But another part of that publicity effort is reflected in the June 1940 cover of *Thrilling Wonder Stories*, along with several interior images, all illustrating what was billed as Henry Kuttner's "novelet of men in miniature," "Dr. Cyclops."[8] More than simply imaging a scene from Kuttner's story, the Brown illustration closely corresponds to a specific shot from the Paramount film—and appropriately so, as a piece on "This Month's Cover" explains. In what the magazine terms a "confidential lowdown" (119), the editor discloses that Brown painted the cover *after* seeing a preview screening of the soon-to-be-released film (Figure 5.6). Moreover, another editorial offering, "The Story Behind the Story," explains that Kuttner too had received such privileged access and that while he had not originated the story, he had been "assigned . . . the job of fictionalizing this thrilling drama for T. W. S. [*Thrilling Wonder Stories*]" ("Story" 125). Besides the preview screening, both Brown's and Kuttner's "assignments" gave them entry to the studio where they supposedly observed the film in production. The implication is that Paramount, or its new external promotional agent, the Tom Fizdale Agency, had probably struck a publicity deal with Better Publications,[9] the parent company of *Thrilling Wonder Stories*—a deal further underscored by a two-page running footer attached to the story, urging the pulp audience to "Read It Now—Then See It at Your Local Theatre!"

The nature of that deal is worth considering a bit further, though, for the Brown cover represents not just some of those "common iconological reference points" that Winter describes or the colonizing of the cultural unconscious that Carter notes. Like Paul Orban's interior illustration as well, the cover reprises a very specific shot from the film version of *Dr. Cyclops*, suggesting that both cover and interior art were probably copied directly from publicity stills provided by Paramount. In fact, in what seems to have been a first for the SF pulps, the story was also partly illustrated with production stills from the studio, one showing a close-up of Albert Dekker as the title character and another demonstrating one of the film's special effects compositions, a composite shot in which the victims of the Doctor's experiments in miniaturization strike back at him. The dynamic color cover painting, interior black and white artwork, and multiple publicity stills not only provide a more elaborate pattern of illustration than usual for any single pre-war pulp story, but they also emphasize a sense of partnership with the movies, with both pulp magazine and film offering their own,

Figure 5.6. Howard V. Brown adapts an image from Paramount's *Dr. Cyclops* for *Thrilling Wonder Stories* (June 1940).

equally attractive, and supposedly complementary takes on a typical SF narrative, as each set about doing the work of the SF imagination.

While the Kuttner adaptation was well received by readers, with numerous letters praising it in "The Reader Speaks" column, the specifically cinematic approach that the editors took to illustrating it drew surprisingly little attention. The most detailed letter remarking on the feature did suggest that *Thrilling Wonder Stories* should "make *Dr. Cyclops* the first of a series of stories" based on the movies, and requested that subsequent efforts likewise "be illustrated by stills taken from the movies" (July 1940, 119). However, other readers, even as they rated the Kuttner adaptation highly, made no mention of the movie stills or general film connection, even though one would praise the cover and interior drawing instead (Sept. 1940, 120). In any case, no such series would follow the *Dr. Cyclops* multi-media experiment. While prior to America's entry into World War II Paramount would release a few more of its "Weird Chillers"—*The Mad Doctor* and *The Monster and the Girl* (both 1941)—neither would receive a mention in *Thrilling Wonder*. In fact, as the war approached, scientifilms themselves almost disappeared from American studios' offerings, and there would be no other pulp experimentation with film-related covers or publicity stills until, as the final chapter describes, the post-war era ushered in a different attitude toward the movies.

Although the absence of any further *Dr. Cyclops*-like experiments is most likely due to the war and the film industry's scaling back production of certain unsettling types of movies,[10] it also seems possible that the nature of that film/SF relationship was a contributing factor. The various film illustrations employed practically insist on their highly representational nature, with their indexical power pointing to a reality that had been glimpsed on set, photographed, or in some way copied from reality. While a logical extension of the "representational" character of the pulp covers and interior illustrations, that indexical power might almost have been too much for the pulps and the SF imagination, binding their most wondrous or abstract-seeming images to a possible reality and a particular way of seeing that was based on the experience of a live-action cinema, or what Anne Friedberg refers to as film's own "visual vernacular" (*Virtual* 3). Rather than just extending the imaginative "logic" that Cheng identified, such cinematic imagery might well have been seen as potentially overwhelming—or undermining—SF's wondrous dimension as the war's darker realities were starting to come into focus.

And yet, another component of that "representational logic" linked to the cinema lingered and seemed to retain its power. The reflexive elements that surface in so many of the pulp covers and interior images repeatedly argue for the cinema or a cinema-like experience as a part of this envisioned world by privileging the act of looking, depicting different sorts of audiences, offering up images of movie cameras, screens, and projectors, and deploying recognizably generic Hollywood imagery. By foregrounding such instances of a filmic reflexivity—of motion frozen, framed, and tied to the SF story experience—the various sorts of pulp artwork certainly testify to how much film had become, as Casetti offers, "a pivotal element of the modern landscape" (172), something from which not even an SF literature could escape. Besides staking out a path to that new visuality of the age, helping us see what the SF imagination might hold in store, those cover images that seem by turns representational and abstract function rather like what Walter Benjamin described as the "lightning flash" that was implicit in the truly modernist text, a shock prompting readers/viewers to see things in a novel way, in a context that he described as "the Now of recognizability" (qtd. in Smith 64).

Benjamin, probably the most important commentator in this period on the new world of mechanical reproduction, thought it was important to map the sort of impact that film was having on modern life. Its appearance and great popularity corresponded to what he would describe as "profound changes in the apperceptive apparatus—changes that are experienced on an individual scale by the man in the street in big-city traffic, on a historical scale by every present-day citizen," and, we should obviously add at this point, even by the casual browser ("The Work of Art" 250), who could not help but see that impact drawn large—sometimes embarrassingly so—on the various pulp covers he perused at the local newsstand. Those gaudy images, with their highly saturated red, blue, yellow, and green color schemes, with their bizarre SF iconography, with their frequently imperiled beautiful women, with their energetic promise, and often with their obvious reminders of the cinematic mechanism itself, managed to draw readers out of the everyday experience and to dispel the "aura" to which the world commonly subjected them. Their "representational logic," despite their attendant sensationalistic seeming, starkly visualized the work of both the SF and cinematic imaginations, advertising—and at least partly paying off on—their similar promise to let us see other worlds, other beings, and other technologies. If these illustrations could so convincingly represent the wonders of the SF imagination, this logic seemed to argue, then they could indeed come to pass.

CHAPTER 6
Of War and Beyond

There was nothing more functional than a threaded spool of photo-film. Projected images were inseparable from civilization. In fact, it was impossible to think of any advanced culture, in any age or dimension, without cinematographic recordings.

—Frank Belknap Long, "The World of Wulkins" (114)

In his futuristic story "The World of Wulkins," one of Frank Belknap Long's characters observes just how fundamental to modern life—or "advanced culture," as he puts it—motion pictures had become. That commentary provides a useful starting point for considering the film-pulps relationship during the war and early post-war years when Long was one of the central figures in SF, and coincidentally a script reader for 20th Century-Fox Studios. While this 1948 story, like a number of others in the period, incorporates into its plot the importance of film as a historical record, it also describes film as largely "functional" or mundane, an everyday tool that evokes little of the science fictional excitement that was commonplace in stories and in the culture just a decade before. By deploying film's ability to record, store, and project images, the future culture Long describes has not only fully mobilized the "mobile gaze" of modernity, but also effectively drained it of any modernist associations. It is on that shift, on the recession of the cinema from its frequently foregrounded status in the pre-war pulps to a mundane position in the post-war period, that this chapter will focus.

In this later period the literature of SF was coming of age, finding a more prominent status as a long form offered by specialized publishers, such as Ace Books and Ballantine Books.[1] In terms of content that development was marked by what Edward James characterizes as "a greater maturity in the writing . . . a freshness in the writing and an enthusiasm for the possibilities of the genre" (88), particularly as demonstrated by a number of authors who essentially came of age in the war and early postwar period—figures like Isaac Asimov, Ray Bradbury, Robert A. Heinlein, and Arthur C. Clarke, among many others, and for all of whom "projected images" were indeed a part of everyday culture. At approximately the same time, the SF film was, after many earlier predictions of success, finally exploding on the scene in what Joyce A. Evans describes as "one of the most interesting developments in . . . the history of motion pictures" (75). With the possible exception of film noir in the 1940s, her judgment that, never before had a film genre "developed and multiplied so rapidly in so brief a period" (75), is fairly accurate. Yet the dual success of SF literature and film would also be marked by something that must have seemed almost "impossible" during the pre-war years, as these two fellow travelers, previously seen in much the same light, as embodying a comparable modernist spirit, as similarly driven by and reflecting the latest scientific and technological developments, would increasingly move in different directions.

That sense of taking separate paths is, of course, partly due to the very maturity of each form. While the "pulp tradition," as it is often termed, continued during this period and was even bolstered by the appearance of a great number of new magazines—*Captain Future, Comet, Fantastic Universe, Out of This World, Space Stories, Stirring Science Stories, Worlds Beyond*, and others, most of which would have relatively brief runs—SF literature was just beginning to bulk beyond these popular pulp outlets with, as the previous chapter discussed, their often "undignified" covers. From an eclectic fan base, largely dominated by young males in the 1920s and 1930s, SF would in the late 1940s and early 1950s attain what Adam Roberts terms "an unprecedented kind of cultural prominence for the genre" (196). And as James chronicles, this change had a great many causes: the simple growth of SF readership, accompanied by a new interest in the genre; a cold-war inspired fascination with science, technology, and the future they were heralding; a rise in paperback publishing, along with the emergence of new hardcover SF series; and an increase in disposable income among the reading public (84). All of these causes, and others, were in various ways linked to a growing sense in the period that SF, if not yet, as James deems, fully "respectable," was certainly "becoming significant" (55). And that sense of significance was due not just to the genre's status as entertainment, but to the perception that it might be a way of directly addressing some of the most pressing cultural concerns, especially those implicated in the latest scientific and technological developments that had been spurred by the war and whose specters increasingly lingered over post-war culture.

A separate SF cinema would take a while longer to achieve a similar level of significance—and artistry—although the sheer number of films that were released in the 1950s certainly argues for their importance to the culture, and an SF cinema would also find added status through various sorts of links to the literature. As the previous chapter noted, the relationship between the pulps and the movies marked so very visibly and intentionally by the connected film and story *Dr. Cyclops* would not produce many similar cooperative efforts with the film industry, and the initial wave of SF narratives that marked the cinema of the 1940s and persisted into the mid-1950s was mainly composed of serials like those of the 1930s, repeating various familiar formulas: mad scientist tales such as *The Monster and the Ape* (1945) and *The Crimson Ghost* (1946); superhero stories like *The Masked Marvel* (1942) and *Superman* (1948); and space operas such as *Brick Bradford* (1947), *King of the Rocket Men* (1949), and *Radar Men from the Moon* (1952) (Figure 6.1). But some SF authors familiar to pulp readers, including Heinlein, Bradbury, and the famed author and editor of *Astounding* John W. Campbell, Jr., among others, would be approached by the film industry and would contribute significantly to both the subsequent outpouring of SF films throughout the 1950s and the genre's growing status, even a measure of critical esteem. These authors would either script or provide the original stories for some of the most significant of the new feature films in this period, most notably *Destination Moon* (1950), *The Thing from Another World* (1951), and *It Came from Outer Space* (1953). However, with a few key exceptions, many of the features that followed in this cinematic outburst were relatively unsophisticated, quickly made films that often, as James suggests, seemed to go "back to the worst of the pulps for their inspiration" (81), particularly with familiar plots about monsters, alien invaders, and space adventuring.

If SF literature at large was reaching for a new level of respectability in the post-war era, SF cinema, in part because of new market paradigms that followed from the Supreme Court's industry-changing Paramount decision,[2] simply faced a more difficult situation. Forced to develop new marketing strategies and faced with an audience that had peaked in 1946 but had begun to shrink during the early post-war years, the film industry sought ways to lure audiences back into theaters—and away from its new rival, television, which was also attracting major SF authors such as Heinlein, Bradbury, Theodore Sturgeon, and Frederick Pohl. One industry strategy to counter this competition was the development of various technological lures, including Cinemascope, Cinerama, and 3-D, while another, perhaps

Figure 6.1. Part of the first wave of post-war SF films, the Republic serial *Radar Men from the Moon* (1952).

more subtle strategy was the exploration of such newly popular genres as SF, which, as the enormous success of early television series like *Captain Video*, *Space Patrol*, and *Tom Corbett, Space Cadet* had quickly demonstrated, seemed a strong and indeed highly topical candidate for exploitation.

But as Bradley Schauer has argued, the larger studios especially found themselves facing what he terms a "pulp paradox" (51), as they tried to fashion generally mainstream features out of what was widely seen as cheap, escapist-type material. *Destination Moon*, an early entry in the new SF wave, had been made on a larger budget than had previously been allotted to such genre efforts—at least in the United States; the studio brought in respected consultants, including noted space artist Chesley Bonestell, to ensure its scientific accuracy; the film employed top writers, including Heinlein; and most important, it proved to be a box office success. However, there were few efforts to duplicate that formula. Instead, a variety of low-budget exploitation films would follow, and as Schauer notes, they managed to "perform just as well or better at the box office" than most of the bigger-budgeted, more sophisticated efforts, while often just adding "flying saucers and little green men to the equation" (51)—that is, the fanciful trappings that were all too often associated with the world of pulp fiction. So while SF may have been seen as holding a major profit potential for a suddenly struggling US film industry, much of that "potential" seemed tied to a cheaper pulp look—and attitude—that "might be effective in attracting spectators looking for SF/horror thrills," but that "also signaled to general audiences that the film was just another cheap exploitation film for kids" (Schauer 66), and in quality not much different from what could readily be found on television. Even as SF literature had incorporated much of film's visual imperatives—what we have repeatedly referred to as the new visuality of the age—and then, during the war and especially in the post-war era, moved on, much of SF cinema, for all of its futuristic trappings, often seemed yoked to the past, and especially the past of the genre's early pulp form, as if it had little more to offer to its literary kin—and a shrinking film audience—than bug-eyed monsters, alien invaders, and apocalyptic scenarios, all effectively standing in for, and sometimes even seeming to shove to the side, the very real international menaces of the present day. We can find these shifting imperatives and uncertain effects reflected in the same pulp components that, prior to the war, afforded just as clear a measure of film's importance to and influence on the SF imagination—the various magazines' advertising, stories, reader/editor discourse, and artwork.

Perhaps the most obvious indicator of this shift in attitudes during the war and post-war years is in the area of advertising. While the earlier pulp ads for bodybuilding courses, music lessons, rupture relievers, and mail-order false teeth still appeared regularly in most of the pulp magazines, gone were the sort of notices that had once suggested the lure of and relatively easy access to the film industry, such as those frequent solicitations for stories that might be turned into film scripts, the promise of screen tests, and contract contests sponsored by the industry, affiliated magazines, or body-building programs. Gone, too, were the constant ads offering instruction to those wanting to make "big money" as movie cameramen, editors, or sound technicians—jobs that, in the post-war era, had largely fallen under union control. They were replaced by reworded ads placed by some of the same companies—Coyne Electrical School of Chicago, J. E. Smith's National Radio Institute of Washington, DC, National Schools of Los Angeles, and others—all touting the new and less controlled field of television, while often striking a note of urgency as they addressed ex-servicemen and a quickly tightening post-war job market. Thus a Coyne ad in *Thrilling Wonder Stories* counseled readers to "Get Ready Quick!" for the future (Apr. 1947, 101), while a National Schools spot in the same issue likewise urged readers to "Act at Once!" (109). These and others were obviously trying to tap the large market of anxious veterans, as we see in Coyne's admonition in a *Startling Stories* spot telling readers to "Get Ready Quick for a Peacetime Future" (Mar. 1946, 105), as well as ads commonly noting the possibility of government financing for television schooling. In any case, it seemed like jobs in the film industry, which by 1946 was already beginning a long process of retrenchment, were no longer a ready part of the future that was being sold by the SF pulps.

Despite the apparent closing off of that promise, the pulps still hosted a variety of ads aimed at what we might broadly describe as film fans. Thus a number of classifieds offered home versions of Hollywood movies, while several companies advertised the availability of movie cameras and projectors (both 8mm and 16mm, probably drawn from massive post-war government surpluses) for sale or rental, and others, like the enticingly titled Hollywood Film Studios, offered film and photograph processing services. In its full-page ad, the General Camera Company (Figure 6.2) combined all of these possibilities with its thirteen-piece "Keystone Home Movie Outfit," which came complete with a collection of 8mm films and the promise of mail-order processing for home movies (*Super Science Stories*, July 1950, 2). However, there was also a distinct shift in tone in some of these post-war notices that speaks to a changing audience as well as audience attitudes. Signaling its increasingly titillating thrust in this period and an effort to play off of film's own scopophilic attraction—which, as the previous chapter reminded, was easily seen on the pulps' covers—*Amazing*

Figure 6.2. Movies become domesticated with ads for the Keystone Home Movie Outfit (*Super Science Stories*, July 1950).

would feature a series of ads offering "Tall Girl Movies," that is, films of "showgirls" six feet and taller, readers were assured, available from the aptly named "Skyscraper Films" of New York. In this same adult vein, the "Hollywood Pin-Ups Company" would place a similarly suggestive notice, offering the "world's largest collection of pin-up photos, slides, and movies" (July 1951, 157). But in contrast to such coarse appeals, *Amazing* would also include notices from a different sort of specialized provider, the "Historic Cinema Service," which announced it had available "Fantasy Movie Stills" from a wide variety of films, but notably from such well-known SF/fantasy efforts as *Frankenstein, Things to Come,* and *Beauty and the Beast* (Aug. 1951, 160). Rather like the upstart television and following the pattern of radio, film, it seems, was making a move into the domestic space.

Far more telling evidence that there was still a general targeting of film fans among the SF readership, though, was the regular appearance of something that, as chapter 2 noted, had largely gone missing from the pre-war pulps: actual feature film advertising. The RKO murder mystery *Nocturne* (1947), for example, would receive a full-page treatment in *Thrilling Wonder Stories* (Feb. 1947, 2) that almost seemed like a continuation of that magazine's often sexualized cover imagery (Figure 6.3). Building upon the scopophilia built into such covers, it featured an outsized set of women's legs dangling above a murdered body, ten photographs of beautiful women, and a headline challenge to the readers—and potential moviegoers— asking, "Whose Legs Are These?" Of course, *Nocturne* had nothing to do with SF, even if it did foreground the same sort of visual concern that had become a regular part of the genre, while further suggesting that the pulps remained largely directed at a male readership. Moreover, there were still few instances of specifically SF film advertisements to be found in any of the pulps, and the exciting—or enticing—imagery was certainly in tune with much of that found in the general run of popular magazines during the early post-war period.

Although less sensational than the *Nocturne* posting and usually patterned on the standard posters or lobby cards for the films, similar full-page ads would make regular appearances in *Thrilling Wonder's* post-war issues, touting such movies as the Republic B-westerns *Plainsman and the Lady* (1946) and *Wyoming* (1947), Columbia's release *Renegades* (1946), the Warner Bros./Mickey Rooney racing drama *The Big Wheel* (1950), the Paramount westerns *El Paso* and *Whispering Smith* (both 1949), RKO's *Blood on the Moon* (1949), and dual ads for the novel and film versions of *Duel in the Sun* (1947) and *The Edge of Doom* (1950). Comparable ads would crop up in several other pulps. For example, in the pages of *Startling Stories*, a sister publication to *Thrilling Wonder* and also edited by that magazine's editor Mort Weisinger, we can find full-page promotions for the John Wayne western *Angel and the Badman* (1947), Republic's *In Old Sacramento* (1946), RKO's adventure film *Tarzan and the Leopard Woman* (1946), its western *Badman's Territory* (1946), and the film noir *The Racket* (1952), the MGM

Figure 6.3. A typical post-war film ad, but for a film noir not SF (*Thrilling Wonder Stories*, Feb. 1947).

crime drama *Black Hand* (1950), Warner Bros.' Alfred Hitchcock murder mystery *Rope* (1949), as well as another of those dual ads for the novel and "Smash-hit Movie" from 20th Century-Fox *Leave Her to Heaven* (1945). The flood of such full-page advertisements seems symptomatic of the film industry's efforts in the immediate post-war period to reach out to other, previously neglected audiences, especially with action-oriented and visually rich genres such as the western and the film noir, although the absence of notices even for the SF serials of the 1940s or for many of the SF features of the early 1950s again seems noteworthy, underscoring the fact that the film industry, at least into the early 1950s, was still unsure of how to market or advertise SF—or perhaps, as some SF commentators have suggested, unsure of whether it actually constituted a distinct genre that might have a real market identity.[3]

Of course, we might hesitate at making too much of this sort of connection—or disconnection—or of suggesting that the film industry might have perceived SF, perhaps because of the legacy of the serials, to fall largely within an action genre context and thus to draw in an audience that was mainly attracted by such action efforts. As David M. Earle reminds, the way that much pulp advertising was placed probably played some role in this linkage. In chapter 2 we noted that many of these pulp ads were supplied by advertising services that offered large ad packages to whole publishing groups, often resulting in an accidental disjunction between a magazine's subject matter and its ads (Earle 202). As members of the Thrilling Publications family of offerings, both *Thrilling Wonder* and *Startling Stories* would probably have shared in the ads with other publications in that group, although a sampling of sister publication *Exciting Western*'s issues of the post-war period shows surprisingly few film ads, and one of the most famous of the pulps *Weird Tales*, while at times publishing SF stories and repeating many of the same ads found in the SF magazines, has practically no film notices. Consequently, we might suppose that at least some of these advertisements may have been placed with an eye to the specific readership of the SF pulps. While focusing more on the class-directed nature of much of this advertising, John Rieder arrives at a similar conclusion, suggesting that it makes "sense . . . to observe that the ads and the fiction fit together precisely to the extent that advertisers succeeded in choosing to place their ads in magazines that were targeting the audiences they hoped to speak to" (*Science Fiction* 53).

One of those multiple ad placements—and special "fits"—deserves special comment, as both *Thrilling Wonder* and *Startling Stories* would feature the first advertisements for an SF film to appear in any of the pulps. Curiously, though, these ads were not for one of the most anticipated SF films of the period such as *Destination Moon* (1950); rather, they were for what would prove to be one of the most successful, *The Thing from Another World* (1951). Moreover, they differed markedly in style from those for the usual run of such film advertisements, such as those cited earlier for the various westerns, noirs, and adventure narratives with their visual designs featuring legs, guns, cars, and other exciting or titillating imagery that echoed the visual pleasures of the pulp covers. In fact, what is especially interesting about these ads is how little they do show. Offered with only minimal graphics and billed in each typically quarter- or eighth-page spot as "Howard Hawks' *Amazing* Movie," "Howard Hawks' *Startling* Movie," or "Howard Hawks' *Astounding* Movie" (the italicized modifiers almost seeming to evoke specific pulp titles), *The Thing* was the subject of an intense promotional push by its distributor RKO, although it was a push that presented it not as SF, but as essentially an unknown subject, a mystery neatly bound up in its mysteriously allusive title.

An article in the industry publication *Motion Picture Daily* sheds some light on the nature of this publicity effort. As it outlined, the film was one of three "exploitation specials" for which the studio in 1951 planned "extensive campaigns based on maximum use of publicity, advertising, and local showmanship" ("RKO" 5). As part of this effort, *The Thing* received special midnight premieres in several cities; RKO conducted a contest among exhibitors, offering a $1,500 prize "for the best exploitation" effort ("Trade" 4); and ads were placed in a wide variety of national magazines, including "slick" outlets like *Collier's* and *Redbook*, industry publications, including *The Film Bulletin*, *Motion Picture Daily*, and *Variety*, and, as noted earlier, several of the SF pulps. Moreover, the ads did not follow the usual model of lifting scenes from the film, depicting its stars, or offering the sort of exaggerated or lurid imagery previously noted.[4] Even more to the point, none of the ads frames *The Thing* specifically as SF. Instead, the initial campaign ads, including those in *Thrilling Wonder Stories* and *Startling Stories*, were all remarkably plain and, compared to most other US film advertising of the period—or, for that matter, compared to the typical imagery of the pulps—were relatively understated, essentially a white box, inside of which all work a variation on the question, "What is *The Thing*?" Some incorporated a slightly different, roughly drawn graphic element, such as a large question mark, a gun firing through the film title (Figure 6.4), or a shadowy figure looming behind the title, and all used fur letters for the title while identifying the movie not by its director or writer, but by its famous producer—typically linked to adventure and noir films—as a Howard Hawks picture.[5] With no major stars involved in the film, the neophyte director Christian Nyby, and few precedents for effectively exploiting examples of SF, RKO had clearly decided to emphasize the mysterious element of the film's title, thereby presenting it not so much as an SF work, but rather as a mystery or horror film—as indeed it was repeatedly referred to in various *Motion Picture Daily* reports. In fact, large two-page spreads in

Figure 6.4. One of the first SF film advertisements in the pulps, *Startling Stories'* announcement for *The Thing* (May 1951).

Motion Picture Daily and *Variety* that appeared at the time of the film's premiere underscored that mystery/horror character by printing "*The Thing*" in letters dripping blood. With no hint of science or technology to be found anywhere in these ads, they seem to identify and reach for a broad thrill-seeking audience, apparently of the sort that the film industry at this time most associated with much SF and, we might assume, with the pulp readership as well.

That several SF pulps would be included in this rather different sort of exploitation campaign is thus telling. Certainly, the pedigree of *The Thing* would seem to justify this particular outreach. After all, the film was based on the story "Who Goes There?" that had first been published in *Astounding Science Fiction* (Aug. 1938), it was written by famed pulp editor John W. Campbell, Jr. (using the pseudonym Don A. Stuart), and it effectively bound together in its plot a variety of what Bradley Schauer terms popular "pulp tropes"—the flying saucer, the isolated scientific station, the monstrous alien, the rugged pilot protagonist, the cool, strong woman, etc. (64). It must have seemed precisely the sort of film that might tap into what was a growing and increasingly visible SF readership. Yet despite being well received in the popular press and proving to be the most profitable SF film of the early 1950s,[6] *The Thing* would find only minor support in the pulps; for example, an *Astounding* reader would close his letter to that magazine's "Brass Tacks" column offering his "congratulations" to editor Campbell "on a fine picture in 'The Thing'" (Dec. 1951, 169). But it would be reviewed in none of the major magazines, it sparked—surprisingly—little commentary in the various editors' and letters' columns,[7] and it would be followed, at least through the early 1950s, by just a few other Hollywood SF efforts that sought to directly address the genre's pulp audience.

A second dimension of the pulp/film intersection, stories involving the film industry or drawing its technology into the narrative, would also shrink in importance, particularly as a new technology like television increasingly bulked into the cultural foreground, much as the training ads we have previously noted might suggest. Certainly, the various technologies that were commonly employed in film production, those involved in image capture, sound reproduction, color, and even three-dimensionality, were no longer seen in quite the new and exciting context that had marked their representation during the pre-war years when sound recording devices and 3-D projectors would be depicted as powerful technologies capable of opening up dimensional or temporal portals. Still, an explorer in Frank Jones' story "Arctic God" would, after coming upon a primitive civilization, measure their archaic status by observing the *absence* of "movies or talking pictures or television," much less other "rudiments of modern science" and signs of a *truly* modern culture (197). As this chapter's epigraph taken from "The World of Wulkins" suggests, the equipment employed in such "science" had generally come to be viewed as simply "functional," part of the technological landscape of any modern—or future—society. As a result, we find fewer stories treating the specific technologies involved, the cameras, microphones, screens, etc., as mysterious devices or gateways to another time, dimension, or alien world, much less as new tools that might be used as aids in scientific inquiry or discovery.

Nevertheless, both a cinematic way of thinking and the lure of the movie industry would continue to have some impact in war-era and post-war SF narratives. As chapter 4 observed, the movies had, even in the pre-war period, filtered into the very rhetoric of SF storytelling, providing easy references, metaphors, and similes that underscore just how much film resonated with the genre audience and, just as significantly, the extent to which it had become a common part of popular—and pulp SF—discourse. That sort of easy evocative use of film would persist in the post-war era, and we might once again note a few examples to underscore this point. In one instance, a character in Roger Dee's *Thrilling Wonder Stories* piece, "Girl from Callisto," observes another figure acting strangely and, in trying to explain his behavior to a companion, notes that he was "moving his lips like an actor in a silent movie. He looked normal . . . but he wasn't" (74). Describing a courtroom scene gone wrong in another *Thrilling Wonder* contribution, "The Sky Was Full of Ships," Theodore Sturgeon would offer one of his typically wry comparisons, suggesting that the incident "was like a movie short. It needed only a comedy dance number and somebody playing a jug" (55). P. F. Costello in his "Whom the Gods Destroy" describes a fantastic mind control device developed by a former Nazi scientist as something that at least "appeared" relatively harmless; in fact, in trying to convey that nonthreatening appearance, one character notes that it "looked somewhat like a motion picture projector" (83). Stephen Marlowe's *Amazing* space opera "The Last Revolution" would attempt to modernize a familiar saying, tellingly by framing it in cinematic terms, as one of his star-traveling characters recalls hearing that "in the moment before death your whole life runs through your mind like an impossibly fast motion picture" (86). Evoking the movies as a touchstone of the past, Keith Winton of Fredric Brown's "What Mad Universe" tries to make sense of the seemingly surreal future world in which, as a time traveler, he has found himself, observing that another character "looks like Errol Flynn" and speculating that, given the sort of "Mad Universe" in which he is apparently trapped, one that seems so much "like a fantastic movie," the figure "might even be Errol Flynn" (46). And Henry Kuttner in one of his later pieces, "The Well of the Worlds," would draw out a familiar allusion to the film version of *The Wizard of Oz* (1939) when one of his characters describes a startling shift in his environment as being "like a film . . . changing from technicolor to drab black and white" (69)—and at a time when the film experience was still predominantly a black and white one. These and many other examples of similar rhetoric or familiar allusions remind us of the extent to which a cinematic way of talking—and, as the reference to *The Wizard of Oz* suggests, of thinking—had by mid-century become commonplace in the SF pulps, just as it was throughout much of modern American culture.

Another link to the pre-war pulps shows up in the reprinting, during the late war and early post-war years, of some of the earlier pulp stories that were focused on the movie industry, as evidence the *Startling Stories* republication of C. Sterling Gleason's "The Radiation of the Chinese Vegetable" (Winter 1945), Henry Kuttner's "Hollywood on the Moon" (July 1949), Arthur K. Barnes' "The Hothouse Planet" (Sept. 1949), and the Kuttner and Barnes collaboration "The Energy Eaters" (Sept. 1950). Similarly, the *Avon Fantasy Reader* would reprint Laurence Manning and Fletcher Pratt's pre-war piece about a zombie culture created by an addiction to visual media, "The City of the Living Dead" (1947). Referring to such reprints as "Scientifiction Hall of Fame Stories," the editor of *Startling Stories* explained that these features were being "reprinted by popular demand" (Winter 1945). But while offering no evidence of such "demand"—letters, petitions, fan club inquiries—he invited readers to "Nominate your own favorite!" (80) for what he promised would be an ongoing series.

Several of the more prominent authors of the pre-war period, particularly Kuttner and Barnes, would add a few more episodes to their Tony Quade and Gerry Carlyle series respectively, both of which, as we previously noted, usually centered on the operations of the futuristic film industry dubbed "Hollywood on the Moon." The Carlyle story "Siren Satellite" (1946), though, would shift focus from the continuing efforts to involve the "interplanetary huntress," as Carlyle was known, in Nine Planets Films' productions to a plot that plays on her well-known susceptibility to publicity, including that promised by the new medium of television, in order to steal her rocket ship. While the comic-adventure tone of the series remained, the narrative incorporated only the sort of cinematic rhetoric noted in various other authors' works, as when Carlyle describes a fight on Neptune's moon Triton as like "an ancient movie—jerky action, but no accompanying sound" (77). In his last Tony Quade tale, "Trouble on Titan" (1947), Kuttner would include a homage to Carlyle, as he recounts how the head of Nine Planets, Ludwig Von Zorn, had produced a series of *Gerri Murri* cartoons based on Gerry Carlyle's character and, as a result, was being sued for libel. But most of the story recounts the difficulties Quade faces in trying to finish an ethnographic documentary about the inhabitants of Titan.

Accompanying this contribution to *Thrilling Wonder Stories*, Kuttner would provide a commentary in the magazine's "The Story Behind the Story" column that casts some light on why this piece would be the last appearance of Tony Quade and the final entry in his popular "Hollywood on the Moon" series. In it he says little about his story, but rather discusses the ongoing development of the movies, including their history, their evolving technology, and their primary need, like any entertainment form, to "reflect the cultural background of the period" (Feb. 1947, 113). It is a revealing overview, especially since there is little about movie technology or—apart from brief references to the landmark documentaries *Grass* (1925) and *Chang* (1927)—movie history within the story proper. Instead, "Trouble on Titan" focuses on the difficulty Quade faces in shooting *Sons of Titan*, as his film is titled, in a strange place and while surrounded by strange, humanoid types known as Zonals. In effect, the story takes the shape of a clash of cultures and a reflection on the sort of cultural understandings that the new, post-war world would require, even from those in the movie industry. More specifically, Quade encounters two types of Zonals, beings he dismissively refers to as almost "sub-human" (39). One is curious about humans, has been taught a rudimentary level of English, and is even willing to work on—and in—his film. The other is very unfriendly, even war-like, primitive and inarticulate, and a constant menace. Yet both groups of Zonals, as Quade discovers, are descended from the same ancient and advanced culture, "a plenty intelligent race before" a plague decimated their great civilization (48). During that earlier cultural stage, we learn, the Zonals had produced a modern society with advanced technology and had even built impressive castles. As Quade manages to vanquish the hostiles and, with the aid of the friendlies, finish filming *Sons of Titan*, it becomes clear that this story is not just another of Kuttner's cinematically themed space operas, but a reflection on America's post-war cultural experience, particularly with Europe, a land of ancient castles and intellectuals that, over the centuries, has been ravaged by both real plagues and the plagues of war. That Quade, like the United States, manages to defeat one group and find allies in the other, even introduce them to modern—cinematic—culture, speaks to the quite different aims Kuttner may have had for his stories in the immediate post-war period and might help explain why he would leave behind the popular character of Tony Quade, the futuristic, even resonant landscape of his Hollywood on the Moon, and the modernist emphasis on new modes of seeing that had prominently featured in these stories. At one point Kuttner describes his space Hollywood as "the strangest city in the solar system," a city "artificially created" and "germ-free" (38), but that sort of artificial, antiseptic culture could hardly correspond to the chaotic, complex, and far from problem-free post-war culture that he and his readers were already having to confront. What he offers in "Trouble on Titan" is an image of that troubled confrontation with reality, as Kuttner set aside his fascination with the possibilities of cinematic illusion in order to address the difficult circumstances of the new, more complex post-war world.

But closely following the early lead of Kuttner and Barnes was another frequent pulp contributor, Walt Sheldon (aka Seldon Walters), who would offer a new SF take on the film industry. Originally a writer of detective fiction (at one time even penning an Ellery Queen novel), as well as a frequent author of "jungle" stories, Sheldon would branch into SF starting in 1948 with "Perfect Servant" (*Startling Stories*, July 1948), a robot tale centered on the Hollywood director/producer Jonathan Gamble. And he would produce numerous stories of time and dimensional travel—such as "Music of the Spheres" (1950) and "A Bit of Forever" (1950)—most with an O'Henry-like ironic twist ending. But he is most noteworthy in the context of this study for the way in which, like Kuttner and Barnes, he would repeatedly work the world of the popular media into his stories, as we might see in several of his *Fantastic Adventures* contributions. For example, the story "Operation Decoy" uses the conceit of a "visaphone transcript" of an encounter with aliens whose planned attack on the Earth is foiled by planted misinformation. After the fashion of some of Kuttner's Tony Quade stories, it adopts a cinematic model, providing italicized set descriptions and indicating fade-ins and dissolves to mark scene changes, along with cut indicators to mark the shot changes in each scene, describing particular images by noting whether they are medium shots, close-ups, or "big close-ups," and, of course, assigning dialogue to each character—human and alien. In effect, it reads much like a finely detailed film script of this brief yet momentous encounter between two antagonistic civilizations, and suggests that the human emphasis on visualization, on surveilling and accurately recording actions, might well prove humanity's saving grace. Similarly chronicling a planned alien attack, his "Mission Deferred" story sets in parallel two conflicts, the first between two aliens, the leader of an Earth invasion force and his irritating, always questioning subordinate, and the second a more routine disagreement between a television writer/ director and his demanding producer. Working for the television series *Time and Space*, which, we are told, specializes in "thrilling drama of the future" (98), Gerald Finch creates an episode, "Defense of the Planet," that his boss dismisses as a botched effort. As he is told, the broadcast "wouldn't have convinced even a little three year old kid—it wouldn't have fooled anybody!" (98). And yet ironically the televised images of an Earth rocket armada, together with Finch's dramatic script, when intercepted by the aliens just a few thousand miles from their target, do fool them, prompt them to abort their invasion, and thus prove powerful enough to save the planet. In effect, they suggest that there might be a value in the various visually oriented space operas, such as *Captain Video*, *Space Patrol*, and *Tom Corbett, Space Cadet*, that had begun to dominate television screens at this time.

Sheldon would further follow in Kuttner's cinematic path with a series of stories focused not on a space cinematographer but rather on a futuristic film director/producer. His *Startling Stories* piece "Perfect Servant," noted above, would be followed by another contribution to the same pulp, "Replica," and a *Fantastic Universe* story, "Jimsy and the Monsters," all of them describing the difficulties his character, a European immigrant filmmaker, encounters as a producer and director working in postwar Hollywood. Although "heralded as Europe's greatest producer of musicals," in Hollywood Jonathan Gamble is typically assigned to produce routine genre programmers, as he offers, "westerns, detectives, semi-type documentaries, family pictures, epics—in short, everything but a musical" ("Replica" 96). The story "Perfect Servant" finds Gamble in the midst of shooting a new SF film *Space!* appropriately adapted from a pulp magazine story, and, as usual, he is unhappy with both the subject and his progress on the production. Gamble notes that "years ago" he dreamed that "he'd find real happiness in Hollywood where things were done right," but nothing has turned out right in his career ("Perfect" 116). While the sudden and mysterious appearance on his set of Tobor, "a mechanical perfect servant from a future time" ("Perfect" 121), offers some hope for the current production, the robot servant's all too "perfect" nature, like Hollywood's general rightness, only proves irritating and disappointing, and instead of helping him inject greater reality into his fantastic production, it eventually results in Gamble being thrust into a time warp where, ironically, he finally finds "a great peace" as his "gleaming office," "the lot, and Hollywood . . . were for him no more" ("Perfect" 122).

"Replica" would reintroduce the always disappointed Gamble and his entrapment in a world of Hollywood illusions as he works on another depressing assignment, shooting the formulaic western *Trigger Tom.* Unable to find any drama in the final and predictable shootout between two western gunslingers, Gamble once again accepts the offer of a time traveler, in this case a scientist who has created a time machine with which, Gamble believes, he will be able to properly research the latest of the "two-bit westerns" that he has been assigned to shoot ("Replica" 102). Inspired by his ability to time travel, Gamble decides to try to "change history" ("Replica" 99) in order to come up with a more interesting climax for his horse opera. Yet because of what is simply described as "the paradox of time travel" ("Replica" 102), he proves unable to change anything, at least within his own time line, and is eventually returned to his set where he has to resign himself to his own unchangeable fate: to continue shooting a bad scene in a bad movie in a long line of other bad movies.

Sheldon's "Jimsy and the Monsters," done for *Fantastic Universe,* would explore the same despairing character, although it gives the producer/director a different name while maintaining the same backstory and dispiriting Hollywood setting, even using language lifted from the earlier stories. Taking the place of Sheldon's previous protagonist is Maximilian Untz, but Untz is a not too thinly disguised version of Jonathan Gamble. He, too, "had been brought to Hollywood heralded as Vienna's greatest producer of musicals" and so far, while being "assigned to westerns, detectives, documentaries, a fantasy of the future," he had done, to his consternation, "no musicals" ("Jimsy" 50). In this instance his primary source of conflict—and of frustration—is a horror film assignment in which he must deal with unconvincing rubber monsters and an uncooperative, even monstrous child star, little Jimsy LaRoche. As in Sheldon's previous Hollywood stories, here too the producer/director believes that if he had more realistic material, "some *really* horrible monsters," he might yet make a good film from another bad script ("Jimsy" 50). Again a scientist unexpectedly appears with an offer to help, not via time travel, but rather with the results of his recent experiments in dimensional teleportation, which have allowed him to trap creatures from another dimension that he believes might merit photographing—and that Untz immediately recognizes might enliven his new film. When the monsters prove uncontrollable and dangerously hungry, though, Untz's plan for a more realistic genre film again falls apart, and the studio itself is only saved when, in one of Sheldon's typical ironic twists, the monsters prove to be "terrified by tiny Jimsy"; as the narrator puts it, at the sight of this small and seemingly uncontrollable child, they "began to quiver" and "paled to a lighter shade of brown and green" ("Jimsy" 60). That Untz would ultimately triumph, not only over the monsters but over his studio bosses, who finally assign him to direct a musical, seems a fitting send-off for this strange character who invariably seems out of place, more probably a denizen of pre-war Hollywood, rather like an Ernst Lubitsch, than part of the post-war world.

Yet the creation and persistence of this character also offer an interesting commentary on the place of that cinematic consciousness in a post-war SF. The figure of Gamble/Untz, who is firmly embedded in the film industry but also constantly at odds with it, readily suggests the troubled relationship between the pulps and film that emerges in the post-war period, with each story offering a variation on the way in which its central character, and indeed the culture, seems caught within a dispiriting realm of cinematic illusion. And while he vaguely recalls Kuttner's longer-lived Tony Quade, he is not the sort of embodiment of film's mobile and revealing gaze that Quade was, nor does he suggest that earlier figure's sense of curiosity, adventure, or appetite for the new. No fan of space travel or space opera—in fact, in "Perfect Servant" he rails about having to film a story taken from the supposed pulp *Atomic Space Fiction*— the filmmaker constantly recalls the "old days" of the movies and chides himself for the mistake of moving from the Old World to the New. And advanced technology, whether it be robots, time machines, or dimensional transporters—typical signposts of SF narratives—always seems to play tricks on him. Thus in many ways he appears almost the opposite of Quade, as a nostalgic figure whom Hollywood, popular film, and post-war culture have snatched from his comfortable European situation, and whose appeal seems to lie in the humorous frustrations and ironic reversals that the film industry, as one troublesome arm of that modern world, repeatedly works on his life.

While the pulps would publish a few other stories set within a present-day or future movie industry, that modernist stimulation and sense of an SF kinship would start to disappear. For example, while Oscar J. Friend's 1942 *Thrilling Wonder Stories* piece "This Is Hell" describes True Depth Pictures' filming on Mars of an epic about the destruction of Atlantis, the adventurous undertaking quickly dissipates into a kind of horror story that obviously reflects war-time anxieties. For the cinematic recreation of the Atlantean catastrophe nearly leads both the film crew and the rest of humanity to, as one character puts it, "the brink of disaster" (112) when the filming process unwittingly unleashes a deadly plague of "silicosis." And Ray Bradbury, one of the new stars of the genre, would use the movies to sound a warning about the direction of future culture in his "Carnival of Madness" (1950). It details a twenty-third-century world wherein all books "and, of course, films" (96), are carefully controlled by the government, which has outlawed anything that suggests the workings of "the imagination" (98). Fantasy is the especially dangerous element that the government has sought to wring out of the lives of the people, and the movies have become a key part of its mind-control strategy, with film producers being forced "to make and re-make Ernest Hemingway," apparently the epitome of literary realism, until there were thirty different versions of *For Whom the Bell Tolls*, and "all realistic" (98). Determined to express his outrage at a world that sets the real at odds with human fantasy, a Mr. Stendahl—his name suggesting how that crusade for the real has even affected identities—recruits as an ally the former horror film star Pikes, whom he describes as "better than [Lon] Chaney. Better than . . . Karloff," and "far better" than Lugosi, but who has been forbidden to perform anymore, and whose films have all been seized and burned by the government (99). Working together, Stendahl and Pikes take revenge on the government bureaucrats tasked with enforcing the ban on fantasy by fashioning an audioanimatronic compendium of various Poe stories that, when government inspectors come to investigate, provides an ironic, fantastic, and horrific retribution on those who have tried to twist the nature of both literature and film, here seen as fundamentally linked, against the human desire—and indeed need—for fantasy.

That sense of alliance or common cause, though, completely disappears in a slightly later story such as Robert Bloch's "Terror Over Hollywood." Through the character of a budding starlet, Kay Kennedy, it reveals that Hollywood is ruled by a covert group—"the walking shadows, the dreams that never die . . . the immortals" (89). By means of a secret robotic technology, this group turns the most favored actors and directors into automatons, keeping them vital, attractive, and employed for decades by harnessing their brains and vital organs "to a synthetic nervous system in a synthetic body" (87), turning them into zombie workers in a zombie-like industry. Almost as dark in conception and tone as Bloch's more famous novel *Psycho* (1959), "Terror Over Hollywood" is a kind of technological Faust story, exploring what those in the movie industry might do for the promise of success and longevity, while critiquing a culture that is so easily seduced by the "walking shadows" of the movies.

The various sorts of internal discussion occurring in the war-era and immediate post-war pulps reflect a similar shift in attitude. While generally not as critical of the film industry as Bloch's story, they show little of the excitement and curiosity about film that we noted in pre-war commentaries. Certainly, there are fewer calls for adaptations of specific pulp stories, hopeful reports about the major studios' forthcoming SF efforts, or anticipations of what had in the pre-war years often been termed the "deluge" of SF films that Hollywood was expected to begin producing to feed the appetites of the growing numbers of pulp readers. However, there would be a variety of film reviews and a developing discourse about several film releases that together crystalize some of the more prominent attitudes toward both the genre and film itself in the post-war period. Particularly significant in this regard is a contribution to *Astounding* by noted SF author Robert A. Heinlein that offers a behind-the-scenes account of the filming of *Destination Moon* (1950), which was adapted from his novel *Rocket Ship Galileo*. Although it was a relatively rare discussion of the movies in the pages of *Astounding*, which had previously established itself as the most "literary," science-oriented, and least concerned with popular media of the many pulps, it points to a continuing interest in the scientifilm, if not of the same intensity that we observed in the pre-war era.

While less common than in that earlier period, there were still sporadic calls for the film industry to do more in an SF vein. For example, an *Amazing Stories* (1945, 19.2) reader would once again question why there were not more SF productions coming from Hollywood and, as a result of a "brain storm," suggest that the magazine's readership should "flood the movie studios with letters demanding more science fiction films" (197). But rather than lead the charge, as *Wonder Stories* had earlier tried to do with its "Do You Want Science Fiction Movies?" petitions of 1931–32, the *Amazing* editor (Raymond A. Palmer) simply urged his readers to accept the correspondent's challenge, to "write letters to all the studios," and noted, in a way that seems to suggest a less than enthusiastic editorial attitude, that "it's up to you" (197). Hardly more enthusiastic was a rather condescending editorial comment in *Thrilling Wonder Stories* (1950, 36.2) that would lay part of the blame on moviegoers, implicitly including the pulp readership, as it laments "that both Hollywood and the popcorn public are still a long way from large-scale production and acceptance of the more abstruse and intriguing . . . aspects of science fiction. We only hope this lamentable condition is extremely brief" (150).

But just as the pre-war era was marked by a much-anticipated and highly publicized SF film, H. G. Wells' *Things to Come* (1936), widely discussed in the various pulp magazines as well as the popular press, so too did the post-war period have its cinematic yardstick for the development of, and interest in, the scientifilm—or rather two such efforts, *Destination Moon* and *Rocketship X-M* (both 1950). Coming at the beginning of the decade and at a time when television was already demonstrating the culture's fascination with SF themes and imagery, thanks to a variety of space operas that followed in the wake of *Captain Video*'s early broadcast success, these films, while similar in concept, would illustrate two different approaches— and reactions—to an SF cinema that was, as Joyce Evans noted, about to blossom "rapidly" and would assume an unexpected prominence in the following years.

Both *Destination Moon* and *Rocketship X-M* would, at least on the surface, seem to offer much that the SF community had long been asking for in the nature of scientifilms. Their accounts of a rocket flight to the moon and a trip to Mars, respectively, had a highly documentary flavor that heavily emphasized scientific details; they eschewed fantastic space opera adventuring to instead draw much of their narratives from the difficulties involved in space travel; and they would receive some pre-release attention in the wider media, suggesting that the film industry was anticipating a ready audience for such SF works. *Destination Moon*, though, was by far the more ambitious of the two productions. Although made by the B-studio Eagle-Lion, the film had a healthy budget of $586,000 (Warren 223) and an advertising budget nearly as large at a reported $475,000 ("Eagle-Lion" 4). It drew on the writing talents of Robert A. Heinlein, the skills of space artist Chesley Bonestell, and scientific advice from the astronomers at the Hayden Planetarium, who, as one account noted, "cooperated with the film's technical staff in order to make the outer space and lunar landscape scenes as realistic as possible" (Herbstman 3). In terms of publicity, it also benefited from preview pieces in such popular magazines as *Life* and *Parade*, as well as from a number of special screenings, including one for a group of industrial leaders and members of the Atomic Energy Commission ("Screen" 3), and another at the Adler Planetarium in Chicago that was accompanied by a presentation from R. L. Farnsworth of the American Rocket Society. In contrast, *Rocketship X-M* was budgeted at approximately $94,000, employed limited special effects—including the already commonplace stock footage of V-2 rockets—and for a Martian setting it relied on the stark landscapes of the Mojave desert and Death Valley. Shot in just eleven days and rushed into release to capitalize on the large publicity campaign that had been mounted for *Destination Moon*, it too received favorable press in film publications, with one pre-release review noting that "exploitation possibilities are good" and that "children especially will find" the film "absorbing" ("Rocketship" 6). A similar prediction was made for *Destination Moon*, with a *Variety* reviewer suggesting it could "be ballyhooed to stout grosses," and that its "novelty" should help to establish "a new interplanetary film cycle" ("Destination" 6). Moreover, both films performed as suggested, with *Destination Moon* earning an estimated $1,800,000 in the United States and *Rocketship X-M* over $600,000 in the same box office, returns that prompted another *Variety* article to predict what many of the pulp readers had long anticipated: "plenty of science fiction ahead" ("Predict" 22). Together, these films seemed to herald what Eric Leif Davin refers to as the "Second Genesis of science fiction" (371).

However, the pulp reception clearly differentiated between these two pioneering efforts. Obviously responding to advance publicity (since *Destination Moon* had not yet been released) and with more than a hint of the sort of hopeful anticipation that had marked *Things to Come*, a *Thrilling Wonder Stories* letter writer urged fellow readers to support the forthcoming film and described *Destination Moon* as "the first really serious movie about interplanetary flight to be made in this country," thanks especially to the contributions of Heinlein and Bonestell (June 1950, 141). Echoing that notion, a letter to *Astounding* would tout the film's appearance because of Heinlein's contribution, while also noting—with tongue in cheek—that an adaptation of "Who Goes There" "by a fellow named Campbell" was also in production (Sept. 1950, 162). Supporting these forecasts, a *Startling Stories* reader would later praise the film as having "the impact of a documentary film—blessedly relieved of the generally objectionable commentator present in too many such productions" (Nov. 1950, 6). And *Astounding*'s editor Campbell would eventually weigh in with his own summary observation, one that also strikes a note of hope about his own film project, that "'Destination Moon' seems to be starting a new series of serious, carefully handled science-fiction pictures" (Mar. 1951, 160).

The formal reviews in the various pulps would prove even more enthusiastic than the readers' comments. *Marvel Science Stories* featured a piece by longtime fan Forrest J. Ackerman, praising the film for its realism and announcing that finally "science fiction enthusiasts have the opportunity to experience the vicarious thrill of a fantastic trip to the moon" (Nov. 1950, 61). The unnamed reviewer for *Thrilling Wonder Stories* would, like several readers, proclaim that *Destination Moon* has "all the impact of a documentary film," an effect the writer attributed to the fact that "the photography and sets are so good they register as reality rather than tricks" (Oct. 1950, 157). Even more unrestrained praise would come from Charles Recour in his review for *Amazing Stories*. Tellingly titled "Destination Perfect!" it describes *Destination Moon* as "the film which every one with the slightest bit of interest in s-f *must* see!" And while acknowledging that "it has little story to it," he suggests that this is a "minor flaw," since *Destination Moon*, unlike "all s-f films to date," is "real science-fiction, incredibly accurate, with no anachronisms, with no obvious ridiculous faults" (139).

The emphasis on "reality," "documentary" character, and technical accuracy that marks all these commentaries would, however, be notably missing from the pulp discourse about *Rocketship X-M*. Perhaps because it lacked the pedigree of *Destination Moon*—no Heinlein source novel, no Bonestell matte paintings, no astronomer advisors, and no special screenings for the scientific or military elite—it received little formal attention in the pulps, although it was mentioned, usually negatively, in several letters to the various readers' columns. *Amazing* offered the sole review, which Leslie Phelps tellingly structured as more of a comparison to *Destination Moon* than a straightforward assessment of *Rocketship X-M*. Describing it—fairly accurately—as "a quickie without particular concern for scientific accuracy," Phelps declared that *Rocketship X-M* is basically "a novelty" and "not to be compared with such an accurate scientific film as 'Destination Moon,'" even though "it offers a pleasant couple of hours of entertainment" ("Rocketship" 94).

However, the general run of pulp readers was less inclined to grant the film a pass on the weight of its "entertainment" value. A British correspondent to *Amazing*, for example, claimed that he "can't describe 'Rocketship X-M' without fear of annoying the censor" (Oct. 1951, 152). A writer to *Thrilling Wonder Stories* noted that the film's inaccuracy is "likely to be sneered at" by serious SF fans and called for more "films that lean towards science" and "thus minimize characterization" (Feb. 1952, 150). SF author Algis Budrys, writing in the following issue, was even less kind, declaring that *Rocketship X-M* "smelled to high heaven" and that its lack of scientific rigor "stigmatized the whole cycle [of SF films] before it was even on the way" (Apr. 1951, 145). And an *Astounding* correspondent, noting the numerous technical inaccuracies in the picture, wondered why the magazine could not offer more reviews so he could have "been spared sitting through" such a picture (May 1952, 162). It seems that the primary concern of most SF fans—or at least of most pulp readers—at this point was not really with the sort of narrative being offered or even with film-related aesthetic matters, but rather with scientific accuracy, and affirming that concern, or at least noting its violation, had become a kind of litmus test for the "true believer."

But in light of the split that I have been suggesting and that would become more obvious by the mid-1950s, we should note another take on these two films. Among film historians and critics *Destination Moon* has, in the course of time, come to be seen as somewhat lacking, while *Rocketship X-M* has gained admirers—and for approximately the same reasons each was originally valued or devalued. John Baxter's early account of SF cinema, for example, scores the former's "artistic aridity" and "generally tepid air" (102) due to its more pronounced documentary styling, while numerous commentators, including some of those in the pulps, have acknowledged its narrative shortcomings. For others, *Rocketship X-M*'s characterizations and plot, particularly its discovery of a Mars desolated by atomic warfare (Figure 6.5), made it the far more interesting and even timely film—or as Bradley Schauer assesses, "a much livelier film than [George] Pal's stolid production" (63). In contrast to *Destination Moon*'s cast of all-male astronauts, Rocketship X-M offers one of the first major woman characters in post-war SF with Dr. Lisa van Horn, a research chemist who, we learn, developed the rocket fuel that made the space flight possible. With her scientific credentials

Figure 6.5. Earthmen—and a woman—survey an atomic-war-devastated Mars in *Rocketship X-M* (1950).

and importance to the narrative, Dr. van Horn's character constitutes, as Dean Conrad points out, "an important role in the history of female representation in science fiction cinema" (85). Moreover, in extrapolating Cold War hostilities to a neighboring planet, *Rocketship X-M*, which had been partially scripted by blacklisted writer Dalton Trumbo, took on a serious edge and a political dimension that, in a way few had previously credited to SF cinema, pointed up its potential for significant social critique.[8]

In response to that letter complaining about the lack of SF film reviews like those appearing in many other pulps, *Astounding*'s editor John W. Campbell, Jr. promised that the magazine "will start reviews," and explained that "until recently, the crop was too small to discuss" (May 1952, 162). But while Campbell, as we have seen, had called attention to *Destination Moon*'s appearance, even suggesting that it could herald the start of "seriously, carefully handled science-fiction pictures" (Mar. 1951, 160), *Astounding* would, at least through the mid-1950s, provide none of those promised reviews. In fact, when *Forbidden Planet*, one of the most popular and successful post-war SF films, appeared in 1956, *Astounding* would review a novelization by W. J. Stuart (aka Philip MacDonald) but not the film itself, and reviewer P. Schulyer Miller made clear that he had not bothered to see the movie version (Aug. 1956, 149). However, the pulp would publish numerous book reviews in each issue and devote a continuing series of essays to broad technology concerns, such as nuclear reactors, robotics, and the development of thinking machines—all subjects that were finding a ready place in the period's SF films. But in keeping with this broad emphasis on technical concerns, the magazine did eventually feature an irregular but particularly noteworthy series of essays that approached film from this vantage. Groundbreaking for the pulp idiom, this series about the "making of" several of the decade's most important SF films includes pieces on *Destination Moon, When Worlds Collide* (1952), *The War of the Worlds* (1953), and *The Conquest of Space* (1955).

The first entry in the series, "Shooting 'Destination Moon,'" is especially significant because, as we earlier noted, it was authored by one of the most important SF writers of the post-war years, Robert A. Heinlein. Since he co-wrote and served as a technical advisor on the film, Heinlein was able to draw on his own experience to describe how the film industry went about dealing with standard SF concerns, such as rocketry, space flight, and planetary exploration. Perhaps taking his lead from the many earlier letters wondering why Hollywood seemed hesitant to take up SF as a major genre, Heinlein concentrates on what he sees as the major hurdles "to producing an accurate and convincing sf picture" (7). These include "finding someone willing to risk the money" on SF writers "with wild ideas" (6);

dealing with "the 'Hollywood' frame of mind," that is, "people in authority who either don't know or don't care about scientific correctness and plausibility" (7); and overcoming "the *technical* difficulties of filming a spaceship picture" (8). While lauding the people involved in creating *Destination Moon*, especially producer George Pal, director Irving Pichel, space artist Chesley Bonestell, as well as various skilled technicians who helped create "movie magic," Heinlein emphasizes two reasons that he believes there had been, to that time, so few major SF features, as he describes the difficult eighteen-month production schedule that this film involved and confesses that "realism is confoundedly expensive" (12).

In light of the general enthusiasm with which the SF pulp community greeted *Destination Moon*, it seems only natural that *Astounding* would in the following year follow up with a similar piece on the shooting of another George Pal production *When Worlds Collide* (1952). Authored by astronomer and SF writer R. S. Richardson, this article, "Making Worlds Collide," was illustrated with a number of production stills courtesy of Paramount Pictures, and it was accompanied by an endorsement from editor Campbell in which he notes that *Astounding* was "cooperating to the fullest with Paramount in promoting" the film (Nov. 1951, 114). While that cooperation extended little further than allowing Paramount to place a full-page ad for the film in the December issue of *Astounding*, this "making of" article effectively followed the lead of Heinlein's earlier piece, focusing largely on the complex and time-consuming technical details involved in telling a story about the evacuation via rocket of a soon-to-be-destroyed Earth, while also acknowledging those same budgetary imperatives that Heinlein had noted. As Richardson observes, because of the cost, "if you insist upon strict scientific accuracy, then the picture could never have been made at all" (90).

However, the main focus of the essay, as might be expected from a scientist, is on this issue of accuracy. Early on in the piece Richardson explains his criteria, noting that, for the film to be effective, "the science must be authentic, the characters and situations convincing, and the trick stuff done with careful attention to detail. There is no critic so hostile as the amateur scientist hot on the trail of a technical error" (84). That light-hearted jab at the overzealous SF fan notwithstanding, Richardson for most of the article documents how such concerns dominated the thinking of those involved with the project, as he says almost nothing about the shape of this apocalyptic narrative, but rather emphasizes the "attention to detail" involved in the film's treatment of space and rocketry. To that end, and again following Heinlein's lead, he gives much credit to space artist Chesley Bonestell and producer George Pal, both of whom, because of their insistence on an astronomically precise look and plausible presentation of how a picked group of humans abandon Earth by rocket, played key roles in achieving a solid SF appeal. In fact, the last third of the essay is largely an interview with Pal, wherein he describes his own attention to scientific detail throughout the production and his hope that the result will help draw in not just SF fans but also a wider audience, thereby allowing him to bring other such realistically framed stories to the public.

Fittingly, the third article in this series, about the adaptation of H. G. Wells's *The War of the Worlds*, was written by Pal himself, who, as if in answer to his previous speculation about doing other such stories, had produced this film too. He reveals that Paramount—seemingly the only one of the *major* studios then pursuing a regular SF agenda—had owned the film rights to Wells's story for twenty-six years, but only decided to greenlight production in the 1950s because of "the big vogue for films of a science-fiction nature" (100), a development that, the studio felt, would finally make an adaptation a viable and profitable undertaking. Demonstrating the same concern with a level of accuracy that had been carefully established in the previous "making of" essays, Pal here describes the guiding philosophy in all of his projects, his belief that "Realism is earned; it doesn't just happen" (107). And the article underscores that policy with five production stills that illustrate not the film itself, but rather the elaborate model work, set construction, and other behind-the-scenes film activities that, he says, attest to the "infinite pains with details" that were required to create a film like *The War of the Worlds* (107). In further testimony to that concern with the "details," he evokes a name that, by this point, had become one of the most respected in the SF community, as he singles out the contributions of artist and adviser Chesley Bonestell, who, as Pal offers, "kept us on the right track" (110) with his precise matte paintings and constant technical advice.

At the end of his commentary on making *The War of the Worlds* Pal announced that he was already planning his next SF production, an adaptation of the Willy Ley and Chesley Bonestell book about the future of space travel, *The Conquest of Space* (1949). Following up on that announcement, *Astounding* would offer in its May 1955 issue not another "making of" article, but a brief illustrated piece that might be seen as a hint of the magazine's (and perhaps the editor Campbell's) flagging interest in cinematic SF. Slightly more than an announcement of the new Pal film's forthcoming release, this unattributed visual essay offers little more than a slight commentary attached to descriptions of each of the Paramount-provided publicity stills used to illustrate the piece: one a staged shot of Pal, director Byron Haskin, Bonestell, and Ley apparently in conference; a second depicting the three "principal props" or models used in *The*

Conquest of Space—a rocket, a circular space station, and a Mars lander; the third a production still showing astronauts being transferred from the space station to the lander; and the fourth illustrating a landing on Mars. As the unnamed author offers, the hope is that these illustrations will demonstrate how Pal's latest SF effort is "as close to the facts-as-they-are-believed-to-be as possible, with a minimum of story-plot hokum" (94). This largely perfunctory piece, which reveals little of what that "story-plot hokum" involves, once again underscores the primary concern with scientific accuracy, as it suggests that Ley and Bonestell's participation—as on previous Pal SF efforts—should ensure that the film "holds as close to the line of exact science planning as is possible" (96).

In his piece on *The War of the Worlds* Pal had also offered a telling description of the SF filmmaking process, noting that it involves "technical feats that any laboratory man can appreciate" (100). The comment suggests that he well understood the pulp audience, or at least the readers of an *Astounding* which always gave more attention to technical facts—as we have noted in various letters to its "Brass Tacks" column—than did most of the other pulps. Many of those readers would probably have appreciated that technical sobriquet of "laboratory man"; and the consistent emphases throughout this series on "scientific accuracy," "attention to detail," and "plausibility," while hardly surprising, only underscore the sense that the "science" in such scientifilms was, at least for *Astounding* and its readers, their principal attraction and the primary evaluative measure. Thus as the SF films of the later 1950s, marked by an increasing fascination with monstrous mutations, predatory aliens, and what Susan Sontag has famously described as an "aesthetics of destruction" (216), began to veer from such criteria, it seems no wonder that this magazine, like most of the other pulps, would find less and less in common with the popular SF cinema, and articles such as these would disappear from its pages.

One counterpoint to this shift occurs in a pulp that had often been seen—somewhat unfairly—as being aimed at younger readers, *Startling Stories*, the sister publication to *Thrilling Wonder Stories*. While Mike Ashley judges that the magazine more often emphasized "science fantasy" than hard-core SF (138) and suggests that some readers found its stories "a little less technical and a lot more fun" (138), *Startling Stories* for a while published a "Video-Technics" column by Pat Jones that described new developments in television, especially emphasizing how they related to hard science. His piece in the March, 1953 issue is particularly noteworthy for its commentary on science education via television, as it offered an overview of the work of the pioneering science series, *The Johns Hopkins Science Review*. During this pulp's last years Jones would also contribute reviews of a variety of new SF films, including *When Worlds Collide* (1951), *The Day the Earth Stood Still* (1951), *The Beast from 20,000 Fathoms* (1953), *Donovan's Brain* (1953), *The Magnetic Monster* (1954), and *Riders to the Stars* (1954). While still suggesting an interest in the flourishing SF film industry, these reviews show little of the effort to come to grips with the specifically cinematic nature of the works that we noted in a number of the earlier commentaries by such figures as C. A. Brandt and Mort Weisinger. Rather, they mainly focus on describing the films' plots and noting links to key SF stories, such as original works by Ray Bradbury, Curt Siodmak, and Harry Bates, and even in the case of films that Jones singles out for special achievement, they often offer a superficial critique of their films' visual approach; thus the review of *The Day the Earth Stood Still* culminates in the observation that "the props were effective enough—but so palpably faked!" ("*Day*" 146). But with the disappearance of both *Startling Stories* and *Thrilling Wonder Stories* in 1955, even such half-hearted appreciations of the very visible SF film industry of the period would become scarce.

That change would also be visible in the dominant covers and interior illustrations for the pulps throughout the war and early post-war era. For those media-reflexive illustrations that had been so popular earlier— illustrations that quite naturally depicted film or elements of the film apparatus as memes of the genre and thus as evocative of the larger SF imagination—would be replaced by a variety of other images more symp- tomatic of the changing cultural climate that World War II and the Cold War would bring in. For example, in contrast with the pre-war emphasis on what Paul A. Carter slightingly terms "the Gernsback art tradition" (176) or what Yaszek and Sharp refer to as "technophilic" art (331), that is, covers mostly featuring males and powerful mechanisms of various sorts engaged in exciting or unusual action, the succeeding period would more often depict scenes of dramatic conflict, typically involving imper- iled women. Carter satirically describes this subject matter, a specialty of cover artist Earle K. Bergey, as "the eternal triangle: the man, the woman, and the monster all sharing space on the cover more or less equally" (176), as they reflected a culture that had grown familiar with extreme conflict, while also sporting a newly sexually charged character. But even that tri- angular design would gradually change its dynamic on the covers of such magazines as *Thrilling Wonder Stories, Planet Stories, Startling Stories, Captain Future*, and *Fantastic Adventures* to emphasize partially clad women in action poses, exaggerating the sort of "visual pleasure" that, as we earlier observed, was typical of conventional film, while also suggestively evoking, as Ron Goulart in his study of pulp covers offers, more "the decorations of *Spicy Detective*" magazine (Figure 6.6) than the world of an earlier SF (141).

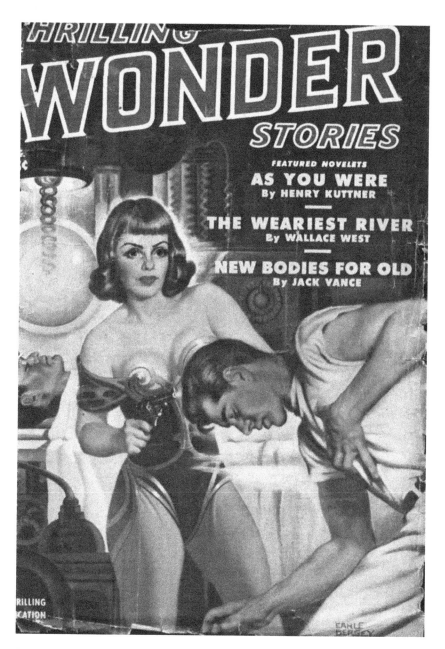

THRILLING
WONDER
STORIES

FEATURED NOVELETS

AS YOU WERE
By HENRY KUTTNER

THE WEARIEST RIVER
By WALLACE WEST

NEW BODIES FOR OLD
By JACK VANCE

Figure 6.6. One of Earle Bergey's post-war spicy detective-type covers for *Thrilling Wonder Stories* (Aug. 1950).

Certainly, somewhat less emphatically "charged" illustrations had also been popular in the pre-war period, as the many readers' comments about sensationalistic even lurid covers cited in chapter 5 attest. As Yaszek and Sharp have observed, a cross-genre magazine such as *Weird Tales*, particularly with the cover art done by Margaret Brundage, had already established a reputation for covers depicting semi-nude damsels in distress in the 1920s and 1930s.[9] But while *Weird Tales* would actually rein in its racy images during the war years, several of the SF pulps would move in the opposite direction, with the looser enforcement of various forms of censorship, especially in the film and publishing industries during the war, leading to far more of those *Spicy Detective*-type covers and, predictably, a continuation of the sort of readers' comments we have often noted. Thus one correspondent to *Amazing* complained how "each month I have to smuggle the magazine into the house" (Aug. 1943, 204), while another confessed that he "felt like hiding the lurid cover of the magazine while walking down the street" (Jan. 1951, 148). Meanwhile, even a reader of *Astounding*—easily the pulp least given to such "spicy" illustrations—admitted that while he did not like to leave some covers exposed "where my uninitiated friends can see" them, he often found a "dignity and aptness to the illustrations" (Oct. 1950, 132). And that point would become especially appropriate for *Astounding*'s post-war covers, which are far more often characterized by images expressing amazement or wonder than sexual predation and peril—images that speak to the magazine's reputation for publishing a more sophisticated vein of SF.

However, even that level of "aptness" noted by the *Astounding* correspondent typically did not translate into the sort of illustrations depicting the cinematic gaze or the technologies involved in producing it that had been relatively common in the pre-war years. Neither *Thrilling Wonder Stories* nor its companion publication *Startling Stories* would disrupt their sensationalistic trajectory to offer many covers in this vein from the war years to the time of their mutual demise in 1955. And while the last of Henry Kuttner's Tony Quade stories, "Trouble on Titan," would be the subject of the cover illustration on the *Thrilling Wonder* issue for February, 1947, the image offers no allusion to Quade's cinematic occupation. Rather, it depicts his fiancée, the actress Kathleen Gregg, underwater and, like so many other women of the period pulps, only partially dressed and in peril. Even the interior illustration for the story omits Quade's special glass-nosed camera ship, so prominently featured earlier, in favor of a more conventional rocket. It seems that film and its trappings no longer immediately evoked the SF context that they once did—or at least did not evoke enough of what the editors thought might be most appealing to the readers of *Thrilling* and *Startling Stories* in this later period, as the magazines swapped their film-related imagery for a more subtle kind of cinematic resonance: various constructions of the sort of scopophilic pleasure in which popular film so frequently traded.

Still, some of those later covers and illustrations deserve mention for the way—as scant as it is—that they recall the modernist emphasis on what Fredric Jameson describes as a world that we "can possess visually" (1). A new generation of illustrators, including such figures as Frank Kelly Freas, Hubert Rogers, Arnold Kohn, and Chesley Bonestell would lend a more realistic and less sensationalistic flavor to many of the covers, while at times recalling the spirit of those cinematic images from the pre-war era, as when a *Fantastic Adventures*' cover illustrates a headlined story about "Flying Saucers: Russia's Secret Weapon?" (Mar. 1952) with an image of Stalin and an alien conferring together on a video screen; an *Amazing* cover for P. F. Costello's "The Illusion Seekers" story shows rocket passengers viewing a hovering ball of light within which they see, as if projected, a beautiful woman's image (Aug. 1950); and *Astounding*, to accompany its Heinlein piece on "Shooting 'Destination Moon,'" used for its cover a publicity still from the film itself, depicting astronauts surveying the lunar surface (July 1950). While hardly the sort of iconic images seen in the earlier period, these and a few other cover and interior illustrations still suggest some of the evocative character that attached to the film apparatus and filmic activity, although the relative scarcity of such images is equally telling, pointing up the extent to which film SF and literary SF seemed to be taking separate paths, claiming different rather than shared emphases and identities.

In his pioneering study of the pulps *The Construction of Tomorrow*, Paul A. Carter argues that, throughout the pre-war and early post-war years surveyed here, these magazines were all engaged in nothing less than the "creation" of the modern SF imagination, as they gave voice—and opportunity—to a variety of writers and artists who speculated on what the future of human life, or the possibilities of other life, might be like. It is a considerable claim, backed by the great body of literature published during the pulp era, by the many major SF authors who got their start and/or inspiration in the pulps, by an artwork that colonized the imaginations of readers (as well as those who simply glanced at the covers displayed on newsstands), and by the development of a host of icons and concepts that would not just influence but eventually channel the direction of much of our SF thinking. But it is a creation that was also shaped, as commentators such as Carl Freedman, Fredric Jameson, and Adam Roberts have acknowledged, by the various impulses of modernism, especially by its imperatives to challenge the nature of both the world and the self, and by its implicit invitation to *see* both differently. And as the preceding chapters have chronicled, those challenges and invitations were articulated throughout the pulps in a great many forms, among them advertising, cover and interior artwork, the dialogue between editors and an emerging and highly vocal fandom, and of course the pulp stories themselves.

As we have also seen, these forms often drew in and on a common inspiration and fellow product of that modernist spirit, that of the movies—an influence that has largely gone unexplored and even unremarked in our histories of the pulps. Hugo Gernsback, among others, early on noted that relationship as he sought to situate the new literature of scientifiction within the modernist climate that also included a host of new technology-based forms—radio, television, the telephone, motion pictures—all part of, and contributors to, what he identified as the "science saturated atmosphere" ("Science Wonder Stories" 5) of his day. In this late modernist period when SF was trying to establish its identity, its audience, as well as its name, these other forms, but especially film, became emblematic of that "atmosphere," icons of a world that SF assumed as its own. Screen forms like film and television, both born at approximately the same time as modern SF, would especially be drafted to help convey the modern spirit of SF, even as their world would, as we have several times noted, become woven into the very rhetoric that was used in the new literature of SF. As late as 1951 the new editor of *Thrilling Wonder Stories*, Samuel Mines, noted the importance of this media linkage, arguing that "the impetus given by the movies, radio and television may well provide the take-off velocity [SF] needs to move into the big time" (6). But as this final chapter has sketched out, that long-standing linkage had become strained, almost seeming to dissolve in the course of World War II and the following decade, as modernism itself, with so many of its fundamental challenges seemingly taken up, had come to seem somehow less modern, perhaps in need of a postscript—or what we might even term a postmodern notation that might help explain the various answers at which a modern culture had apparently arrived, or simply, and temporarily, stopped.

In a development that clearly speaks to the changing post-war status of SF, the popular press would report at length on one of the first SF conventions of the period, held in Newark, NJ on March 6, 1946. Writing for the slick magazine *Harper's*, William S. Baring-Gould described the scene in which veteran pulp editors such as Sam Merwin, F. Orlin Tremaine, and C. A. Brandt met with readers and various authors to discuss a crisis in "direction" for the field of SF. As Baring-Gould reports, "never in America had there been such general interest in scientific fantasies" (283) as there was in the immediate post-war years, but with the upswell of technological progress that had accompanied the war, he notes, "almost overnight" the genre's "farthest-into-the-future plots had become the common stuff of the daily headlines," as science "had finally caught up with science fiction" (283–84). His judgment was that SF writers would, in this post-war world, increasingly have to become either more visionary or more like conventional authors, since the usual "trick" of luring an audience with some "new invention" or "strange property" could no longer be adequate when "reality itself" has become "frighteningly unreal, in the world of atom bombs and rocket ships" (288). In the face of what he saw as such an already fantastic and troubling world, Baring-Gould challenged SF authors and editors to address not so much the future as the problems of the present, concluding that "the trick may well be to make the reader believe that in any world where science has outstripped its present powers human life itself is [still] a plausible assumption" (288).

While coming from what we might term a layman's vantage, even what seems a somewhat jaundiced—or worried—one, that assessment suggests a similar sort of leveling out, a similar merging with the present that the epigraph with which this chapter began had attributed to the movies. For Baring-Gould, SF was also, at least in the pulp forms he was familiar with, starting to seem a bit everyday, or as Frank Belknap Long puts it, just another one of the common features "of any advanced culture" (114). But his ironic closing thought, linking advanced science to the seemingly precarious position of "human life"—as if one had somehow put the other in a challenging position—was not far off from the turn that SF literature, perhaps with a sense of human purpose, and certainly with an abiding sense of its special vision, would increasingly take in this period. It is a turn that might help explain the different, even strained relationship with the cinema and those filmic icons that had appeared so prominently in the pre-war SF publications we have surveyed.

The year following Baring-Gould's article would see the last entry in Henry Kuttner's once popular Tony Quade series about "Hollywood on the Moon." More broadly, SF literature would itself start to shift focus from the outer space precincts of works like the Quade stories to what noted SF author J. G. Ballard, writing in the key British pulp *New Worlds*, would term "inner space." While film in the early 1950s was finally taking up some of the possibilities that had intrigued Gernsback, Ackerman, Campbell, and many others—space exploration, alien encounters, robotic creations, and more generally visual spectacle, as *Astounding*'s pieces on George Pal's films might suggest—Ballard in 1962 was calling for the literary genre to look in another direction, to "turn its back on space, on interstellar travel, extra-terrestrial life forms" (117), in effect, on much that a cinematically in-spired or cinematically linked vision had enabled and that the cinema was currently exploiting. In place of the outward gaze that was explicit in such films as *First Man into Space* (1959), *12 to the Moon* (1960), or *Journey to the 7th Planet* (1962), he suggested that "it is *inner* space, not outer, that needs to be explored" (117) if SF wants to take its rightful place as a leader within the literary mainstream, or as what he termed "a complete speculative po-etry and fantasy of science" (118). The result—easily glimpsed on many pulp covers of the 1950s and early 1960s with their depictions of staring eyes, strong, determined faces, curious glances, all seemingly reflective of that "inner" self and a determination to explore its mysteries—is a fiction that seems far more about an inward turn and subjective experience than about following the possibilities of cinema's—and modernism's—mobile gaze.

That "inner landscape," to which Ballard and other authors of what would become SF's New Wave pointed, has been seen by many as the be-ginning of a postmodern SF, one less concerned with the sort of things that film did best—the recording or constructing of a wondrous reality—than with the interrogation of a constructed world, self, and ultimately re-ality itself.[10] In such a context, it was perhaps inevitable that there would eventually be some cleavage between an art like film, *created* by science and technology, and a literature that is *about* science, technology, and their various creations, that there would be an effort to sort out an apparent confusion or conflation that could well be traced back to Gernsback's early enthusiastic if also largely uncritical descriptions of the whole field of SF—a sensibility easily glimpsed in the great variety of advertising hosted by the early pulps, as well as in the wide array of attitudes voiced in their var-ious letters columns. Driven by a modernist energy and abundant enthu-siasm embodied in their editors, authors, and readers, the early pulps had cast the net of SF widely with some of their editors perhaps intuiting a point made several times here, that both modernity and the very modern character of SF might best be understood within a cinematic context.

In fact, it might be helpful to see that early linkage that we have traced out between cinema and pulp SF as an instance of what the philosopher of science Bruno Latour has described as an "impossible modernization" (132). Itself both product and technique, film has always been something of what Latour terms a "hybrid," and in its linkage with SF the cinema became almost invisibly more so. But many who laid claim to the mod-ernist mantle—and who saw SF as part of the larger scientific project of modernism—asserted the necessity for what Latour calls "purification," that is, the need for a more systematic vision and an effort to separate the disparate items of nature and culture, of art and science, so that we might better measure them and assess their impact and meanings (51). Framed in this way, film would eventually come to be seen as not so much a part of the SF world—and certainly not as science—but simply as one more "functional" piece of late modernist, even postmodern culture. The turn suggested by Ballard and others in the post-war period, along with the shift in focus of some pulps and the disappearance of many others, might be viewed as a reaction to the convenient, fruitful, yet "impossible" modernist vision of a sort that had so energized the pulps in their pre-war "Golden" age but that would change character in a new post-war era.

However, within that "Golden" age's vision and in that moment when SF was in the ongoing process of forging its identity and taking a name, the cinema, along with a new cinematic mindedness, played a crucial developmental role. Through its own popularity and especially its cultural pervasiveness, film contributed to the air of currency and excitement surrounding the developing genre, thereby helping it find additional acceptance. And since the cinema acted out one of the central impulses of all SF, telling stories of what might be, even materializing those possibilities, it provided an important level of support or confirmation for SF readers and the greater SF imagination, as the various calls for the production of "scientifilms" to match the new literature of "scientifiction" might suggest. More fundamentally, film on various levels helped the SF genre mobilize the new visuality of the age in order to better envision other worlds, other selves, and other possibilities—possibilities that both a cinematic and literary SF would continue to explore, albeit in their own ways, well beyond those post-war years.

NOTES

CHAPTER 1

1. Freedman's distinction is a particularly useful one, since the comparison we are dealing with is between something typically perceived as a form or medium—film—and something often categorized as a kind of content: SF. While Freedman explains that a "generic tendency" is essentially "something that happens within a text" (20), we should also think of it as the relationship between similar texts and between those texts and their audience or readers. In any case, I want to suggest here that part of the "happening" that goes on in pulp SF, at least through the pre-war period, is a consistent engagement with film or what I more broadly characterize as the cinematic imagination.

2. We should note that there were pulp SF magazines in other countries as well, and of course various national approaches to serious SF writing. Edward James has chronicled the presence and importance of these other bodies of literature, while also acknowledging that the "creation of specialist sf pulps" represented "a significant fact in the publishing history of sf and in the foundation of the sf community" (44).

3. The term "scientifilm," a combination of Gernsback's early name for the literature, "scientifiction," with "film," would have a lingering currency in the pulps and fan magazines throughout the late 1920s and 1930s and even into the early 1940s when "scientifiction" had largely been replaced with "science fiction." Forrest J. Ackerman did a column of film reviews for the fan magazine *Science Fiction Digest* in the 1930s called "The Scientifilms," while movie reviews in *Thrilling Wonder Stories* were often titled "Scientifilm Review," as in editor Mort Weisinger's review of *Things to Come* in the August, 1936 issue, p. 112.

4. We might draw out a further connection between early film and SF by observing that it was Robert Paul who supplied Georges Melies with his first motion picture camera, an Animatograph, in early 1896, thereby making possible his proto-SF films of the 1890s–1900s. See Ezra's account, p. 12.

5. Struck by the way Wells's descriptions of time travel corresponded to early Kinetoscope experiences, Ramsaye corresponded with Wells to determine if the author had been inspired by his first experience with a film device. While Wells claimed that he was "unable to remember details of the relation," Ramsaye offered the assessment that "if the story was not evolved directly from the experience of seeing the Kinetoscope, it was indeed an amazing coincidence" (153). While Keith Williams agrees that *The Time Machine* "is replete with analogies suggestive of the experience of film-watching" (26), he also notes that

Wells's work was already in serialization in the *National Observer* when the first London Kinetoscope Parlor was opened in late 1894. The clear implication is that both Wells's imagined time machine and Paul's film apparatus were similar, yet largely independent products of this heady period and its "new visuality."

6. For a detailed account of the origin and contemporary reactions to the Pan American Exposition's "A Trip to the Moon," see the Winter and Liebermann article of the same title.

7. A highly useful resource for exploring early radio history and especially for examining copies of early radio magazines is retired broadcaster David Gleason's "American Radio History" web site: www.americanradiohistory.com. Accessed July 2, 2018.

8. While there are many histories that might be cited, including a number of specialized treatments of the pulp literature, such as those by Paul A. Carter, Mike Ashley, and John Cheng, throughout this study I have relied most extensively on Edward James' *Science Fiction in the Twentieth Century*, Brooks Landon's *Science Fiction after 1900: From the Steam Man to the Stars*, and Adam Roberts's *The History of Science Fiction*.

CHAPTER 2

1. In an obvious effort to build an advertising base, Gernsback would even include in *Amazing Stories* (July 1926) an ad designed to attract potential advertisers. Proceeding from a rather modernist notion that, as he says in the copy, "America is an advertising nation," he headlined his box announcement with the slogan "Advertising Pays You!" (382). The point is that Gernsback and others, such as Harold Hersey, saw advertising as vitally important to the success of their pulp endeavors, and they were even willing to advertise *for advertisers*, as a way to obtain more advertising.

2. It has often been suggested that exhibitors freely transposed this non-narrative scene, some placing it prior to the start of *The Great Train Robbery*'s narrative as an exciting lead-in and others showing it as a dramatic punctuation at the film's conclusion.

3. We might note that other sorts of pulps offered similar appeals pointedly directed at female readers. Nose shapers, bust enhancers and reducers, and various sorts of physical culture regimens, such as that offered by famed swimmer Annette Kellerman, were commonplace in pulps that were more obviously directed at a female readership.

4. In his history of the Fox Film Corporation, Aubrey Solomon describes the almost unprecedented scale of publicity that 20th Century-Fox was planning for the movie. See Solomon, p. 216. As a prelude to that campaign and partial measure of its scale, a two-page spread was placed in the industry paper *Motion Picture Daily*, proclaiming the studio's goal that "60,000,000 people will soon be reading the full page national magazine ads . . . for this greatest of Twentieth-Century pictures" (Jan. 7, 1935). A similar two-page insert appeared in the January 8, 1935 issue of *Variety*, and in every issue of another trade paper *The Film Daily* for a week (Jan. 7–Jan. 11, 1935).

5. While it is possible that Brown was indeed given access to an advance screening, it is just as likely that the cover, as well as the interior illustrations Brown did, was based on the various publicity stills that Paramount and/or its new outside publicity agent, the Tom Fizdale Agency, made available in support of this elaborate production.

6. *Dr. Cyclops* was not Paramount's first effort at reaching out to pulp readers in a joint effort. For example, to advertise its big budget western *Wells Fargo* (1937), the studio entered into an agreement with the pulp *Wild West Weekly* to serialize a novel version of the film beginning in the magazine's Mar. 12, 1938 issue. Along with the story, *Wild West Weekly* featured pictures of the movie's principal players, including Joel McCrea, Frances Dee, and Ralph Morgan.

CHAPTER 3

1. Gary Westfahl makes a powerful argument that Gernsback might be better known as the true "father" of modern SF, and especially of the SF magazine. The constant use of Gernsback as a touchstone throughout this study testifies to the extent of his impact on the development of SF, but I also want to note the SF community's indebtedness to the work of Westfahl—as well as that of Mike Ashley and Robert A. W. Lowndes—for their efforts in properly chronicling Gernsback's formative influence on the "successful institution" of SF (13) through the venue of the pulps. See especially Westfahl's *Hugo Gernsback and the Century of Science Fiction*.

2. As a small sampling of that growing popular and pulp-delivered discourse about movie technology, we can note such pieces as John J. Furia's "A Stereoscopic 'Movie' Screen," *Electrical Experimenter* 8.2 (1920): 134, 234; Hugo Gernsback's "The Movie Theater of the Future," *Science and Invention* 8.11 (1921): 1172–73; C. H. Claudy's "240,000 'Movie' Photos per Minute—A New Motion Picture Camera and Projector," *Science and Invention* 9.2 (1921): 123, 191; and Joseph M. Kraus's "Perfectly Synchronized Talking Pictures," *Science and Invention* 9.8 (1921): 710.

3. Echoing a number of other commentators on modernism and its impact, Miriam Hansen suggests that one way we might approach cinema is to locate it "within a history of sense perception in modernity, in particular the spiral of shock, stimuli protection, and ever greater sensations" ("America" 363) that seemed to characterize the experience of audiences attending the various sorts of visual presentations—World's Fair attractions, amusement parks, movies—that were so popular in the late nineteenth and early twentieth centuries.

4. While largely superficial and dating to the previous decade when several sound-on-film technologies vied for mastery in the American marketplace, including variable density as well as variable area formats, the technical discussion is accurate and suggests some familiarity with or research into the film-making process.

5. In the same issue of *Thrilling Wonder Stories* Kuttner makes his story's focus on the European conflict quite explicit. He recalls that he had gone to a revival of *The Lost World* with a friend, a war correspondent "just returned from Europe" with whom he then spent some time discussing the war while looking at some battlefield photographs. When he "couldn't get the memory of those pictures" and of his friend's account out of his mind, Kuttner states that he "had to write" a story about that destruction. See Kuttner's comments in "Tomorrow's Battlefield," p. 124.

6. We might note that 3-D film, particularly in the red and blue anaglyph format, was being repeatedly demonstrated on a commercial basis in this period. For example, MGM, as part of its Pete Smith Specials film series, released 3-D shorts in 1935, 1938, and 1941, the first of these receiving a nomination for an Academy Award. It seems highly likely that Kuttner, a film enthusiast, probably

saw at least one of these efforts. For background on these films see Ray Zone's *Stereoscopic Cinema*, pp. 144–49.

7. I offer this judgment based on repeated readers' comments found in "The Reader Speaks" column of *Thrilling Wonder Stories*. Kuttner's stories were consistently well received, with a piece like "Hollywood on the Moon" receiving a great many reader plaudits, one calling it the "stand out" story of its issue (*Thrilling Wonder Stories*, June 1938, p. 125), while even stronger comments were offered in support of the last Quade-Carlyle entry "The Seven Sleepers," co-written by Kuttner and Arthur K. Barnes.

8. The Frank Buck comparison only furthered the cinematic connection of these stories, since Buck was himself a popular movie star of the period. He produced his own highly successful films in the 1930s and 1940s, including *Bring 'Em Back Alive* (1932), *Wild Cargo* (1934), and *Jungle Menace* (1937), all of them about capturing wild animals in exotic locales, usually starring himself.

9. Both *Grass* and *Chang* were highly praised documentaries about exotic cultures made by Merian C. Cooper and Ernest B. Schoedsack, the team later famous for making *King Kong* (1933). While *Chang* was nominated for an Academy Award and both were distributed by Paramount Pictures, their fame, and Kuttner's familiarity with the documentaries, probably traces to their re-introduction in 1941 at New York's Museum of Modern Art. We might see Kuttner's references to these "old" films in part as a homage to the pioneering film work of Cooper and Schoedsack.

CHAPTER 4

1. Based on the number of reports from the Los Angeles chapter and descriptions of its activities, this branch seems to have been one of the most active of the Science Fiction League's chapters, with many of the reports chronicling film discussions or film related events, such as group attendance at a triple feature of scientifilms and the screening of recent movies at various meetings.

2. Of course, given Ackerman's age of fifteen when he wrote this letter about his insider's "campaign," we have to wonder what sort of influence he could have wielded.

3. *Creation* never advanced beyond test footage, since a change in studio leadership brought Merian C. Cooper in as a new lead producer and led to animator Willis O'Brien's efforts being combined with Cooper's idea for a giant ape movie, resulting in the original *King Kong* (1933). For a concise account of how the *Creation* project described by Ackerman became the RKO film *King Kong*, see Carlos Clarens's *An Illustrated History of the Horror Film*, pp. 92–95.

4. Various industry trade papers, for example, *Film Daily, Motion Picture Herald*, and *Variety* reported these films under the titles Ackerman cites as "in production." Shifting titles during production or even just prior to release is hardly uncommon, and in the case of *100 Years to Come* (or, as it was also announced, *100 Years from Now*) Ackerman's enthusiasm seems understandable given the rousing description of United Artists and London Films' plans for the Wells adaptation, including a $1,000,000 budget and a "spectacle" approach depicting "among other things, the destruction of a city by 500 airplanes in five minutes and submarines which are tanks on land" ("$1,000,000 Special" 6).

5. Specific circulation numbers are difficult to calculate, since much pulp activity derived from newsstand sales, but Everett F. Bleiler offers a mid-decade snapshot of the major SF pulps, estimating that in 1935 *Astounding* had a readership of

approximately 65,000, *Wonder Stories* 45,000, and *Amazing*, which was on a decline under the editorship of T. O'Conor Sloane, was down to 20,000. See his *Science-Fiction: The Gernsback Years*, p. 550. Mike Ashley in his *The Time Machines* offers more conservative estimates for *Astounding* ("probably about 50,000") and *Wonder Stories* ("25,000"), but calculates that *Amazing* was a bit higher, "not much more than 25,000" (85–86).

6. It is probably worth noting that Merritt's novel was itself hardly "novel," with a number of its plot elements closely recalling the twice-made and highly popular Lon Chaney fantasy film *The Unholy Three* (1925, 1930), both based on an original novel by Tod Robbins and both produced by MGM, which also released *The Devil Doll*.

7. For background on the financing and distribution of *Things to Come*, see Charles Drazen's biography of producer Alexander Korda, *Korda: Britain's Movie Mogul*, pp. 139–41.

8. Brandt offers this sort of critique on the American film industry in several other film reviews. For example, in his highly favorable review of the German/British/French co-production *F. P. 1*, he cautions that the usual "importer of foreign films dare not import anything but standardized trash" ("Notes on Moving Pictures" 135).

9. Another instance of the pulps' apparent dissatisfaction with Wells's late work shows up in a different *Thrilling Wonder Stories* review the following year. Signed by H. K., the review of the relatively obscure *The Eternal Mask* suggests that "this Swiss production is worth a dozen things like *Things to Come*" (Aug. 1937, 114).

10. Keith Williams in his *H. G. Wells: Modernity and the Movies* offers an extensive discussion of the cinematic characteristics of Wells's fiction, or what he terms the author's "cinematically enhanced vision" (45). See especially Williams's discussion of the original story "The Man Who Could Work Miracles" on pp. 44–45.

11. Chapman and Cull in *Projecting Tomorrow* note that while "the film was the ninth most successful film of the year in Britain," it did poorly in the United States and "because of its enormous expense failed to recoup its production costs" (35–36).

CHAPTER 5

1. While the reader comments here are generally representative, they were all taken from various issues of *Astounding Stories*, specifically Feb. 1932, Nov. 1932, Jan. 1936, and Aug. 1938. A similar array of contrary opinions can be gleaned from the readers' opinions columns in any of the other pulps, or even from single letters, as when a correspondent to *Thrilling Wonder Stories* (Apr. 1939) lauds a recent cover as "a work of art," while noting that most others "have all been too glaring and blatant, mainly because of the violent and painful contrasts of the colors used" (120).

2. While Gernsback announced that the prize-winning design was submitted by A. A. Kaufman, he also notes that it "was a crude design at best," and that "we started to amplify . . . the original idea" ("Results" 519). Everett F. Bleiler in his *Science-Fiction: The Gernsback Years* attributes the final cover design to Frank R. Paul rather than to the contest winner (544). A similar attribution can be found on the *Internet Speculative Fiction Database* at www.isfdb.org/cgi-bin/pl.cgi?56666. Accessed July 11, 2017.

3. We might especially note a brief—and very deliberate—shift in covers starting with the stylized rocket diagonally linking two worlds in the January 1933 issue

of *Amazing Stories* and continuing through the June 1933 issue that depicts a giant dragon in conflict with a rocket and several satellites. Done in subdued colors, tied to none of the stories in the respective issues, and lacking the usual descriptive commentary on the table of contents page, these covers were praised by some of the readers because of the very change they represented. Thus one reader notes that the new cover style "is dignified and symbolic; it removes *Amazing Stories* from the realm of cheap fiction" (282), while another similarly finds that such covers "give the magazine 'class'" (283). Although the editor, probably T. O'Conor Sloane, responds that "the new covers have met with great appreciation" and assures the readers that "there is no danger of our giving them up" (284), before the end of the year *Amazing* would return to its conventional brightly colored and representational approach.

4. See Koszarski's history of this formative period, *An Evening's Entertainment*, especially pp. 36–40 where he discusses early film industry publicity and promotional activities.

5. As briefly noted in Chapter 3, the film industry was in this period already experimenting with 3-D technology, so Kuttner—as well as many of the pulp readers—probably had seen some of the popular short films produced as 3-D demonstrations. MGM, for example, produced several 3-D shorts as part of its "Pete Smith Specials" series: *Audioscopiks* (1935), *The New Audioscopiks* (1938), and *Three Dimensional Murder* (1941), the last of which even includes a version of the Frankenstein monster. The 1939–1940 New York World's Fair also included a number of 3-D shorts, generally done in this format to suggest how audiences might see movies in "The World of Tomorrow"—the fair's theme.

6. Mulvey's notion that classical film narrative typically placed the spectator in a masculine viewing position was a key intervention in film theory. Although since challenged by other theorists and even altered by Mulvey, her approach aligned then-current psychological mechanisms with feminist readings of the film experience, allowing for a new vantage on the female image and female performance, a vantage that seems similarly pertinent to reading the artwork of the SF pulps.

7. Paramount announced that its large-scale advertising campaign for *Gulliver's Travels* was costing $250,000 and that it would reach "more than 100,000,000 readers" of various national publications, including *Collier's*, *The Saturday Evening Post*, and *Look* magazines. Information on this campaign can be found in a two-page color spread placed in several trade papers, including *Motion Picture Daily* (Dec. 7, 1939): 7–8.

8. Veteran screenwriter Tom Kilpatrick is credited with writing the original screenplay of *Dr. Cyclops* and was subsequently nominated for a "Retro-Hugo Award" for his work on the film. Kuttner's effort was, as he explains in "The Story Behind the Story," simply "writing a fictionalization of a photoplay," after having "seen it in production at the studio" (126). While Kuttner's version of the story would eventually be published in several collections, Will Garth, probably under commission by Paramount, would also produce a full-length novelization that appeared at the same time as the film's premier. In fact, this book version was reviewed in the issue of *Thrilling Wonder Stories* (July 1940, 124) following the number that contained Kuttner's version.

9. In addition to hiring additional "exploiteers" for *Dr. Cyclops*, Paramount had also brought in a New York advertising company, the Tom Fizdale Agency, to "handle and plant all publicity on the *Dr. Cyclops* picture . . . including tie-ups, stunts,

radio hook-ups, etc." As an article in *Variety* explains, Paramount executives were "dissatisfied with the publicity and exploitation results on various features lately, notably *Gulliver's Travels*" ("Par Experiments" 5, 20). The "tie-up" with *Thrilling Wonder Stories* is most likely part of the concerted effort to ramp up publicity for this and other forthcoming Paramount films, and might serve as a reminder of how the pulps and their SF content were seen as a kind of exploitative context.

10. A report in the trade paper *The Film Daily*, "Crime and Horror Films Decline 3%," notes that the category of "crime and horror" films—a category that would have also included science fiction—had already seen a significant decline in production throughout the US film industry in 1940.

CHAPTER 6

1. For background on this change, see Gary Westfahl's article "The Marketplace" in *The Oxford Handbook of Science Fiction*, especially pp. 84–87.

2. The Paramount decision refers to an antitrust case against the major motion picture studios in the United States. Five studios, MGM, RKO, Warner Bros., 20th Century-Fox, and Paramount—collectively known as the Big Five— had been accused of trust-like activity due to their ability to produce films, distribute them, and exhibit them at their corporately owned theater chains, while also setting the terms for independent theaters and theater chains to gain access to their films, and for other film companies to exhibit in their larger and more profitable movie houses. As a result of the Supreme Court ruling against this monopolistic activity, starting in 1948 the Big Five were required to divest themselves of their theater chains, eventually forcing a number of changes in the film industry. With this change, smaller and less capitalized independent companies moved into the market, often producing exploitation-type films; youth or specialized audiences were specifically targeted; and genres that linked to current cultural trends—as did SF in the 1950s—were more heavily emphasized. For additional background on the Paramount decision and its impact, see Bernard Dick's history of the studio *Engulfed*, especially pp. 37–41.

3. John Rieder, among others, makes this argument in his *Science Fiction and the Mass Cultural Genre System*.

4. For examples of typical SF film advertising in the 1950s and a discussion of some of its common visual components, see Telotte's "Sex and Machines: The 'Buzz' of 1950s Science Fiction Films."

5. Hawks officially served as producer of *The Thing* for his own company, Winchester Films, while Christian Nyby, who had previously served as an editor on several of Hawks's films, was billed as the director. However, it was widely known in the film industry that Hawks was heavily involved in the day-to-day shooting process as he sought to help his protégé Nyby move into directing.

6. As *Variety* reports, the film grossed approximately $2,000,000 and was the second highest earner the month it premiered. See "Top Grosserss of 1951."

7. In "The Editor's Notebook" column of *Fantastic Adventures* (Aug. 1951, 6), *The Thing* would receive a few passing comments, lauding the film for "its tight plotting, and its really excellent characterizations," while also suggesting that there was "nothing new" in the movie, and that it failed to offer the sort of "suspense" found in a great many "old thrillers," including *Frankenstein* (1931), *Dracula* (1931), *The Werewolf of London* (1933), and *Dr. Jekyll and Mr. Hyde* (1932). Dismissing it as a failed suspense film and comparing it to an older horror

tradition seem symptomatic responses to the film's failure to connect with the hard-core SF audience of the pulps.

8. For a discussion of Dalton Trumbo's participation in the writing of *Rocketship X-M*, see Bill Warren's treatment of the film in his *Keep Watching the Skies*, especially pp. 708–10.

9. For background on Margaret Brundage's work for *Weird Tales*, see the section on "Artists" in Lisa Yaszek and Patrick B. Sharp's collection *Sisters of Tomorrow*, pp. 331–35.

10. Carl Freedman has suggested that, particularly in the case of SF literature, a "formal line between modernism and postmodernism cannot be clearly drawn" (196), that what he terms a "stylistic periodization" of modern and postmodern SF is relatively easy "to dismantle" (194).

A SELECT SCIENTIFILM FILMOGRAPHY

The following list provides production details (director, producer, cast, studio, and date) for films that were frequently or prominently cited by readers and editors of the various pulps, as well as those that were reviewed in the same magazines during the pre-war and early postwar periods. While hardly a comprehensive listing of SF films made during these years, these are many of the works that were on the minds of the pulp audience, thus forming a recurrent and essential part of pulp discourse about the scientifilm.

The Beast from 20,000 Fathoms. Dir. Eugene Lourie. Prod. Jack Dietz and Hal E. Chester. Perf. Kenneth Tobey, Cecil Kellaway, Paula Raymond. Warner Bros. 1953.

The Bride of Frankenstein. Dir. James Whale. Prod. Carl Laemmle, Jr. Perf. Boris Karloff, Elsa Lanchester, Colin Clive, Ernest Thesiger. Universal. 1935.

Buck Rogers. Dir. Ford Beebe and Saul A. Goodkin. Prod. Barney A. Sarecky. Perf. Buster Crabbe, Constance Moore, Jackie Moran. Universal. 1939.

The Conquest of Space. Dir. Byron Haskin. Prod. George Pal. Perf. Walter Brooke, Eric Fleming, Mickey Shaughnessy. Paramount. 1955.

The Day the Earth Stood Still. Dir. Robert Wise. Prod. Julian Blaustein. Perf. Michael Rennie, Patricia Neal, Sam Jaffe. 20th Century-Fox. 1951.

Death from a Distance. Dir. Frank R. Strayer. Prod. Maury M. Cohen. Perf. Russell Hopton, Lola Lane, Wheeler Oakman. Invincible Pictures. 1935.

Deluge. Dir. Felix E. Feist. Prod. Sam Bischoff. Perf. Peggy Shannon, Sidney Blackmer, Lois Wilson. RKO. 1933.

Destination Moon. Dir. Irving Pichel. Prod. George Pal. Perf. John Archer, Warner Anderson, Tom Powers. Eagle-Lion. 1950.

The Devil Doll. Dir. Tod Browning. Prod. Edward J. Mannix. Perf. Lionel Barrymore, Maureen O'Sullivan, Frank Lawton. MGM. 1936.

Donovan's Brain. Dir. Felix E. Feist. Prod. Allan Dowling and Tom Gries. Perf. Lew Ayres, Gene Evans, Nancy Davis. United Artists. 1953.

Dr. Cyclops. Dir. Ernest B. Schoedsack. Prod. Dale Van Every and Merian C. Cooper. Perf. Albert Dekker, Thomas Coley, Charles Halton, Janice Logan. Paramount. 1940.

End of the World (*La Fin du monde*). Dir. Abel Gance. Prod. K. Ivanoff. Perf. Victor Francen, Colette Darfeuil, Abel Gance. L'Ecran d'Art. 1931.

The Eternal Mask (*Die Ewige Maske*). Dir. Werner Hockbaum. Perf. Mathias Wieman, Peter Petersen, Olga Tschechowa. Progress Film. 1935.

Flash Gordon. Dir. Frederick Stephani. Prod. Henry MacRae. Perf. Buster Crabbe, Jean Rogers, Charles Middleton. Universal. 1936.

F. P. 1 Does Not Answer (F. P. 1 Antwortet Nicht). Dir. Karl Hartl. Prod. Erich Pommer. Perf. Hans Albers, Paul Hartman, Sibylla Schmitz, Peter Lorre. UFA/ Gaumont. 1933.

Frankenstein. Dir. James Whale. Prod. Carl Laemmle, Jr. Perf. Boris Karloff, Colin Clive, Edward Van Sloan. Universal. 1931.

Gold. Dir. Karl Hartl. Prod. Alfred Zeisler. Perf. Brigitte Helm, Hans Albers, Michael Bohmen. UFA. 1934.

The Invisible Man. Dir. James Whale. Prod. Carl Laemmle, Jr. Perf. Claude Rains, Gloria Stewart, E. E. Clive. Universal. 1933.

The Invisible Ray. Dir. Lambert Hillyer. Prod. Edmund Grainger. Perf. Boris Karloff, Bela Lugosi, Frances Drake, Frank Lawton. Universal. 1936.

Island of Lost Souls Dir. Erle C. Kenton. Perf. Charles Laughton, Bela Lugosi, Leila Hyams, Richard Arlen. Paramount. 1933.

Just Imagine. Dir. David Butler. Prod. Buddy DeSylva. Perf. El Brendel, Maureen O'Sullivan, John Garrick. Fox. 1930.

The Lost World. Dir. Harry Hoyt. Prod. Earl Hudson. Perf. Lewis Stone, Wallace Beery, Bessie Love. First National. 1925.

The Magnetic Monster. Dir. Curt Siodmak. Prod. Ivan Tors and George Van Marter. Perf. Richard Carlson, King Donovan, Jean Byron. United Artists. 1954.

The Man Who Could Work Miracles. Dir. Lothar Mendes. Prod. Alexander Korda. Perf. Roland Young, Joan Gardner, Ralph Richardson. London Film/United Artists. 1937.

Metropolis. Dir. Fritz Lang. Prod. Erich Pommer. Perf. Brigitte Helm, Gustav Froelich, Rudolf Klein-Rogge. UFA. 1927.

The New Gulliver. Dir. Aleksandr Ptushko. Perf. Vladimir Konstantinovich Konstantinov, Ivan Yudin. Mosfilm. 1935.

Riders to the Stars. Dir. Richard Carlson. Prod. Ivan Tors, Herbert L. Strock, and Maxwell Smith. Perf. Richard Carlson, William Lundigan, Herbert Marshall, Martha Hyer. United Artists. 1954.

Rocketship X-M. Dir. Kurt Neumann. Prod. Robert L. Lippert. Perf. Lloyd Bridges, Osa Massen, John Emery, Hugh O'Brien. Lippert Pictures. 1950.

The Thing from Another World. Dir. Christian Nyby. Prod. Howard Hawks. Perf. Kenneth Tobey, Margaret Sheridan, Robert Cornthwaite, Douglas Spencer. RKO Pictures. 1951.

Things to Come. Dir. William Cameron Menzies. Prod. Alexander Korda. Perf. Raymond Massey, Ralph Richardson, Sophie Stewart. London Film/United Artists. 1936.

Transatlantic Tunnel. Dir. Maurice Elvey. Prod. Michael Balcon. Perf. Richard Dix, Leslie Banks, Helen Vinson. Gaumont. 1935.

The War of the Worlds. Dir. Byron Haskin. Prod. George Pal. Perf. Gene Barry, Ann Robinson, Les Tremayne, Robert Cornthwaite. Paramount Pictures. 1953.

When Worlds Collide. Dir. Rudolph Mate. Prod. George Pal. Perf. Richard Derr, Barbara Rush, John Hoyt, Larry Keating. Paramount Pictures. 1951.

Woman in the Moon (Frau im Mond). Dir. Fritz Lang. Perf. Gerda Maurus, Willy Fritsch, Fritz Rasp. UFA. 1929.

A SCIENTIFILM BIBLIOGRAPHY

Abel, Richard. "*A Trip to the Moon* as an American Phenomenon." *Fantastic Voyages of the Cinematic Imagination: Georges Melies's Trip to the Moon.* Ed. Matthew Solomon. Albany: SUNY Press, 2011. 129–42.

Ackerman, Forrest J. "Another Science Fiction Movie." *Wonder Stories* 3.6 (Nov. 1931): 806.

———. "More Scientifilms." *Wonder Stories* 5.3 (Oct. 1933): 286.

———. "Science Fiction Movies." *Wonder Stories* 5.7 (Feb. 1934): 800.

Ashley, Mike. *The Time Machines: The Story of the Science-Fiction Pulp Magazines from the Beginning to 1950.* Liverpool: Liverpool UP, 2000.

———, and Robert A. W. Lowndes. *The Gernsback Days: A Study of the Evolution of Modern Science Fiction from 1911 to 1936.* Rockville, MD: Wildside Press, 2004.

Attebery, Brian. "The Magazine Era: 1926–1960." *The Cambridge Companion to Science Fiction.* Ed. Edward James and Farah Mendlesohn. Cambridge: Cambridge UP, 2003. 32–47.

Ballard, J. G. "Which Way to Inner Space?" *New Worlds* 118 (May 1962): 2–3, 116–18.

Baring-Gould, William S. "Little Superman, What Now?" *Harper's* 193 (Sept. 1946): 283–88.

Barnes, Arthur K. "The Seven Sleepers." *Thrilling Wonder Stories* 16.2 (May 1940): 93–116.

———. "Siren Satellite." *Thrilling Wonder Stories* 28.1 (Winter 1946): 64–78, 82.

———. "Trouble on Titan." *Thrilling Wonder Stories* 19.2 (Feb. 1941): 14–51.

———, and Henry Kuttner. "The Energy Eaters." *Thrilling Wonder Stories* 14.2 (Oct. 1939): 16–32.

Baxter, John. *Science Fiction in the Cinema.* New York: Paperback Library, 1970.

Benjamin, Walter. "The Work of Art in the Age of Mechanical Reproduction." *Illuminations.* Ed. Hannah Arendt. Trans. Harry Zohn. New York: Schocken, 1969. 217–51.

Berman, Marshall. *All That Is Solid Melts into Air: The Experience of Modernity.* New York: Penguin, 1982.

Bleiler, Everett F., with Richard J. Bleiler. *Science-Fiction: The Gernsback Years.* Kent, OH: Kent State UP, 1998.

Bloch, Robert. "Terror Over Hollywood." *Fantastic Universe* 7.6 (June 1957): 70–89.

Boddy, William. *New Media and Popular Imagination: Launching Radio, Television, and Digital Media in the United States.* Oxford: Oxford UP, 2004.

Bould, Mark. "Film and Television." *The Cambridge Companion to Science Fiction.* Cambridge: Cambridge UP, 2003. 79–95.

———, and Sherryl Vint. "There Is No Such Thing as Science Fiction." *Reading Science Fiction*. Ed. James Gunn, Marleen Barr, and Matthew Candelaria. New York: Palgrave, 2009. 43–51.

Bradbury, Ray. "Carnival of Madness." *Thrilling Wonder Stories* 36.1 (Apr. 1950): 95–104.

Brandt, C. A. "A Coming Prophesy [sic]." *Amazing Stories* 10.13 (Dec. 1936): 135.

———. "The Man Who Could Work Miracles." *Amazing Stories* 11.6 (Dec. 1937): 135.

———. "Notes on Moving Pictures." *Amazing Stories* 8.10 (Feb. 1934): 134–35.

———. "Notes on Moving and Talking Pictures." *Amazing Stories* 9.1 (May 1934): 134.

Brown, Fredric. "What Mad Universe." *Startling Stories* 18.1 (Sept. 1948): 11–71.

Burks, Arthur J. "The Mind Master." *Astounding Science Fiction* 9.2 (Feb. 1932): 238–63.

Carter, Paul A. *The Creation of Tomorrow: Fifty Years of Magazine Science Fiction*. New York: Columbia UP, 1977.

Casetti, Francesco. *Eye of the Century: Film, Experience, and Modernity*. Trans. Erin Larkin with Jennifer Pranolo. New York: Columbia UP, 2005.

Chapman, James, and Nicholas J. Cull. *Projecting Tomorrow: Science Fiction and Popular Culture*. London: I. B. Tauris, 2013.

Charney, Leo. "In a Moment: Film and the Philosophy of Modernity." *Cinema and the Invention of Modern Life*. Ed. Leo Charney and Vanessa R. Schwartz. Berkeley: U of California P, 1995. 279–94.

———, and Vanessa R. Schwartz. "Introduction." *Cinema and the Invention of Modern Life*. Ed. Leo Charney and Vanessa R. Schwartz. Berkeley: U of California P, 1995. 1–12.

Cheng, John. *Astounding Wonder: Imagining Science and Science Fiction in Interwar America*. Philadelphia: U of Pennsylvania P, 2012.

Christie, Ian. *The Last Machine: Early Cinema and the Birth of the Modern World*. London: BFI, 1994.

Clarens, Carlos. *An Illustrated History of the Horror Film*. New York: Capricorn, 1967.

Cohen, Lizabeth. *A Consumer's Republic: The Politics of Mass Consumption in Postwar America*. New York: Knopf, 2003.

"The Conquest of Space." *Astounding Science Fiction* 55.3 (May 1955): 94–96.

Conrad, Dean. *Space Sirens, Scientists and Princesses: The Portrayal of Women in Science Fiction Cinema*. Jefferson, NC: McFarland, 2018.

Corn, Joseph J., and Brian Horrigan. *Yesterday's Tomorrows: Past Visions of the American Future*. Baltimore: Johns Hopkins UP, 1996.

Costello, P. F. "Whom the Gods Destroy." *Amazing Stories* 25.3 (Mar. 1951): 80–122.

"Crime and Horror Films Decline 3%." *The Film Daily* (Apr. 1, 1941): 1, 6.

Cummings, Ray. "The Story of the Cover." *Thrilling Wonder Stories* 13.3 (June 1939): 37.

Custen, George F. *Twentieth Century's Fox: Darryl F. Zanuck and the Culture of Hollywood*. New York: Basic Books, 1997.

Davin, Eric Leif. *Pioneers of Wonder: Conversations with the Founders of Science Fiction*. New York: Prometheus Books, 1999.

Dee, Roger. "Girl from Callisto." *Thrilling Wonder Stories* 38.2 (June 1951): 73–77.

"Destination Moon." *Variety* (June 28, 1950): 6.

Dick, Bernard F. *Engulfed: The Death of Paramount Pictures and the Birth of Corporate Hollywood*. Lexington: UP of Kentucky, 2001.

"Do You Want Science Fiction Movies?" *Wonder Stories* 3.7 (Dec. 1931): 904.

"Dr. Cyclops." *The Film Daily* Mar. 8 (1940): 8.

Drazen, Charles. *Korda: Britain's Movie Mogul*. London: I. B. Tauris, 2011.

"Eagle-Lion Classics Set to Market an 'A' Film Monthly." *Motion Picture Daily* (June 1, 1950): 1, 4.

Earle, David M. "Pulp Magazines and the Popular Press." *The Oxford Critical and Cultural History of Modernist Magazines*, Vol. II. Ed. Peter Brooker and Andrew Thacker. Oxford: Oxford UP, 2012. 199–216.

Evans, Joyce A. *Celluloid Mushroom Clouds: Hollywood and the Atomic Bomb*. Boulder, CO: Westview, 1998.

Ezra, Elizabeth. *Georges Melies: The Birth of the Auteur*. Manchester: Manchester UP, 2000.

Fielding, Raymond. "Hale's Tours: Ultrarealism in the Pre-1910 Motion Picture." *Film Before Griffith*. Ed. John L. Fell. Berkeley: U of California P, 1983. 116–30.

Frayling, Christopher. *Things to Come*. London: BFI, 1995.

Freedman, Carl. *Critical Theory and Science Fiction*. Hanover, NH: Wesleyan UP, 2000.

Friedberg, Anne. *The Virtual Window: From Alberti to Microsoft*. Cambridge: MIT Press, 2006.

———. *Window Shopping: Cinema and the Postmodern*. Berkeley: U of California P, 1994.

Friend, Oscar J. "This Is Hell." *Thrilling Wonder Stories* 21.3 (Feb. 1942): 108–14, 125–29.

Gaudreault, Andre. *Film and Attraction: From Kinematography to Cinema*. Trans. Timothy Barnard. Urbana: U of Illinois P, 2011.

Gernsback, Hugo. "Baron Munchausen's Scientific Adventures." *Amazing Stories* 3.2 (May 1928): 148–56.

———. "Experts Join Staff of 'Amazing Stories.'" *Amazing Stories* 1.4 (July 1926): 380.

———. "$500.00 Prize Story Contest." *Amazing Stories* 1.9 (Dec. 1926): 773.

———. "A New Sort of Magazine." *Amazing Stories* 1.1 (Apr. 1926): 3.

———. "Results of $300.00 Scientifiction Prize Contest." *Amazing Stories* 3.6 (Sept. 1928): 519–21.

———. "The Science Fiction League: An Announcement." *Wonder Stories* 5.9 (Apr. 1934): 933.

———. "Science Fiction Movies." *Wonder Stories* 5.7 (Feb. 1934): 800.

———. "Science Wonder Stories." *Science Wonder Stories* 1.1 (June 1929): 5.

———. "Wanted: A Symbol for 'Scientifiction.'" *Amazing Stories* 3.1 (Apr. 1928): 5.

Gleason, C. Sterling. "The Port of Missing Airplanes." *Radio News* 9.12 (June 1928): 1322–23, 1373–74.

———. "The Radiation of the Chinese Vegetable." *Science Wonder Stories* 1.7 (Dec. 1929): 618–23.

———. "Silent Dynamite." *Radio News* 9.3 (Sept. 1927): 214–15, 264, 266–67.

Goulart, Ron. *Cheap Thrills: The Amazing! Thrilling! Astonishing! History of Pulp Fiction*. Neshannock, PA: Hermes Press, 2007.

Gray, Jonathan. *Show Sold Separately: Promos, Spoilers, and Other Media Paratexts*. New York: NYU Press, 2010.

Gunning, Tom. "The Cinema of Attraction: Early Film, Its Spectator and the Avant-Garde." *Wide Angle* 8.3-4 (1986): 63–70.

———. "Now You See It, Not You Don't: The Temporality of the Cinema of Attractions." *Velvet Light Trap* 32 (1993): 3–12.

Hansen, Miriam. "America, Paris, the Alps: Kracauer (and Benjamin) on Cinema and Modernity." *Cinema and the Invention of Modern Life*. Ed. Leo Charney and Vanessa R. Schwartz. Berkeley: U of California P, 1995. 362–402.

———. *Babel and Beyond: Spectatorship in American Silent Film*. Rev. ed. Cambridge: Harvard UP, 1994.

———. "The Mass Production of the Senses: Classical Modernism as Vernacular Modernism." *Modernism/Modernity* 6.2 (1999): 59–77.

Heinlein, Robert A. "Shooting 'Destination Moon.'" *Astounding Science Fiction* 45.5 (July 1950): 6–18.

Herbstman, Mandel. "*Destination Moon*." *Motion Picture Daily* (June 26, 1950): 3.

Hersey, Harold Brainerd. *Pulpwood Editor: The Fabulous World of the Thriller Magazines Revealed by a Veteran Editor and Publisher*. New York: Frederick A. Stokes, 1937.

H. K. "Scientifilm Review—*The Devil Doll*." *Thrilling Wonder Stories* 8.3 (Dec. 1936): 119.

———. "Scientifilm Review—*The Eternal Mask*." *Thrilling Wonder Stories* 10.1 (Aug. 1937): 114.

"Hold Wells Preview." *Motion Picture Daily* (Apr. 7, 1936): 2.

"Huge Black Boots Used for 'Cyclops.'" *Motion Picture Daily* (Apr. 29, 1940): 8.

James, Edward. *Science Fiction in the Twentieth Century*. Oxford: Oxford UP, 1994.

Jameson, Fredric. *Signatures of the Visible*. New York: Routledge, 1992.

Jones, Frank. "Arctic God." *Amazing Stories* 16.5 (May 1942): 192–208.

Jones, Idwal. "Over the Make-Up Box." *New York Times* Jan. 20, 1935. p. X4.

Jones, Pat. "*The Day the Earth Stood Still*." *Startling Stories* 24.3 (Jan. 1952): 145–46.

———. "Worlds at War in Technicolor." *Thrilling Wonder Stories* 42.3 (Aug. 1953): 92–93.

"*Just Imagine*, a Musical, Talking Film." *Wonder Stories* 2.9 (Feb. 1931): 1054–55.

King, Vance. "'Dr. Cyclops.'" *Motion Picture Daily* Mar. 7 (1940): 4.

Kittler, Friedrich. *Optical Media*. Trans. Anthony Enns. Cambridge: Polity Press, 2010.

"Korda-Wells Film Debated in Legislatures of World." *Motion Picture Daily* (Apr. 7, 1936): 8.

Kostkos, Henry J. "North God's Temple." *Amazing Stories* 9.4 (Aug. 1934): 99–110.

Koszarski, Richard. *An Evening's Entertainment: The Age of the Silent Feature Picture, 1915–1928*. Berkeley: U of California P, 1990.

Kuttner, Henry. "Dr. Cyclops: A Novelet of Men in Miniature." *Thrilling Wonder Stories* 16.3 (June 1940): 14–33.

———. "Hollywood on the Moon." *Thrilling Wonder Stories* 11.2 (Apr.1938): 12–31.

———. "No Man's World." *Thrilling Wonder Stories* 17.2 (Aug. 1940): 42–50.

———. "The Shadow on the Screen." *Weird Tales* 31.3 (Mar. 1938): 320–30.

———. "The Star Parade." *Thrilling Wonder Stories* 12.3 (Dec. 1938): 26–45.

———. "Tomorrow's Battlefield." *Thrilling Wonder Stories* 17.2 (Aug. 1940): 124.

———. "Trouble on Titan." *Thrilling Wonder Stories* 29.3 (Feb. 1947): 36–52.

———. "The Well of the World." *Startling Stories* 25.2 (Mar. 1952): 10–90.

Landon, Brooks. *Science Fiction after 1900: From the Steam Man to the Stars*. New York: Routledge, 2002.

Lefebvre, Thierry. "*A Trip to the Moon*: A Composite Film." *Fantastic Voyages of the Cinematic Imagination: Georges Melies's Trip to the Moon*. Ed. Matthew Solomon. Albany: SUNY Press, 2011. 49–63.

Leinster, Murray. "The Runaway Skyscraper." *Amazing Stories* 1.3 (June 1926): 250–65, 285.

Long, Frank Belknap. "The World of Wulkins." *Thrilling Wonder Stories* 32.1 (Apr. 1948): 102–17.

Macpherson, Kenneth. "As Is." *Close Up* 2.2 (Feb. 1928): 4–16.

"The Man Who Could Work Miracles." *The Film Daily* (Feb. 24, 1937): 6.

Manning, Laurence, and Fletcher Pratt. "The City of the Living Dead." *Science Wonder Stories* 1.12 (May 1930): 1100–07, 1136–37.

Marcus, Laura. *The Tenth Muse: Writing about Cinema in the Modernist Period.* Oxford: Oxford UP, 2007.

Marlowe, Stephen. "The Last Revolution." *Amazing Stories* 26.1 (Jan. 1952): 84–110.

Milner, Andrew. *Locating Science Fiction.* Liverpool: Liverpool UP, 2012.

Mines, Samuel. "The Reader Speaks." *Thrilling Wonder Stories* 39.2 (Dec. 1951): 6, 130.

"More Scientifilms." *Wonder Stories* 5.3 (Oct. 1933): 286.

Moskowitz, Sam. *Seekers of Tomorrow: Masters of Modern Science Fiction.* New York: Ballantine, 1967.

Mountain, Joseph D., and C. Sterling Gleason. "The Voice of the People." *Radio News* 9.5 (1927): 479, 564–69, 572–73.

Mulvey, Laura. "Visual Pleasure and Narrative Cinema." *Film Theory and Criticism*, 3rd ed. Ed. Gerald Mast and Marshall Cohen. Oxford: Oxford UP, 1985. 803–16.

Musser, Charles. *Thomas A. Edison and His Kinetographic Motion Pictures.* New Brunswick: Rutgers UP, 1995.

Nevins, Jess. "Pulp Science Fiction." *The Oxford Handbook of Science Fiction.* Ed. Rob Latham. Oxford: Oxford UP, 2014. 93–103.

Nevins, W. Varick, III. "Cosmic Calamity." *Wonder Stories* 6.1 (June 1934): 61–63.

———. "The Mystery of the -/-." *Wonder Stories* 7.1 (June 1935): 40–47.

"$1,000,000 Special in London Films Lineup." *The Film Daily* (May 16, 1934): 1, 6.

Pal, George. "Filming 'War of the Worlds.'" *Astounding Science Fiction* 52.2 (Oct. 1953): 100–11.

"Par Experiments with 'Cyclops.'" *Variety* (Jan. 24, 1940): 5, 20.

"Para. Adds Exploiteers for 'Cyclops' Key Runs." *The Film Daily* (Mar. 21, 1940): 2.

Phelps, Leslie. "Hollywood in Space." *Fantastic Adventures* 12.2 (Feb. 1950): 115.

———. "Rocketship X-M." *Amazing Stories* 24.12 (Dec. 1950): 94.

Pierson, Michele. *Special Effects: Still in Search of Wonder.* New York: Columbia UP, 2002.

"Predict More Science Fiction Pix, Sparked by Increasingly Big Grosses." *Variety* (Oct. 3, 1951): 22.

Przyblyski, Jeannene M. "Moving Pictures: Photography, Narrative, and the Paris Commune of 1871." *Cinema and the Invention of Modern Life.* Ed. Leo Charney and Vanessa R. Schwartz. Berkeley: U of California P, 1995. 253–78.

Rabinovitz, Lauren. *Electric Dreamland: Amusement Parks, Movies, and American Modernity.* New York: Columbia UP, 2012.

Ramsaye, Terry. *A Million and One Nights: A History of the Motion Picture Through 1925.* New York: Simon & Schuster, 1926.

Ray, Rice. "Today's Yesterday." *Wonder Stories* 5.6 (Jan. 1934): 608–17.

Recour, Charles. "Destination Perfect!" *Amazing Stories* 25.4 (Apr. 1951): 139.

Richardson, R. S. "Making Worlds Collide." *Astounding Science Fiction* 48.3 (Nov. 1951): 83–97.

Rieder, John. "On Defining SF, or Not: Genre Theory, SF, and History." *Science Fiction Studies* 37.2 (2010):191–209.

———. *Science Fiction and the Mass Cultural Genre System.* Middletown, CT: Wesleyan UP, 2017.

"RKO to Stress Three Exploitation Films." *Motion Picture Daily* (Mar. 20, 1951): 5.

Roberts, Adam. *The History of Science Fiction*. New York: Palgrave MacMillan, 2005.

"Rocketship X-M." *Motion Picture Daily* (May 3, 1950): 6.

Rosborough, L. B. "Hastings—1066." *Amazing Stories* 9.2 (June 1934): 53–63.

Schauer, Bradley. *Escape Velocity: American Science Fiction Film, 1950–1982*. Middletown, CT: Wesleyan UP, 2017.

"Science Fiction Movies." *Wonder Stories* 5.7 (Feb. 1934): 800.

Sconce, Jeffrey. *Haunted Media: Electronic Presence from Telegraphy to Television*. Durham, NC: Duke UP, 2000.

"Screen *Destination Moon*." *Motion Picture Daily* (June 21, 1950): 3.

Sennwald, Andre. "Pageant of Empire at the Rivoli in 'Clive of India.'" *The New York Times*. Jan. 18, 1935. www.nytimes.com/movie/review. Accessed Feb. 13, 2017. Web.

Shaver, Richard S. "We Dance for the Dom." *Amazing Stories* 24.1 (Jan. 1950): 8–36.

Sheldon, Walt. "Jimsy and the Monsters." *Fantastic Universe* 1.4 (Jan. 1954): 49–61.

———. "Mission Deferred." *Fantastic Adventures* 13.7 (July 1951): 94–98.

———. "Operation Decoy." *Fantastic Adventures* 12.6 (June 1950): 110–17.

———. "Perfect Servant." *Startling Stories* 17.3 (July 1948): 115–22.

———. "Replica." *Startling Stories* 22.3 (Jan. 1951): 95–103.

"'Shoot the Works' for *Destination Moon*." *Motion Picture Daily* (Oct. 10, 1950): 16.

Skal, David J. *Screams of Reason: Mad Science and Modern Culture*. New York: Norton, 1998.

Skidmore, Joe W. "The Velocity of Escape." *Amazing Stories* 9.4 (Aug. 1934): 55–89.

Smith, Erin A. *Hard-Boiled: Working Class Readers and Pulp Magazines*. Philadelphia: Temple UP, 2000.

Smith, Gary, ed. *Benjamin: Philosophy, Aesthetics, History*. Chicago: U of Chicago P, 1989.

Solomon, Aubrey. *The Fox Film Corporation, 1915–1935: A History and Filmography*. Jefferson, NC: McFarland, 2011.

Stableford, Brian. "Science Fiction Between the Wars: 1918–1938." *Anatomy of Wonder: A Critical Guide to Science Fiction*. 3rd ed. Ed. Neil Barron. New York: Bowker, 1987. 49–62.

"The Story Behind the Story." *Thrilling Wonder Stories* 11.2 (Apr. 1938): 6.

"The Story Behind the Story." *Thrilling Wonder Stories* 16.3 (June 1940): 125–26.

Sturgeon, Theodore. "The Sky Was Full of Ships." *Thrilling Wonder Stories* 30.2 (June 1947): 55–60, 65.

Telotte, J. P. "Sex and Machines: The 'Buzz' of 1950s Science Fiction Films." *Science Fiction Film and Television* 8.3 (2015): 371–86.

"This Month's Cover." *Thrilling Wonder Stories* 16.3 (June 1940): 119.

"Top Grossers of 1951." *Variety* (Jan. 2, 1952): 70.

"Trade Press Writers on RKO Promotion." *Motion Picture Daily* (June 1, 1951): 4.

"Transatlantic Tunnel." *Wonder Stories* 7.7 (Feb. 1936): 893–94.

Vincent, Harl. "Cat's Eye." *Amazing Stories* 8.12 (Apr. 1934): 10–32.

Virilio, Paul. *The Vision Machine*. Trans. Julie Rose. Bloomington: Indiana UP, 1994.

Warren, Bill. *Keep Watching the Skies! American Science Fiction Movies of the Fifties*. 21st Century Edition. Jefferson, NC: McFarland, 2010.

Weaver, William R. "*Dr. Cyclops*." *Motion Picture Herald* (Mar. 9, 1940): 56.

Wegner, Philip E. *Imaginary Communities: Utopia, the Nation, and the Spatial Histories of Modernity*. Berkeley: U of California P, 2002.

Weisinger, Mort. "Scientifilm Review: *The Man Who Could Work Miracles*." *Thrilling Wonder Stories* 9.3 (June 1937): 127.

———. "Scientifilm Review: *Things to Come*." *Thrilling Wonder Stories* 8.1 (Aug. 1936): 112.

Westfahl, Gary. *Hugo Gernsback and the Century of Science Fiction*. Jefferson, NC: McFarland, 2007.

———. "The Marketplace." *The Oxford Handbook of Science Fiction*. Ed. Rob Latham. Oxford: Oxford UP, 2014. 81–92.

Whissel, Kristen. *Picturing American Modernity*. Durham: Duke UP, 2008.

Williams, Keith. *H. G. Wells, Modernity and the Movies*. Liverpool: Liverpool UP, 2007.

Winter, Frank H., and Randy Liebermann. "A Trip to the Moon." *Air & Space Smithsonian* 9 (Oct./Nov. 1994): 62–67.

Winter, Jerome. "Art and Illustration." *The Oxford Handbook of Science Fiction*. Ed. Rob Latham. Oxford: Oxford UP, 2014. 196–211.

Yaszek, Lisa, and Patrick B. Sharp, eds. *Sisters of Tomorrow: The First Women of Science Fiction*. Middletown, CT: Wesleyan UP, 2016.

Zone, Ray. *Stereoscopic Cinema and the Origins of 3-D Film, 1838–1952*. Lexington: UP of Kentucky, 2007.

INDEX

Figures are indicated by an italic *f* following the page number

Gleason, C. Sterling 15, 55–56, 58, 61–62
    "The Port of Missing Airplanes" 56–57
    "The Radiation of the Chinese
        Vegetable" 56–57, 142–43
    "Silent Dynamite" 56–57
    "The Voice of the People" 57
Gold (film) 89–90
Goulart, Ron 158
Gray, John 109–11
Griffith, D. W. 111
Gulliver's Travels (film) 123, 172n7
Gunning, Tom 4–5, 20, 27, 31,
    108–9, 111

Hansen, Miriam 8, 169n3
    late modernism 67–68
    spectatorship 51–53
    visuality 8, 48
Harper's (magazine) 25, 162–63
Haskin, Byron 156–57
Hawkins, Ward 123
Hawks, Howard 138–40, 173n5
Hayden Planetarium 150–51
Heinlein, Robert A. 129–30, 131–33, 155
    and *Destination Moon* 133, 149, 151,
        152, 161
    Rocket Ship Galileo (novel) 149
Hersey, Harold Brainerd 30, 31, 168n1
Hetzel, France Pierre 12
High Modernism 4, 112
Hollywood 48–50, 149–50, 154–55
    as cultural attraction 33–37, 68, 122
    as fictional setting 48–50, 51, 56–57,
        58, 65–66, 146–47, 148–49
Hornig, Charles 85–86, 87
Horrigan, Brian 20–21
House of Rothschild (film) 39–41

Illustrated Detective Magazine 39
Inventor's Secret, The (film) 20
Invisible Man, The (film) 17–18, 39, 80,
    89–90, 91–93
Invisible Ray, The (film) 80–82, 85–86
Island of Lost Souls (film) 41, 85–86
It Came from Outer Space (film) 131

James, Edward 5, 22–23, 130–31, 167n2
Jameson, Fredric 161–62
Johns Hopkins Science Review, The
    (television series) 157–58

Jones, Frank 141
Jones, Pat 157–58
Journey to the 7th Planet (film) 163–64
Jowett, George F. 28–29
Just Imagine (film) 17–18, 89–90,
    109–10f, 109–11

Kateley, Walter 73
Keaton, Buster
    Cameraman, The (film) 53–54
Kilpatrick, Tom 42–43, 172n8
King Kong (film) 41–42, 80, 123, 170n3
King of the Rocket Men (film) 131
Kittler, Friedrich 112–13
Kohn, Arnold 161
Korda, Alexander 95–96, 97–99, 171n7
Kostkos, Henry J. 76
Koszarski, Richard 109, 172n4
Kuttner, Henry 41, 64–74, 116, 143–45,
    147, 163–64, 170n7, 172n5
    "Doom World" 66, 121–22
    Dr. Cyclops 42–43, 123–24,
        125–26, 172n8
    "The Energy Eaters" 66,
        70–71, 142–43
    Galloway Gallegher series 65–66
    "Hollywood on the Moon" 41, 64–68,
        82–83, 119f, 119, 142–43
    "No Man's World" 63–64, 117–21
    partnership with Arthur K.
        Barnes 65–66, 144–45
    Pete Manx series 65–66
    "The Seven Sleepers" 66, 70–72
    "The Shadow on the Screen" 65–66
    "The Star Parade" 66, 68–70
    "Trouble on Titan" 66, 143–44,
        160–61, 163–64
    "weird" stories of 65–66, 85–86
    "The Well of the Worlds" 141–42
    and World War II 143–44, 169n5
    See also Moore, C. L.

Landon, Brooks 4, 7–8, 22–23
Lang, Fritz
    Metropolis (film) 38, 82
    Woman in the Moon (film) 82
Lasser, David 3–4, 82, 84–86, 87
    film petition 87–89
Latour, Bruno 164–65
Lefebvre, Thierry 10–12